KINGS
OF THE HILL

Power and Personality in the
House of Representatives

RICHARD B. CHENEY
LYNNE V. CHENEY

A TOUCHSTONE BOOK
Published by Simon & Schuster
NEW YORK LONDON TORONTO
SYDNEY TOKYO SINGAPORE

TOUCHSTONE
Rockefeller Center
1230 Avenue of the Americas
New York, NY 10020

TOUCHSTONE and colophon are
registered trademarks of Simon & Schuster Inc.

Manufactured in the United States of America

1   3   5   7   9   10   8   6   4   2

Library of Congress Cataloging-in-Publication Data
is available.

ISBN 0-684-82340-3

All photos not credited below are from The Library of Congress Collection:

Copyright 1960 by Herblock in the *Washington Post,* 13
AP, 16

Acknowledgments

Many people provided aid and advice to us as we worked on an updated version of this book. For their scholarly counsel, we would like to thank William F. Connelly, Michael Malbin, and John J. Pitney, Jr.; for his insights based on long experience working in the House of Representatives, Bill Pitts; for her patient attention to detail, research assistant Lynne Munson; and for keeping us on schedule, executive assistant Amy Rash. We would also like to thank our literary agent, Robert Barnett, and our fine editor at Simon and Schuster, Sarah Baker.

For Liz and Mary

Contents

Introduction

In November of 1800, when members of Congress began to gather, they found themselves in a wilderness town of mud and mire and half-finished buildings. The seat of national government had been moved from Philadelphia even though Washington, the new federal city, was far from ready. A newly arrived member of the House of Representatives who took a carriage up to inspect the capitol would have found the stonemasons still at work. Only one wing of the building had been completed, a dismaying discovery for the representative, no doubt, but at least he found himself in a magnificent setting. The Capitol crowned Jenkin's Hill, and westward from it, the broad vistas being planned by Pierre L'Enfant were beginning to emerge from the forest. Shifting his gaze a little to the north, the representative could see the president's house, sparkling white in the distance below.

But if looking down on the seat of executive power gave the early-arriving representative a moment of satisfaction, he would soon learn that the president had an awesome advantage over the Congress. He was one and they were many. He had merely to decide and act, while they had a multitude of viewpoints on what should be done. The problem of numbers was particularly acute for the branch of Congress in which our representative served. With its membership elected according to population, the House that was about to assemble had 142 members, as opposed to a Senate of only 34. Virginia alone sent 22 representatives in 1800, while, like the other sixteen states no matter what their population, she had just two senators. Because its numbers made decisions difficult, the House would frequently be criticized, sometimes by its own members. John Randolph of Roanoke called it "a temple of confusion," and his successors would find it even more chaotic as membership increased to 186 in 1810, 242 in 1830, 357 in 1890, and, finally, to 435 in 1910.

Adding to the difficulty of orderly decision-making was the intensity with which representatives reflected the sentiments of the electorate. Running for election every two years made them much less aloof than their colleagues in the Senate, who served six-year terms and were, until 1913, appointed by state legislatures. Members of the House arrived in Washington freshly imbued with the concerns of their countrymen. They brought all the passion of the larger society to the chamber in which they served, and although this concentration made for much drama, it fostered little efficiency. Lord Bryce, an English observer, remarked, "When you enter [the House], your first impression is of noise and turmoil, a noise like that of short sharp waves in a Highland loch, fretting under a squall against a rocky shore."

As one might suspect, the task of leadership in such an institution has seldom been easy or predictable. Persuading ambitious and competitive individuals to follow another's lead is hard work under any circumstance, but in the House, where there are so many members all pressured by intense and diverse forces, it is an especially formidable undertaking. There have been periods when no one was able to master the institution, but from time to time certain representatives have built the necessary coalitions, found ways to keep them together, and succeeded in riding the tiger, at least for a while. Despite its tumultuous nature, the House has had strong rulers, and this book is about them. It focuses on nine men who dominated the House of Representatives and shows how they managed the not inconsiderable feat of controlling it.

A more varied group than these nine is hard to imagine. Short and tall, thin and fat, Republican and Democrat, they are as different as the parts of the United States they represented. Two of them were born in log cabins in Tennessee; another grew up in a Cincinnati mansion. Two were confirmed bachelors; a third was married to one of the most beautiful and talked-about women of his day. One of them, a slender, fair-skinned man, became known as the Great

Compromiser. Another, a crippled man in a brown wig, was one of the harshest, most uncompromising figures in American history.

Most of the men we consider were Speakers of the House, but one held sway from the chairmanship of the Appropriations Committee. All showed a willingness to take on tough foes—Clay had his Randolph, Polk his Adams, Reed his McKinley—and they confronted their rivals with personalities that ranged from charming to dogged, from seemingly agreeable to undeniably acerbic.

All but one of them—a history professor from Georgia—studied law. And all of them, once they became Kings of the Hill, had to deal with the matter of the mountain. The presidency was the only position more powerful than the one they held, and several were tempted to seek it. In the first two hundred years of the Republic, only one, James K. Polk, succeeded in becoming president, but others came to wield more influence than the man in the White House.

One characteristic they invariably shared was a love for the institution they served. The tartest-tongued of them sometimes waxed sentimental about it, and there was no surer way to provoke them than to suggest, as their countrymen all too often did, that the House was an ignoble institution, somehow inferior to the Senate or the presidency. Nicholas Longworth expressed a feeling common to all of them when he declared, "I want to assist in bringing about universal recognition of the fact that the House, closer as it is to the people than any similar body and more directly responsible to their will, is in very truth, as it ought to be, the great dominant, legislative body of the world."

But the House is not an institution given to unbroken stretches of philosophizing; its members have had other ways of expressing their fondness for it. The men we have chosen often used a clear-eyed humor to acknowledge the realities of power within the organization. Joe Cannon, who developed the Speaker's power to recognize whom he pleases into an awesome force, answered a minority inquiry about whether a certain bill could be passed by observing, "This House could pass an elephant if the gentleman in charge of it could catch the Speaker's eye." Another Republican Speaker, Tom Reed, had a formula he liked to use when notifying the Democratic members of the Rules Committee of his intentions. "Gentlemen," he would drawl, "we have decided to perpetrate the following outrage." The House has, Nicholas Longworth observed, "the saving grace of humor. It continually hovers over the Chamber and often comes to save a situation which seems dark indeed."

There are other moods as well. "In its inner life," journalist Neil MacNeil has accurately observed, "the House has had a mind of its own . . . sometimes sullen, sometimes whimsical, sometimes reckless, sometimes cautious . . . frequently boisterous, occasionally violent, sometimes impetuous." It is a place of deep frustrations and great satisfactions, of mind-numbing tedium and edge-of-the-seat drama. Almost in an instant, it can move from pettiness to the most profoundly moving nobility.

It is a complex institution, one that can be difficult—even for a member of it—fully to understand. Woodrow Wilson, who made one of the most heroic efforts, wrote, "Like a vast picture thronged with figures of equal prominence and crowded with elaborate and obtrusive details, Congress is hard to see satisfactorily and appreciatively at a single view and from a single stand-point." Wilson's simile is psychologically apt. In the House one does feel at times as though he has stumbled into a gigantic nineteenth-century painting whose cast of characters he will never fully comprehend. But the problem is both more and less complicated than Wilson indicates. The House is not a painting so much as a moving picture with new characters constantly entering as others leave, and a description of it at any moment is no more than a freeze-frame, which will change as soon as we start the film rolling again. One response to this situation has been for students of the House to ignore individual members and talk in terms of abstractions like "the Speaker" or "committee chairmen" on the theory that they are longer lasting. But this approach captures none of the vitality of the institution, none of the drama which led Sam Rayburn to call it "the highest theater that anyone plays in upon this earth today."

In explaining the House by way of abstractions, one must also keep in mind the power of strong individuals to reshape the forms they find. The House has often had such individuals, and it is they who make the institution less complicated than Wilson's simile suggests. Not all the figures in the painting are of equal prominence; some stand out, and they have been most responsible for what the House of Representatives is. They have often determined whether the public admires or disdains it. They have given it its inward form, shaping the speakership, determining where other sources of power lie, and from time to time altering the entire configuration by changing the rules of the game. The intricate, ritualistic body known as the House of Representatives is largely their creation. Their stories are not only a part of the drama that makes it fascinating, they are a key to understanding what it is and how it works.

To paraphrase Robert Heilbroner, whose book *The Worldly Philosophers* has been an inspiration for our own, we are embarked not on a lecture tour of principles, but on a journey to consider the individuals who have created—and re-created—an institution.

"But what is government itself but the greatest of all reflections on human nature?"

James Madison,
The Federalist

1

MR. CLAY'S WAR

In November 1811, six young representatives, most of them new, roomed at Mrs. Dawson's boardinghouse on Capitol Hill in Washington City. They were from the South and what was then called the West. Finding one another's company quite congenial, they usually chose to sit around the common parlor fire after dinner rather than retire to their private quarters. Perhaps a few women joined them, since two of the congressmen were accompanied to Washington by their wives. There may have been a child sitting by the fire whittling and folding paper scraps, since one of the group had brought his young son, and the boy liked to make toy boats. One thing certain is that as the men talked late into the evening, the conversation sooner or later got around to the subject of England. Everyone in the room believed that the British were fomenting Indian attacks on frontier settlements, and as they saw it, such activity was more than sufficient cause for war.

One of the congressmen, Langdon Cheves of South Carolina, had grown up hearing how his aunt had been murdered and scalped near Bulltown Fort. It was a tragedy all the more fixed in family memory because as she had died, he was being born inside the fort, where his parents had managed to find refuge from Cherokees determined to drive out white settlers. Another of the group, John C. Calhoun, he of the burning eyes and icy emotions, had lost a grandmother, an uncle, and two cousins in an Indian raid. Such experiences were only too familiar to Mrs. Dawson's boarders, and each new report of the British supplying the Indians with money and weapons fed their passion for war. Even the gentlest spirit among them, the tall, thoughtful William Lowndes, was ready to fight England.

Feeling strongly as they did, these men could have been a hard group to lead; but it was not many evenings before a slender, fair-skinned congressman from Kentucky was dominating the fireside discussions. Young like the rest of them, equally full of energy and certitude, he was distinguished by a truly awesome political talent. He not only knew what he wanted to have happen, he saw ways of bringing such things about; and as the child fell asleep and the women sewed, the men in the room would have shifted their chairs to face him and leaned forward to listen as he spoke. The Kentuckian's name was Henry Clay and his plans involved the House of Representatives. He was about to turn his extraordinary skill upon the institution, and in a matter of days would be elected its Speaker. That achievement was astonishing in itself, since he was just beginning his first term as a representative; but he would go further. He would transform the post of Speaker, which had previously been largely ceremonial, into a power center—and he would use it to propel the country into war.

This spirited man who would do so much had already accomplished a great deal. His father had died when he was four; his mother and stepfather, anxious to leave Virginia and move west, had arranged for him to clerk in the High Court of Chancery and then left him on his own when he was fourteen. In his twentieth year, he joined the endless stream of emigrants heading west on the Wilderness Road, and possessing little besides a license to practice law, he crossed through the Cumberland Gap and rode on to Lexington, where he quickly became a successful member of the bar. He also proved adept at hard drinking and high-stakes gambling, questionable accomplishments for a lawyer today, but in early Kentucky they enhanced Clay's reputation. He was invited to the finest homes, including Colonel Thomas Hart's, where he met the colonel's pretty, dark-eyed daughter Lucretia. The two were married, and in the years ahead, Lucretia would prove herself an adaptable and generous-spirited helpmate. She would frequently pack up their children (eleven in all) and undertake the arduous journey to Washington with her husband. At other times, she would spend long months by herself overseeing home and family while Henry was off politicking. Throughout, she retained an equanimity which made her remarkably tolerant of Henry's drinking and gaming. "Isn't it a pity your husband gambles so much?" a prim New England lady once said to her. "Oh, I don't know," Mrs. Clay replied. "He usually wins."

Lexington had a population of sixteen hundred when Clay first settled there. It boasted two newspapers, a library, a university, and a set of statutes that outlawed some of the more boisterous frontier customs. It was forbidden to light a fire with a rifle, for example, or to keep a pet panther, but they still knew how to appreciate a good cockfight in Kentucky—or a good duel. Henry Clay, who would fight two duels in his lifetime, fit in splendidly. In his person, he epitomized the vigorous, enterprising westerner. And when he began to use his quick wit to speak out in public, it was clear to all who listened that he had the gift of a bold, defiant oratory. When he spoke, even a rowdy frontier crowd would fall silent to hear him. He could hold even that most cynical of listeners—the news reporter—spellbound. During one of Clay's speeches, Abraham Lincoln wrote, "The reporters forgot their vocation, dropped their pens, and sat enchanted from the beginning to quite the close. The speech now lives only in the memory of a few old men, and the enthusiasm with which they cherish their recollection of it is absolutely astonishing."

Clay decided to go into politics, and while still a young man became a United States senator. In fact, he became a senator at age twenty-nine, a year short of the constitutional requirement, but this detail seems not to have troubled him or anyone else very greatly. In later years, Clay would shrug it off as one of his "supposed juvenile indiscretions."

When his term expired, he returned to Kentucky and won a seat in the state assembly, where he had previously served. Feelings were running high against Britain by this time, and in January 1809 Clay got into a scuffle on the floor of the assembly with Humphrey Marshall, a Federalist who opposed action against England. Clay challenged Marshall to a duel, and on a cold January morning the two stood at ten paces and fired three rounds. Both ended up with minor wounds, a detail that was quickly obscured as the duel became part of Kentucky lore. Marshall, no doubt disgusted with the hyperbole that came to surround his encounter with Clay, tried to deflate the episode. "We were kept on the ground, trying to kill each other," he said, "until a skillful duellist would have killed both, with less powder and fewer balls."

After Clay had rested a few weeks (and won large sums at cards, it was reported), he returned to the assembly. A year later, in 1810, he was again sent to Washington to fill out an unexpired term in the United States Senate.

Now, in 1811, he was a freshman member of the House, because the Senate, with what he called its "solemn stillness," had bored him. Senators were not elected by popular vote as they are today, but chosen by state legislatures. The Constitution's framers, many of whom distrusted the voting public, had decided on this method as a way of distancing senators from public opinion. The effect, however, was to remove them from the mainstream of national concern. Their droning debates lacked the passion and immediacy of those that occurred in the House, a fact the Senate recognized by frequently adjourning so its members could go to the representatives' chamber and listen to their deliberations. James Madison, president in 1811, had once declared that "being a young man and desirous of increasing his reputation as a statesman, he could not afford to accept a seat in the Senate." Clay, who would disagree with Madison on other things, saw eye to eye with him on this one. He had yielded readily when urged to leave the Senate for the House, to "fill the more honourable and important appointment of an immediate Representative of the People," as a Kentucky newspaper put it.

Clay's experience was one reason he dominated the gatherings at the boardinghouse. Indeed, it had already given him something of a national reputation, as William Lowndes acknowledged when he wrote to his wife, "Mr. Clay ... they call 'the Western Star.'" But another aspect of Clay's leadership was his personality. He was an ebullient, life-loving man who charmed almost everyone who knew him. He liked people, liked being with them, and they responded in kind. William Plumer of Massachusetts, who met Clay when they both served in the Senate, quickly became an admirer of the young Kentuckian and noted in his diary how rapidly Clay was taken up by Washington society. He "is in all parties of pleasure," Plumer recorded in 1807, and "out almost every night."

Plumer observed that Clay was especially favored by the ladies. It was not because he was particularly handsome. Except for an unusually large mouth (which he joked was so constructed that he could never learn to spit), he was rather plain featured. But when he spoke, Clay was animated by an inner fire, and when he listened, it was with caring and careful attention. Mrs. Samuel Harrison Smith, a Washington bluestocking who knew him through most of his long political career, talked about his "soul-speaking eye and persuasive voice" and said she found in him "an openness, communicativeness, an affectionateness and warmth and kindness which were irresistibly captivating." Eliza Johnston, a beautiful Senate wife who was smitten with Clay, wrote to him, "It is not the display of talents, of the highest kind, which have endeared you to your friends, no, no, it is the display of *heart*, in all you do and say."

But the pull of his personality was felt by men too. When General Glasscock of Georgia was given the opportunity to be introduced to Clay, he refused for fear of falling under his influence. Even John C. Calhoun, whom Harriet Martineau called "the cast-iron man," was not impervious. In later years, Calhoun and Clay became fierce rivals, but even then Calhoun found Clay difficult to resist. "I don't like Henry Clay," he said. "He is a bad man, an imposter, a creator of wicked schemes. I wouldn't speak to him, but, by God, I love him."

With his warmth and magnetism, Clay possessed in abundance the ability to enlist people in a cause. He seemed almost instinctively to know how to make others follow where he wanted to lead, and it seems reasonable to suppose that during the long evenings by the boardinghouse fire he suggested to his messmates ways of persuading others in Congress that the time had come for war. Although the group in the boardinghouse had powerful personal reasons for regarding the British connection with the Indians as England's most hostile activity, they also needed to advance other reasons for war. They couldn't seem too parochial in their concerns, not if they wanted representatives from all around the country on their side. Though he had probably never seen the ocean, Clay had become well practiced in talking about "freedom of the seas" and had caused many a Kentucky crowd to become incensed over the outrageous way the British were treating the United States. Far removed as Kentuckians were from it, they had the frontiersman's acute sensitivity to insult, and what the British were doing on the high seas was an affront to national honor. England behaved as though she owned the ocean, dictating where American ships might go and where they might not, and seizing those that violated her orders. When she had difficulty finding sufficient manpower to conduct her war with France, her sea captains adopted the tactic of stopping American ships, claiming their crews were full of British deserters, and impressing men they found on board into British service. Most of the time, the hapless sailors set to working the English guns were, in fact, American citizens.

The most dramatic instance had happened in 1807 when the British warship *Leopard* fired on the American frigate *Chesapeake*, wounding or killing twenty-one men and forcing the commodore to give up four crew members, only one of whom, it turned out, was an Englishman. The affair was a blow to national pride, a blood insult; one had only to mention it in front of an audience and the cries for revenge would begin.

This is the way we need to frame the matter, Clay might have said to the group at Mrs. Dawson's, for that was the way he himself had begun presenting it. When he stood on the Senate floor and declared himself for "resistance by the sword," he spoke of Britain's violation of "the sacred personal rights of American Freemen" before he passed on to talk of conquering Canada in order to extinguish "the torch that lights up savage warfare."

.Structuring the debate in the House, focusing that body on the issue of war, seemed all the more important when the young hot-bloods in the parlor considered the president, James Madison. Although he was kind and conscientious, with a considerable intellect, which made itself felt in intimate gatherings, he was not a bold leader, not the risk taker they wanted. Over the years, his achievements had been impressive: he had shaped the Constitutional Convention, been responsible for the Bill of Rights. But to the young congressmen that was ancient history. Now Madison was sixty years old, and he looked much older. ("He is but a withered little apple-John," Washington Irving rather unkindly declared.) Added to that, he was shy. Not until his thirtieth year had he been able to bring himself to address a gathering of any sort, and he still became stiff and unsmiling when people he didn't know well were introduced to him. He was quiet, cautious, steady, a man of unshakable integrity; but he could be so diffident that even his advocates at times had doubts about him. House Clerk John Beckley, who helped Madison secure his party's nomination, worried that he was "too timid and indecisive as a statesman."

On first assuming office in 1809, Madison had continued Jefferson's policies of economic coercion against England. When that proved ineffective, he left the decision on a new course up to Congress; but the House of Representatives, the leading body of Congress, was unprepared for the task. It was divided into factions—Federalists, Madisonians, Clintonians, Quids, to name a few—and it was unaccustomed to looking within itself for leadership that could unite the various elements. Though members liked to complain about executive influence, they were nonetheless in the habit of receiving guidance from the executive branch. During Jefferson's time, certain among them had been informally appointed by the president to see that the administration's policies were implemented. One of these congressmen, William Giles, was referred to as "the premier" or "prime minister"—not necessarily a compliment, but it did reveal a truth. It was members like Giles, chosen by the president, who directed the House; not the Speaker, whom the members themselves elected.

Thus, when Madison left the matter of what to do about England to Congress, confusion ensued, with a leaderless House trying in vain to lead the nation. Though cries for war were loud across the country, there were also pressures for accommodation. New England Federalists, whose constituents were economically dependent on maritime trade, cringed at the idea of doing anything that would jeopardize it. That was "cutting one's throat to cure the nosebleed," as they saw it, and although they were a minority, they were influential, and Congress was able to pass only the most innocuous legislation. When Congress adjourned in May 1810, a self-satisfied British envoy wrote in his diary, "Thus ends this famous session. It began in 'blood and thunder' and ended in drunken frolic. . . . One thing, however, is certain—they have covered themselves with ridicule and disgrace."

But the young congressmen gathered at Mrs. Dawson's boardinghouse in the fall of 1811 were resolved that the Twelfth Congress would be different. They hadn't gone to the trouble of getting themselves elected and then traveling all the way to Washington by saddle horse and coach and flatboat over muddy roads and swollen rivers simply to continue the national humiliation. The House of Representatives could lead the country, lead it right to war, if it had "some controlling or at least some concentrating influence," as William Lowndes put it in a letter to his wife. And no one was better suited for that than Henry Clay, the man who had stood on the floor of the Senate and so eloquently proclaimed, "No man in the nation desires peace more than I. But I prefer the troubled ocean of war . . . with all its calamities and desolations, to the tranquil, putrescent pool of ignominious peace."

No one recorded the details of exactly how Clay came to be elected Speaker, but if one assumes that convincing political victories seldom come about by accident, it seems reasonable to conclude that a plan was developed in the boardinghouse parlor. Perhaps it involved secrecy, since Clay's name was not publicly mentioned for the Speaker's post until the night before the election. Probably it included a special appeal to other new members. They would have been especially receptive to the idea of electing a freshman to the speakership—and they comprised well over half of this particular House.

On November 3, 1810, the Twelfth Congress assembled in the Representatives' chamber, an elliptical room with rich Turkish carpets, gold and scarlet draperies, and Corinthian columns around the perimeter. The members voted for Speaker, and when the totals were announced, Clay of Kentucky was the winner, receiving more than twice the votes of his nearest competitor. At age thirty-four, on his first day as a member of the House of Representatives, he had been chosen to lead it.

Shaking hands, accepting congratulations, he made his way up the aisle to the Speaker's chair, a gilded, ornately carved, thronelike seat located under a fringed velvet canopy. Edward Hooker, a Connecticut squire who visited the Capitol, declared the chair "resembles more the trappings of royalty than the seat of republicanism"; but if the same thought occurred to Clay as he was mounting the rostrum, he would have had to smile at the irony of it. Though the Speaker's chair might look like a caliph's throne, the men who had sat there had been virtually powerless. Muhlenberg, Trumbull, Dayton, Sedgwick, Macon, Varnum—good men all—but they had left little mark on the body over which they had presided. Henry Adams, acidly commenting on one of them, neatly summed all of them up: "No man in history has left a better name than Macon, but the name was all he left."

Clay set out at once to make sure it would be otherwise with him. He began with the committees. The Speaker had the power to appoint the members and the chairman, and Clay exercised that pre-rogative with his own aims in mind. The goal of previous Speakers had been to maintain a stance of objectivity; Clay's was to put men who thought like him into positions where they could translate their convictions into action. He decided to make Langdon Cheves, his messmate from South Carolina, chairman of the Committee on Naval Affairs. To serve on the Foreign Affairs Committee, of crucial importance in the current crisis, he wanted John C. Calhoun, an-other friend from Mrs. Dawson's, as well as a short, red-faced Ten-nessee congressman named Felix Grundy, who had lost three broth-ers to the Indians and was widely known as a war hawk. As chairman of Foreign Affairs, Clay chose Peter Porter, a rotund, thirty-eight-year-old lawyer from the Niagara frontier of New York, who made no secret of his desire to have the United States seize upper Canada.

Plans for these appointments were well under way by the time Mr. Coles, the president's secretary, delivered Madison's message to the new Congress. Confident they were on course to their goal, Clay and his war hawks settled back to listen as the president's message was read. They heard Madison's recounting of familiar grievances, and, more important, his suggestion that the lawmakers "feel the duty of putting the United States into an armor and attitude de-manded by this crisis and corresponding with the national spirit and expectations." On the following Tuesday, after committee assign-ments had been announced, there was a motion to refer the message to committees, and since it was clear they would turn the president's careful words into specific recommendations on preparing for war, one antiwar member, John Randolph of Roanoke, objected, com-plaining at length about having no chance to comment on the mes-sage. His objection was futile, however. The House voted it down, allowing the war hawks to proceed.

Meanwhile, hundreds of miles to the west, an event was taking shape that would increase the momentum toward war. At the center of what was about to happen was a slim, proud Shawnee chieftain who had learned to hate just as fiercely as Clay and his allies. While Langdon Cheves and Felix Grundy had been losing loved ones in Indian massacres, Tecumseh had been watching Indians die at the white man's hand, his father among them. He had seen Indian homes burned and crops razed. He had seen Indian heritage and character debased by the white man's religion and whiskey. To him it seemed clear the time had come for Indians to join together and resist the white man's advance. Dressed in unadorned buckskin, he had taken long journeys on horseback, all the way from the Ozarks to New York and from Iowa to Florida, to encourage different tribes to unite together. He was remarkably successful, in part because he was a compelling orator. Wrote one white man who heard him, "The effect of his bitter, burning words . . . was so great on his companions, that the whole three hundred warriors could hardly refrain from springing from their seats. Their eyes flashed, and even the most aged . . . evinced the greatest excitement." Other white men would say that Tecumseh's eloquence put them much in mind of a certain Kentucky orator, a young man named Henry Clay. Tecumseh also had another gift, a personal magnetism that drew men to him, and historians who try to describe it use words like *warm* and *radiant*, the same words Clay's biographers use in portraying him.

Tecumseh brought more than thirty tribes into his confederacy, an accomplishment white Americans saw as a menace to their frontier settlements. In 1809, when he and his brother, known as the Prophet, founded a settlement at Great Clearing, where the Tippecanoe River empties into the Wabash, Indiana settlers became particularly alarmed. A group of them met at Vincennes and demanded that the Tippecanoe settlement be broken up. And they further declared, "We are fully convinced that the formation of the combination, headed by a Shawnee prophet, is a British scheme, and that the agents of that power are constantly exciting the Indians to hostilities against the United States."

Within two years, the settlement had grown to a thousand warriors, and William Henry Harrison, the aloof and ambitious aristocrat who had become governor of Indiana Territory, decided to move against the Indians. He waited until Tecumseh had gone south to meet with the Chickasaw and Seminole tribes, then marched with an army, which included a contingent of blue-coated Kentucky volunteers, up the Wabash. On the night of November 6, 1811, Harrison and his troops camped near the mouth of the Tippecanoe. They were in Indian country. No treaties had ceded this land to the white man; in fact, the United States was pledged to protect it from incursions. And so on the gray, wet morning of November 7, the Indians attacked. The Fourth Infantry's musician had just gone to Harrison's tent to inquire if he should sound reveille when a rifle shot and war whoop were heard. In the bloody hours that followed, sixty-one of Harrison's men were killed and 127 wounded, but he emerged the victor nonetheless, putting the Indians to flight and destroying their village. He marched his troops back to Vincennes and almost immediately began to write about the battle that would one day make him president. "The Indians have never sustained so severe a defeat since their acquaintance with the white people," he informed William Eustis, the secretary of war.

The news of Tippecanoe electrified Washington. Coming just as members of the House Foreign Affairs Committee were making recommendations to increase the regular army, raise a volunteer militia, and put the country's naval vessels in good repair, word of the battle gave powerful force to their arguments. The Indians weren't acting alone, Felix Grundy rose on the floor to declare:

> It cannot be believed by any man who will reflect, that the savage tribes, uninfluenced by other Powers would think of making war on the United States. They understand too well their own weakness, and our strength. They have already felt the weight of our arms; they know they hold the very soil on which they live as tenants at sufferance. How, then, sir, are we to account for their conduct? In one way only; some powerful nation must have intrigued with them, and turned their peaceful disposition towards us into hostilities. Great Britain alone has intercourse with those Northern tribes; I therefore infer, that if British gold has not been employed, their baubles and trinkets, and a promise of support and a place of refuge if necessary, have had their effect.

Grundy talked about the men who had died, mourned them, eulogized them. "War is not to commence by sea or land," he thundered, "it is already begun; and some of the richest blood of our country has already been shed."

But even the emotion of the moment could not keep Grundy from advancing another argument, this one more pragmatic. "The war, if carried on successfully, will have its advantages," he pointed out. Once the British were driven from Canada, not only would the Indian problem be solved, but the United States could expand its empire to the north. "I am willing to receive the Canadians as adopted brothers," Grundy declared.

As other war hawks took to the floor, John Randolph of Roanoke was getting ready to present the opposition view. His preparations were no simple matter. He would untwist a long silk scarf from around his neck and lay it neatly on the floor, very close to the three large hounds that often accompanied him into the House chamber; then he would take off another scarf, and another, neatly laying them on top of the first one. Next he would remove the greatcoats he was wearing in layers, and one by one add them to the pile on the floor. When he had disrobed sufficiently to suit himself and had rested a few moments at his desk, he would stand—seem to unfold, really, so long were the thin legs on which his emaciated trunk rested. "Mis-ter Speak-er! Mis-ter Speak-er!" he would cry out in his sharp, high voice.

This time when he was recognized and had the floor, he suggested that the war hawks were not being quite candid. They were not debating a war of defense, as they suggested, but one "of conquest, of aggrandizement, of ambition," and the country would not support such an undertaking. "Our people will not submit to be taxed for this war of conquest and dominion," he declared in his shrill voice.

As was so often the case, Randolph had seen his opponents' soft white underbelly and struck. No matter how many times those who wanted war urged it on the ground of England's actions on the high seas, the fact remained that seaboard communities, the part of the country most directly affected by England's depradations, were opposed to war. The frontier states were the ones that produced the war hawks, and committed as they were to securing their communities from Indian attack, it was daily becoming clearer that they had more than defense in mind. The idea of expanding the nation's boundaries, particularly into Canada, animated them as well. From the time the Foreign Relations Committee had reported to the House, Randolph declared, "We have heard but one word—like the whip-poor-will, but one eternal monotonous tone—Canada! Canada! Canada!"

From his point of view, a war of expansion was a threat to democracy, a danger to liberty. Political power always grew at the expense of individual rights, he believed, and it was unthinkable to encourage that growth in the federal government, as a commitment to men and arms would inevitably do, unless there was a grave threat to be met. "The government of the United States is not calculated to wage offensive war," he told the House. "It was instituted for the common defence and general welfare."

But as one reads the speeches of Randolph made over the next few months, experiencing both their vivid insights and strange meanderings, one senses other factors behind his opposition to Clay and his allies. For one thing, he seems to have loved conflict for its own sake, to have craved it even. This characteristic had been apparent when he was growing up, an excitable, brilliant boy, on a plantation home called "Bizaare." There, his mother's desire for him to be religious was enough to turn him enthusiastically anti-Christian. When he went off to college, he shot another student in a duel—over, it was said, a matter of pronunciation. (On his deathbed, Randolph was reported to have corrected someone who mispronounced *omnipotent*.) He broke off all relations with his stepfather, the amiable St. George Tucker, because of a chance remark, and he added "of Roanoke" to his name to distinguish himself from another kinsman whom he came to despise.

His nearest companion and most trusted friend during his youth was his brother Richard. But when John was barely into his twenties, Richard was involved in a scandal of the first magnitude. It concerned his wife's sister and the bloody corpse of an infant, and it led to Richard being put on trial for murder. He was acquitted, but he was a broken man; within three years he was dead.

Thus was extreme pressure brought to bear on John Randolph, who was not strong either psychologically or physically. A long-time acquaintance of his suggested he never knew a single day of good health in his life, and a catalog of his infirmities would fill pages, indeed, do fill the pages of the letters he wrote. In 1808, he described his health after a fall: "I can walk after a fashion, but the worst of my case is a general decay of the whole system. I am racked with pain and up the better part of every night from disordered stomach and bowels. My digestive faculties are absolutely worn out. When to all this you add spitting of blood from my lungs and a continual fever, you may have some idea of my situation."

His continued ill health took a toll. Although, from a distance, his thin frame made him look like a boy, from up close, wrinkled and sallow-skinned, he appeared twice his age. He was also beardless, a condition believed by his contemporaries to signal his impotence, and Randolph did little to alleviate this impression. When one of his enemies alluded to his lack of manhood, he spewed forth the venom of his times: "You pride yourself on an animal faculty in respect to which the negro is your equal and the jackass infinitely your superior."

Before he died in 1833, Randolph was undeniably mad, an end all the more tragic given the ability he had displayed as a young man. In 1800 at age twenty-eight, he had become chairman of the Ways and Means Committee. Recognizing his brilliance, Jefferson used him as his personal representative in the House for a time and gave him the task of guiding administration legislation. But it was not Randolph's way to work with someone for long. He preferred the role of opponent, of adversary, finding in it, perhaps, some release for the tensions inside him. He broke with Jefferson, lost his committee chairmanship, and by the time of the Twelfth Congress, was a man of much-diminished influence. This fact no doubt added to his resentment of Clay—whom he dubbed "the Cock of Kentucky"—and the other war hawks, "that horde of upstart patriots," he called them. Young and bright, they were running the House of Representatives as he once had.

Clay exerted his authority over the Virginian early on by ordering the doorkeeper to remove the dogs Randolph habitually brought into the chamber with him. No Speaker before Clay had dared do that, even though the dogs sometimes started barking when members rose to debate. The hesitation of these other Speakers is thoroughly understandable in light of Randolph's volatility. When a member in the previous Congress had angered him, Randolph had attacked him with his cane.

But Clay ordered the dogs out, and no violence followed, possibly because Clay also reprimanded other members. When Congressman Smilie, an older member from Pennsylvania, was out of order, Clay ordered him to take his seat, stating the command so forcefully that Smilie dropped his glasses. A nodding member was told either to wake up or go to bed. Congressmen who had their feet on their desks were told to put them down.

Clay's success in getting Randolph's dogs out of the House chamber without a scene no doubt also owed something to Clay's manner. He had a way of gracefully removing the venom from an opponent's sting without any diminishment of his own authority. Once when he reproved Randolph for his conduct on the floor, the Virginian shot back the accusation that Clay was paying no attention. "Oh, you are mistaken, Mr. Randolph," cried Clay. "I frequently turn away my head, it is true, and ask for a pinch of snuff ... but retentive as I know your memory to be, I will wager that I can repeat as many of your speeches as you can."

But if Randolph yielded on the matter of the dogs, he was steadfast when it came to opposing the war. During the debate on the resolutions recommended by the Foreign Affairs Committee, his speeches consumed hour after hour. Not only did he make the obvious points, he went on to talk of Shakespeare and Milton, of Attila, Tamerlane, and Kublai Khan. Hour after hour he went on, seeming to ramble, but then honing in with a point that would shock his listeners to attention. There was the black population, for example. Recently there had been "repeated alarms of insurrection." Who knew what would happen in a war? "While talking of Canada," he said, "some of us were shuddering for our own safety at home."

But the resolutions had the impetus of Tippecanoe behind them, and they passed overwhelmingly. Clay and his war hawks were still in control, and the new Speaker wanted to insure they would stay that way. When the bill to enlarge the regular army came back from the Senate, he took the opportunity to set up a counter to Randolph's rhetoric. With the House in the Committee of the Whole, Clay took to the floor and made a two-hour address. Previous Speakers of the House, convinced their proper role was to moderate, had not entered into debate; but Clay did so enthusiastically. He argued for the Senate version, which provided an increase of twenty-five thousand regulars. The ten thousand troops that the House had previously approved and that the president was known to want were "too great for peace, and ... too small for war," he declared. He also used his speech to breathe fire into the fainthearted. "What are we to gain by war?" he asked rhetorically. "What are we not to lose by peace?—commerce, character, a nation's best treasure, honor!"

Clay got the army bill he wanted. It passed ninety-four to thirty-four, inspiring Randolph to take to the floor and sarcastically demand to know who was running the country, the president or the Speaker? "After you have raised these twenty-five thousand men ... shall we form a Committee ... of Public Safety," he asked. "Or shall we depute the power to the Speaker ... to carry on the war? Shall we declare that the Executive, not being capable of discerning the public interest, or not having the spirit to pursue it, we have appointed a committee to take the President and Cabinet into custody?"

But when the Committee on Naval Affairs reported to the House, the war hawks' string of victories was broken. Not even Clay's eloquence could persuade the congressmen to vote for more ships. His own party had traditionally been opposed to naval forces since they could not, like an army, be disbanded the moment war was over and so were seen as a permanent threat to liberty. "Navies have been and always will be engines of power and employed in the projects of ambition and war," Richard M. Johnson declared—and he was one of Clay's most hawkish allies. The matter was lost.

And then came the issue of paying for the war. The Reverend Samuel Taggart, a corpulent Federalist with a penchant for gustatory metaphor, called the budget report "very chokey meat," and smugly observed, "I find many of our war hawks in and out of Congress, altho' they may relish war as a feast, yet do not love to pay the reckoning." The debate over policies to recommend to the Ways and Means Committee was bitter and divisive. It was finally decided to recommend certain taxes, but this was a far cry from actually levying them, and time was passing. By now spring was approaching. The war movement seemed to have lost its momentum, and Clay and his allies, so exultant at first, now began to wonder if war would ever come.

In their frustration, some of them blamed the president. If he failed to show a firm course, how was the House ever to gather the majorities it needed? The hawkish George Poindexter, a nonvoting delegate from Mississippi and a card-playing friend of Clay's, wrote, "Mr. Madison is afraid to go to war or to be at peace; and the course he pursues really deserves ridicule."

What the war hawks wanted was a chief executive who would sound the trumpets and inspire martial fervor throughout the country. But to Madison's way of thinking, it was important to build a consensus for war before sounding the battle call, and on March 9 he took a step in that direction. He sent to the Congress papers revealing that a Captain John Henry had been a British spy in New England in 1808 and 1809. Under the command of the governor-general of Canada, he had encouraged antiwar Federalists to resist laws with which they disagreed and even to break with the United

States and join a portion of the Northeast to Canada. Secretary of State James Monroe had paid an intermediary of Henry's, a smooth-talking Frenchman named Crillon, fifty thousand dollars for the papers, and when the president submitted them to Congress, the reaction among those already disposed to fighting England was enthusiastic. They demanded that war be declared immediately. One of Clay's Kentucky colleagues wrote home, "Can any American after this discovery doubt the propriety of ousting the British from the continent?"

But this cannot have been the only audience Madison was trying to reach. He must have hoped the Henry documents would have an effect on the Northeast, perhaps embarrassing representatives from that section into softening their position by showing them how earnestly their antiwar policies were desired by the British. But the opposite happened. After some initial dismay, the Federalists responded angrily, claiming this was an attempt to libel them. And in succeeding weeks, they took great satisfaction from reports that Crillon had been an imposter—actually a gambler named Soubiron and possibly an agent of Napoleon. Being at war with England himself, the French dictator would find it very desirable for the United States to declare war against Britain.

Such perfidy seemed to prove the point of those who argued that France's transgressions were as great as England's and that any war we fought ought to be against both countries. This argument gained further strength on March 23 when news was received that the French were seizing and burning American ships in the Atlantic. Wrote Nathaniel Macon, a firm supporter of war against England, "The Devil himself could not tell which government, England or France, is the most wicked."

Nevertheless, Madison went ahead with a plan that had been worked out with Clay, submitting to Congress on April 1 a proposal for a general embargo. As Clay understood it, the embargo was a device for getting American ships into port and for finalizing preparations for war against England. "It is to be viewed as a direct precursor to war," he proclaimed exultantly in a secret session of the House. "Mr. Clay was a flame of fire," one member reported. "He had brought Congress to the verge of what he conceived to be a war for liberty and honor, and his voice, inspired by the occasion, rang through the capitol, like a trumpet tone sounding for the onset."

But Randolph of Roanoke was not impressed. He began by announcing he would have no part of keeping war deliberations secret, and then he took to the floor to contradict Clay: "The honourable Speaker is mistaken when he says the message is for war.... At the end of 60 days, we shall not have war, and the reason is the Executive dare not plunge the nation into war in our unprepared state."

Randolph was cut off by a demand for the previous question,* and the House passed the embargo measure. Within days, however, there was widespread doubt if the president had meant by it what Clay said he had meant—or was this another instance of Randolph's biting sarcasm cutting through to a bone of truth? On April 9, the *National Intelligencer*, an administration newspaper, declared that embargo "is not war, nor does it inevitably lead to war." And there were rumors that Madison intended to send a peace mission headed by Senator Bayard to England.

Was the president wavering? This close to the final deed, he may well have been. He was the sort who liked to put off irrevocable decisions as long as possible, who liked to make sure that every last consideration had been weighed. When one did that in the matter of war with England, there were factors to give even the stoutest of hearts pause: enlistments were not going well, the country had no navy to speak of, war taxes had not been levied. There were significant numbers of citizens who thought we ought to fight France rather than England and others who didn't want to fight at all. Small wonder if another peace mission to England looked attractive.

Clay and his war hawks went to see the president. As those unfriendly to Clay and Madison liked to tell it, during their meeting, Clay browbeat a reluctant president into taking a prowar stance. Clay's control of the Congress certainly gave him a potent weapon, particularly since presidential candidates in those days were nominated by congressional caucus rather than by convention, and the caucus upon which Madison's renomination depended had been delayed. But it is difficult to imagine Clay being heavyhanded; he genuinely liked Madison, even if he thought him too timid for the times. And in any case, Madison was not opposed to war. He simply thought there ought to be a unified spirit for it and adequate preparation. This was the point of disagreement, for the war hawks had

---

* A motion that the House had decided in 1811 should close debate and bring a vote on the main issue.

concluded that the endless discussions had to stop. There had to be a decision for war, and when that was accomplished, consensus and preparations would follow.

However the war hawks worded their message, the president began to act decisively, and by the middle of April, his administration was sending out consistently bellicose signals. There was to be no peace mission to England, and the *National Intelligencer* declared, "The truth, then, is the undoubted truth, that the Embargo is meant to be the precursor to war. . . ." The Federalists concluded that the war party was now running the presidency as well as the Congress. "He [Madison] . . . is driven by them like chaff before the wind," wrote Samuel Taggart.

When, at the end of May, it became widely known that the president was preparing a war message, it seemed that Clay and his allies, after months of effort, were about to attain their goal. Once more, John Randolph of Roanoke tried to thwart them. He took to the floor and irritatingly, aggravatingly, and with unerring accuracy, pointed out the weaknesses of the prowar position. Why England and not France? he wanted to know. To war with Britain alone would make the American government "the panders of French despotism . . . the tools, the minions, the sycophants, parasites of France." And what was the war to be about? Was it really a matter of freedom of the seas? How odd then that this "war for commerce [is] deprecated by all the commercial portion of our country, by New England and New York. . . ."

Finally, John Calhoun could stand it no longer, and he called Randolph to order. "The question of war is not before the House," he declared. "The gentleman is therefore speaking contrary to rule."

Clay was temporarily out of the chair, and Mr. Bibb, who was presiding, ruled. "The objection is not valid," he stated. "The gentleman from Virginia has announced his intention to make a motion and it has been usual in such cases to permit a wide range of debate."

"I thank the gentleman from South Carolina for the respite that he has unintentionally given me and for which, in my exhausted condition, I am highly grateful," Randolph declared, resuming his diatribe. "This war for commercial rights is to be waged against the express wish of the great commercial section of the United States. . . ."

Calhoun interrupted, "As the gentleman has expressed his satisfaction at the rest given him by the former call to order, I would give him another opportunity to rest himself. I ask that the gentleman from Virginia submit to the Chair the proposition he intends to make."

Clay by now had resumed the Speaker's chair. "It is the duty of the Chair to require the application of observations made on the floor to the subject debated," he said, "and this cannot be performed unless the chair is apprized of the terms of the proposition."

"My proposition," said Randolph, "is one respecting our relations with two great belligerants, and goes to . . . the question of peace or war."

"The gentleman will please take his seat," Clay said. "This motion must be submitted before further debate."

"I . . . appeal from that decision," said Randolph. ". . . The right of prefacing a motion by remarks is almost the last vestige of freedom of debate."

Several members jumped to their feet to support Randolph. Declared Mr. Goldsborough: "On all occasions of appeal from the Speaker's decision on a question of order, the first impulse of my mind is to support the Chair. . . . In the present instance, however, the conviction of my judgment as to the incorrectness of the honorable Speaker's decision is so clear and conclusive that I shall be compelled to declare so by my vote."

But in the end, the House decided to support Clay's ruling. The vote was sixty-seven to forty-two for the Speaker, causing Randolph to lament, "Has it come to this, that members of this House shall grow gray in the service, and in proportion to their experience become ignorant of the rules of proceeding, and receive the construction of them from those who have never been familiar with them? Having been fourteen years on this floor, is a man to be told he knows nothing of the rules of the House?"

The personal battle between Clay and Randolph was not over. They would argue about Clay's ruling in the pages of the *National Intelligencer* until finally Langdon Cheves persuaded Clay that it wasn't fitting for the Speaker, "the second man in the Nation," to quarrel publicly with a member of the House. Randolph would continue to castigate Clay on other matters, and as the years passed, his attacks grew increasingly bitter. In what John Kennedy cited as "the most memorable and malignant sentence in the history of personal abuse," Randolph called Clay "a being so brilliant yet so corrupt, which like a rotten mackeral by moonlight, shines and stinks." Finally, in 1827, after Clay had served five more terms in the House, all of them in the Speaker's chair, he and Randolph met on the dueling field. Randolph, wearing his voluminous greatcoats, misfired in nervousness. Clay's shot went through Randolph's clothing without ever touching him, and the confrontation ended more or less in a draw.

But in 1812, Clay was the undeniable victor, supported by a majority of members who were weary of words and ready to fight. The clearest illustration of the power Clay had gathered to himself and the Speaker's chair came when Madison's war message was delivered to the House and a declaration of war passed the day after it was reported. The Senate also voted approval, and on June 18, 1812, Madison signed the declaration. Henry Clay had achieved what he wanted. He had gained control of the House, even of the country, some said, and now all of the passion and optimism and enthusiasm that had enabled him to gain mastery would be put to the test. The country was at war.

2

WHO IS JAMES K. POLK?

While Henry Clay was directing all his energies toward war, a family living in a log cabin in the Duck River country of Tennessee was reaching an important decision. Their oldest son, Jim, had always been sickly, unable to keep up on long surveying trips or wrestle with other farm boys, and they had recently come to think his weakness had a specific cause: bladder stones. When they heard of a doctor in Danville, Kentucky, who had successfully performed surgery on such cases, they decided to take seventeen-year-old Jim to see him.

Dr. Ephraim McDowell confirmed the diagnosis of stones, and as soon as Jim had rested up from the journey of more than two hundred miles, Dr. McDowell operated. On a Sunday afternoon in a second-floor room of McDowell's frame house, Jim was strapped to a wooden table and given a stiff drink of brandy. McDowell, a florid-faced man with piercing black eyes and a kindly manner, marked the line of incision, and then while Jim was still conscious, he began to cut. Anaesthesia was unknown at the time, as was antisepsis, but the young man somehow came through the operation. In fact, his life was transformed by it, for afterward he was free of the grinding pain that had made him listless and pale. Although he would never be robust, he felt so much better, was so full of energy compared to the way he felt before, that he came to believe he could accomplish anything if only he applied himself with sufficient determination. And he was correct, at least if one judges by the political career he set for himself. He became a member of the Tennessee legislature, a United States congressman, and then rose to the speakership. But that was not the end of it, for he went on to an accomplishment managed by no other Speaker before or since: Jim—or James K. Polk, as history remembers him—became president of the United States.

Many Speakers have wanted to be president, and on the face of it, it seems odd that only one so far should have succeeded. The speakership, after all, is the third highest office in the land, ranking immediately behind the vice-presidency, and fourteen vice-presidents have become president. But if one reflects a moment, it seems clear that for much of our history the speakership and the presidency have required different kinds of political talent. To become Speaker, one had to have the ability to persuade individuals, one-on-one. That is how Speakers are elected and how most of them have succeeded. But presidents must deal with the masses. They must communicate with citizens by the hundreds of thousands, and that is a different art form entirely from the hands-on technique Speakers have traditionally practiced.

And yet James K. Polk did both. He combined these different kinds of political skills and did it so effectively that he would reach the presidency by defeating one of the most naturally gifted politicians the country has ever known—Henry Clay.

What manner of person was it who could accomplish this?

Perhaps first on the list of characteristics distinguishing Polk was an absolutely dogged persistence. He simply refused to quit. After his operation, he convinced his father to send him to school, and though at the outset he was barely able to read and write, he applied himself with such diligence that, within two years, he was accepted by the University of North Carolina as a sophomore. He joined a very active debating society at Chapel Hill, was president of it for two years, and at the same time managed to graduate at the top of his class. Almost as soon as he had delivered the valedictory address in Latin, however, he collapsed, and it was several months before he was able to travel back to his home in Tennessee. The pattern would be repeated several times in his career. It was the obverse side of his extraordinary determination, his strength become a weakness. His will was so strong that at times its demands seemed to overcome his physical self.

Another of his characteristics was astonishingly good judgment. He had the ability to make the right choice at the right time, an asset of incalculable value to a politician. He showed this skill early on, shortly after his college graduation when he was reading law in Nashville with Felix Grundy, Clay's ally in the war cause, now temporarily retired from national politics. On a summer day in 1819, Polk overheard Grundy suggest to Francis Fogg, another lawyer in training with him, that Fogg seek election as clerk of the Tennessee senate. Grundy had recently been elected to the legislature and offered to use his influence to help Fogg attain the post. But Fogg turned him down, feeling that further legal training would be more valuable to him, whereupon Polk volunteered and immediately began seeking additional support from other legislators in his home district. That autumn, he was elected senate clerk, a post that gave a healthy start to his political career. It gave him a chance to meet Tennessee's most influential citizens and brought him together with people who would play crucial roles in the years ahead. Not least of these was a plain, but charming, wealthy, and well-educated young woman who happened to live in Murfreesboro, where the legislature gathered. Her name was Sarah Childress, and she and James Polk were married in 1824.

After clerking a few years, Polk ran successfully for a seat in the legislature. Tennessee politics at the time was a thicket in which more than one political career became hopelessly entangled; but Polk threaded his way through it skillfully, generally choosing to align himself with the reformers. Along with another young legislator named Davy Crockett, Polk carried the banner for the backcountry citizens, for the common folk who had been devastated by the panic of 1819. They were demanding changes in land and banking policies, reforms Polk was soon leading efforts to bring about. On one crucial matter, however, Polk broke with the reform coalition. It had to do with General Andrew Jackson, the hero of the War of 1812.

A group of Tennessee politicians, representatives of land and banking interests, had begun to suspect there might be a certain political capital in Jackson's widespread popularity, and they managed to get the Tennessee legislature of 1823 to nominate him for president. It wasn't that they really thought he could be elected. Rather, they intended by this maneuver to pump the chances of one of their own, an antireform Senate candidate. They were so intent on using Jackson for their own ends, they seem to have had little idea what kind of force they were unleashing. Jackson would ultimately become the archenemy of the interests they represented; he would become the champion of the reform cause, the overwhelmingly popular spokesman of the common man.

But the reformers were equally insensitive to Jackson's potential. They lined up in opposition to him—except for the young representative from Maury County. James Polk supported Jackson from the outset, and as one state political convention after another endorsed Jackson's candidacy, making him one of the chief contenders for the presidency, young Polk's own political position improved. He was a natural to run against Andrew Erwin, the anti-Jackson candidate for the U.S. House of Representatives.

At the outset, he was not an especially imposing candidate. He was slightly built and had an undistinguished face. Commented one contemporary, "He reminded me very much, when I first saw him, of a silversmith in Greenville, South Carolina." Nor did he have a flashing, charismatic personality. He was a cautious and introverted man, not given to revealing emotion—the very opposite, one would think, of the natural politician. But he was as determined in this as he was in all things, and he acquired an impressively upright carriage, which people began to notice more than his small size. In his precise and methodical way, he taught himself to appear relaxed and casual on the stump, and he built up a store of homey anecdotes to make his points. During one campaign, he liked to say that his opponent reminded him of the man captured by a scouting party during the Revolutionary War: when they demanded to know whether he was for king or for country, the captive replied, "You say first, for you are the most." He became skilled at delivering punch lines with a knowing glance of the cool gray eyes, at letting the joke settle on the crowd while a sly smile played on his thin lips. And if he could never be a hail-fellow-well-met, at least he could be sure to remember names. Once he went out of his way to show that he knew a man he had met only briefly in a crowd—ten years before.

He also exhibited astonishing energy. For nearly six months, he crisscrossed Maury County, rushing from one meeting to another, virtually living on horseback. As an acquaintance remembered it, "He dashed from point to point over his district with a rapidity which struck his opponents with surprise and paralyzed them with despair."

His campaign was also aided by the results of the 1824 presidential election. Jackson received the most votes, but not a majority in the electoral college, and so the election was thrown into the House of Representatives. Henry Clay, who had finished just out of the running, said he could not believe that "killing two thousand five hundred Englishmen at New Orleans" qualified a man for the presidency, and he began to lobby actively for John Quincy Adams. When Adams was subsequently elected by the House, he appointed Clay secretary of the state, a position widely perceived to put Clay next in line for the presidency. There were howls of outrage, charges that a corrupt bargain had been made. "The passions of men were running mountain high," as Martin Van Buren remembered it, and nowhere was there more indignation than in Jackson's home state of Tennessee. Polk profited, not only because he was a Jackson man, but because his chief opponent had the misfortune to be related to Clay through marriage. His son had wed Clay's favorite daughter, Anne, a fact greatly to the opponent's disadvantage at a time when the kindest thing anyone in Tennessee could say about Clay was that he had betrayed his fellow westerners. Polk carried the district handily.

As a new congressman, he first addressed the House in a speech advocating that the electoral college be abolished and the president chosen by direct vote. Standing in the high-domed, semicircular Congress Hall, its refurbishing only recently completed after the destruction the British had wrought in 1814, he declared what he believed to be the nation's vital principle: *That this is a government based upon the will of the People; that all power emanates from them; and that a majority should rule.* His proposal to abolish the electoral college did not get far. The House was controlled by administration forces, who rightly regarded it as a slap at the way Adams had come to power. But the speech brought Polk notice from someone else who placed great faith in the people. Andrew Jackson wrote to congratulate the young congressman.

Polk became involved in the efforts of Jackson's supporters to make sure their man would be elected in 1828. It was a long campaign, stretching over four years, and it ended in an overwhelming victory for Jackson. Almost immediately, however, another bitter contest ensued, this one within the ranks of Jackson's adherents. It began with a woman, Peggy Eaton, and would end up not only wrecking Jackson's cabinet, but helping determine the next president. "The Eaton imbroglio," wrote Martin Van Buren, who ended up in the middle of it, ". . . 'tho in no proper sense political, exerted perhaps a more injurious influence upon the management of public affairs than could be ascribed to any of the disturbing questions of [this] excited period." For a time, it turned Washington into a war zone where alliances were shattered and careers blasted.

Daughter of an Irishman who owned one of the boardinghouses in which congressmen usually stayed, the pretty, vivacious Peggy was married to a naval purser named Timberlake. While her husband was off at sea, she stayed with her father, and during one of these periods, her relationship with Senator John Eaton, one of her father's boarders and a longtime friend and supporter of Jackson's, became much talked about. When Timberlake killed himself and Eaton subsequently announced his intention to marry the widow, the gossip escalated—or perhaps *descended* is a better word for it— several levels. To Martin Van Buren, Jackson's choice for secretary of state, a member of Congress wrote, "There is a vulgar saying of some vulgar man, I believe Swift, on such unions—about using a certain household [receptacle] . . . and then putting it on one's head."

But while the gentlemen of Washington might snicker, the ladies were outraged, particularly after Jackson appointed Eaton secretary of war. "A stand, a *noble* stand, I may say . . . has been made by the ladies of Washington," a female observer wrote, "and not even the President's wishes, in favour of his dearest friend, can influence them to violate the respect due to virtue, by visiting one, who has left her strait and narrow path." The women refused to call on Mrs. Eaton. They ignored her if they were at the same gathering, protested if they were placed next to her at dinner. Sarah Polk, who had quickly become a social leader, was as adamant as any of them. Observed one of her husband's colleagues, she "would sooner suffer Randolphs Black John to set at table with her than be [on] any familiarity with a Lady whose only fault is that the Secretary has made her honest—instead of finding her ready made."

Jackson was furious. His beloved wife, Rachel, had died just before his inauguration, and he blamed her death on those who had assaulted her reputation by claiming that she and the general had had an adulterous relationship. He saw similarities to the Eaton case, vowed to restore Mrs. Eaton's reputation, and promptly made matters worse. A cabinet meeting he held, which was in effect a hearing on Mrs. Eaton's chastity, left his cabinet members disgusted. He ordered Mrs. Donelson, the wife of his nephew and his official White House hostess, to visit Mrs. Eaton, and when she refused, gave her the choice of either complying or leaving the White House. She and her husband, the president's private secretary, went home to Tennessee.

Outraged and helpless, Jackson soon concluded that the entire event must have been orchestrated by his archenemy, Henry Clay. And then his suspicions shifted to his vice-president, John C. Calhoun, with whom he was already at loggerheads on a number of issues. Wasn't Mrs. Calhoun in the forefront of the movement to snub Mrs. Eaton? Up to this time, Calhoun was considered Jackson's natural successor; but the calm and smiling Van Buren, who happened to be a widower, was able to entertain the Eatons graciously in his home, and soon he had become Jackson's heir apparent.

Congressman Polk might also have found himself displaced in Jackson's favor, but he managed the hazards of Washington society with the same cool competence he had shown in Tennessee politics. He wisely declined to participate in efforts to drive Eaton from his cabinet and just as wisely refrained from discussing the matter in writing. While he could not expect a wife as properly upright as Sarah to waver in her stand on Mrs. Eaton, he seems to have decided—or perhaps they decided together—that she did not need to continue proving her virtue. In 1830, instead of going to Washington with him as she usually did, Sarah stayed at home in Tennessee. An astute politician herself, she apparently didn't mind removing herself as a source of irritation to the president, and she joked with friends about the money she would save by staying in Columbia for a time.

Thus, when the dust from the Eaton affair had settled, Polk's reputation with the president was undamaged. He was seen as a faithful adherent of Jackson's policies, and he found that role generally easy to play, because on most points he shared Jackson's views. But even when it was painful, he supported the president. When the legislature of South Carolina, following John C. Calhoun, approved the doctrine of nullification (which held that a state might in its own vital interest choose to ignore a federal edict), Jackson demanded a bill that would allow him to use force to enact the law. Polk, a southerner and a states rights man, voted for the Force Bill, but his discomfort was so obvious that it was a source of amusement to John Quincy Adams. The former president, who was now a member of the House, couldn't resist sending along for Polk's notice a particularly bitter southern attack on Jackson's policy.

After Jackson was reelected overwhelmingly in 1832, Polk was moved to a seat on the Ways and Means Committee. Jackson had by now molded a political organization strong enough to reach from the executive into the legislative branch, and there was no question about the direction in which authority flowed through it. The president's power was strengthened by the fact that he did not owe his office to the Congress as his predecessors had: the congressional caucus as a nominating device had been replaced by a convention system. Thus, although Speaker Andrew Stevenson made the appointment of Polk to Ways and Means, he no doubt did so in the full knowledge it was Jackson's wish. The president needed Congressman Polk's judgment and dependability; moreover, Polk was firmly on record as being opposed to the National Bank, and nothing was more important to the president than destroying the bank. He looked on it as a monster that was draining the lifeblood of the masses for the benefit of a privileged few, and he regarded its president, the brilliant Nicholas Biddle, as the devil incarnate. For their part, the banking forces had a scarcely more charitable view of Jackson. To them he was an uncivilized animal whose victory would see economic anarchy loosed in the land.

So far the battle had been a draw. Jackson had opposed rechartering the bank when Biddle proposed it, but Congress had voted to renew the charter. Jackson had used his veto, but Biddle was undeterred. The charter he currently held still had four years to run, and Biddle, never short on self-confidence, was certain he could change government policy. "The Bank . . . does not mean to begin to close its concerns," he announced. "It means to go on in its general business just as if no such event as the President's negative had ever happened." Jackson received intelligence of Biddle's intention to seek an override of his veto and wrote to Polk, "The hydra of corruption is *scotched not dead.*" He suggested the way to kill the monster was with a congressional investigation. "Let this be had," he wrote. The investigation was pushed forward, Congressman Polk aggressively questioned the witnesses, and although the majority of the committee found the bank's practices sound, Polk supplied an exquisitely detailed minority report on the bank's transgressions. It was exactly the ammunition Jackson needed, and at the next Congress, Polk was moved from last place on the committee to the chairmanship.

Jackson announced his intention to remove federal deposits from the bank, and when he acted, Chairman Polk was among those at the center of the storm. Biddle forced a severe contraction of credit to put pressure on Congress, and members were deluged with distress petitions, all of which were sent on to Chairman Polk. Like other members of Congress, he had to make his way each morning through delegations of citizens camped out in the halls of the Capitol. They blamed the financial disasters that had overtaken them on Jackson's bank policy, and one can easily imagine how they reacted to the sight of the Ways and Means Committee chairman. Meanwhile, Polk was working on the speech that would become the administration's justification for the president's action. The bank, he declared on the floor of the House, was a "great irresponsible rival power of the Government," and the issue at hand was "whether we shall have the republic without the bank, or the bank without the republic." Simultaneously, Polk was keeping a close monitor on the House so that votes would come at advantageous times, and it was his responsibility to bring party pressure to bear on wavering members. Ultimately the president triumphed, his victory in large part due to his Ways and Means Committee chairman.

At the same time Polk was managing the bank matter, he was also waging a campaign to become House Speaker, an unsuccessful campaign as it turned out, but one that taught him a valuable lesson. Different political goals, pursued simultaneously, he discovered, may become mutually exclusive. The steps he took to insure Jackson's victory got in the way of his own efforts. There were members of Jackson's own party who worried about the president's obsession with destroying the bank, and they were hesitant to support for Speaker the man who was heading up the assault forces. The Nullifiers, united behind Calhoun, also had their doubts. Polk tried to convince them he was not necessarily committed to Martin Van Buren succeeding Jackson in the presidency, but the Nullifiers went with the public evidence, which argued that Polk wanted what

Jackson wanted, and they voted for Polk's opponent. These votes, added to those of the Whigs, who delighted in doing anything they thought contrary to Jackson's wishes, were enough to elect John Bell as Speaker. Although Bell, like Polk, was a Democrat from Tennessee, Jackson was deeply disappointed at the outcome. He had been counting on Polk's victory. He had even sent a carriage to bring Polk to the White House to celebrate, and when the coachman returned alone with word Polk had lost, the president was in foul humor for days.

At the end of this session of Congress, Polk collapsed. "The labours you have passed through this session are enough to break down a man of iron," Roger Taney wrote to him. Polk recovered, but didn't change his ways. Soon he was working as hard as ever, all his energies focused on the speakership. He and his allies set out to read John Bell out of the Democratic party. Hadn't Bell been elected with Whig votes, after all? And where did he stand on the bank question? In pieces planted in newspapers and in public speeches, they hammered away on these points until they seem to have convinced almost everyone, including Bell himself, that he really belonged with the Whigs. The next time there was a vote on the speakership, the Democrats all stood with Polk, and he defeated Bell convincingly.

The House Polk presided over was in many ways like the House in which Henry Clay had been elected Speaker. The conduct of its affairs seemed as informal as ever. "The members wear their hats, and talk and buzz while business is going on so that much of the time it sounds like a town meeting," a new congressman observed. Perhaps it was a little harder to hear whomever had the floor than it had been when Clay was elected. A new chamber had been built after the British burned the Capitol in 1814, and the semicircular domed ceiling which Benjamin Latrobe had designed was acoustically dreadful, though so lovely to behold, members hadn't the heart to lower it. Washington City, where members spent from three to seven months a year, depending upon whether Congress was in a short session or a long one, continued to amaze those who expected something grander. Observed Harriet Martineau in 1835, "The city itself is unlike any other that ever was seen, struggling out hither and thither, with a small house or two a quarter of a mile away from any other; so that in making calls 'in the city' we had to cross ditches and stiles, and walk alternately on grass and pavements, and strike across a field to reach a street."

But there was an important change since Clay's time as Speaker, and it had to do with the two strong political parties that had formed. Andrew Jackson's friends called themselves Democrats; his enemies, Whigs, and they faced off against each other with all the ardor his controversial personality and policies inspired. Although the House had never been a placid institution, now the violence increased. It was as though the Republic were still in its adolescence when it came to handling partisan emotions, and opposing members of the House of Representatives offered personal insults to one another, even came to blows. Two members engaged in a duel with rifles and kept firing until one of them lay dead.

As Jackson's man, managing the speakership to achieve the president's goals, Polk became a target for all those who despised the president. Almost as soon as he took the chair, John Bell and a few of his Whig colleagues, most notably Henry Wise of Virginia and Bailie Peyton of Tennessee, began a campaign of harrassment against him. They called points of order arbitrarily, appealed his decisions and personally insulted him. Wise, a tall, extremely thin man with a complexion yellowed from too much tobacco, liked to accuse Polk of being an administration tool. He took advantage of a resolution offered by John Quincy Adams to charge the Speaker with participating in a nefarious conspiracy with the president. He had witnesses, he claimed, to prove that during the last session the Speaker had told two members that the president favored a certain bill. "Mr. Speaker," he declared. "I charge you with that fact. You may deny it in your place or not."

Wise went on and on in this vein until finally Polk requested permission to speak from the chair. If members asked, he said, he might well have told them how the president regarded a bill; however, he "would respectfully remark, that he was really unable to conceive how this could be a matter of any sort of importance."

But it was no good arguing with Wise. No matter how calm and reasoned one's reply, Wise could find a way to use it to continue his assault—which in this instance depended almost entirely on insinuation. "Great God, sir," he shot back at Polk, "and this not a matter of importance!" Polk's friends began to worry that he might himself finally be driven to a less than rational response. "*Moral courage* is the highest virtue," his brother-in-law and confidant James Walker wrote to him. "You cannot settle the matter by a personal encounter without degradation, and duelling is clearly a violation of the laws of God and man. . . ."

It soon became clear that Wise's aim was, in fact, to draw Polk into a duel. On a day when the Speaker had to call him to order a number of times for intemperate remarks, Wise waited for Polk at the door when the House adjourned. "Sir, you talked in a damned arbitrary manner to me today," he said, pointing his finger. When Polk tried to pass on without answering, Wise called him a "petty tyrant," and added, "I intend this as a personal insult, and you may pocket it or act in any other way you please!"

In the parlance of southern manhood, this was a clear challenge, but Polk would not let himself be drawn in, not even when a newspaper in his home state suggested his reticence came from knowing Wise was a "dead shot." He continued to preside over the House dispassionately, impersonally—but that did not keep him from being partisan. He used his power of appointment to favor the Democrats, making sure their numbers prevailed on important committees. And to them went the chairmanships, with a few important exceptions. As previous Speakers had done, Polk recognized the special qualifications of John Quincy Adams by making him a chairman, and he appointed his rival Bell to the head of the Committee on Indian Affairs. The Democrats thought these appointments overgenerous, and the Whigs considered them insufficient— which may be the best evidence that Polk had acted as evenhandedly as a partisan Speaker could.

Bell and his allies complained that the Democrats, under Polk's leadership, acted in concert to keep him from giving certain speeches he had prepared on issues harmful to the Jackson administration. They also said that Polk abused the Speaker's power of recognition by refusing to see Bell when he rose to address the House. "He looked over his head or through his body. . . ," they claimed. Doubtless there was some of this, but evidently not so much as Polk's adversaries maintained, since a naval appropriations bill found Bell on the floor delivering a speech that lasted four days. Another appropriations measure gave him the chance to say that he, for one, would certainly not suggest that President Jackson was a "tyrant, a usurper, a crouching sycophant, or a degraded slave," and to add, no doubt with a meaningful glance in the direction of the Speaker's chair, that the president might, nonetheless, "be the master of *slaves* and *menials*." A Boston newspaper editor considered such goings-on and concluded, "Never was man more rigidly and constantly assailed by a pack of untiring pursuers than was Mr. Speaker Polk by his uncompromising assailants."

As if emotions were not running high enough, the Twenty-fourth Congress saw the beginning of a bitter struggle between northern abolitionists and southern radicals. The abolitionists petitioned the Congress to end slavery in the District of Columbia (over which Congress had full power). Southern extremists demanded that Congress not even receive petitions on slavery since doing so would imply purview where there was none. Northern and southern moderates, who formed a majority in the House, believed that continued debate on the subject would inflame the country and threaten the union, and they united behind a measure presented by Henry Pinckney of South Carolina. It provided for the House to receive slavery petitions, but then table them for no further action.

Polk, who was a slaveholder, personally favored this measure, but John Quincy Adams was outraged by it. He was not an abolitionist, but he held slavery to be a great evil, and he felt the Pinckney resolutions violated the right to petition set forth in the Constitution. He rose to voice his objections, but Polk recognized another member who moved the previous question. Adams attempted to speak anyway, and Polk reminded him that a motion for the previous question is not debatable. A parliamentary wrangle followed, with Adams appealing on the grounds that "there is a slaveholder in the chair," and Polk declaring Adams's appeal to be nondebatable. Adams was becoming more and more upset. The top of his bald head was turning red with anger. Finally he shouted, "Am I gagged or not!" It was a unique moment with the only man ever to serve in the House after he had been president challenging the only Speaker who would ever become president. Polk won this particular skirmish when he was sustained by the House, but the battle would continue throughout his speakership, and after he had left Adams would finally triumph.

Polk's enemies abused his reputation and impugned his motives for the way he handled the petition matter, but the record shows him being logical and fair. Had he denied the petition forces all opportunity to present their case, the House would probably have supported him and the southern Democrats would have been immensely comforted. Instead, when the next session convened, he ruled that the Pinckney resolutions had expired. The "gag rule," as it was known by now, would have to be passed again—and debated again. And while it soon became a certainty that Adams would violate the rules of the House whenever the petition matter came up, Polk never cut him off until the ex-president had actually stepped over the line—which usually meant that Adams got to make his point. On January 9, 1837, a Monday and a traditional petition day, Adams rose to present a petition from South Weymouth, Massachusetts. An objection was voiced immediately, but Adams started to read the petition anyway.

"Impressed with 'the sinfulness of slavery, and keenly aggrieved by its existence in a part of our country over which Congress—' "

"Has the gentleman from Massachusetts a right, under the rule, to read the petition?" Henry Pinckney interrupted.

"The gentleman from Massachusetts has a right to make a statement of the contents of the petition," the Speaker said.

"It is a privilege which I shall exercise till I be deprived of it by some positive act," Adams declared.

"You have a right to make a brief statement of the contents of the petition," Polk said, and when Adams started to comment on "my friends from South Carolina," Polk made the point again that he must proceed to the contents of the petition.

"I am doing so, sir," said Adams.

"Not in the opinion of the chair," said Polk.

"I was at this point of the petition," said Adams, and he began to read: " 'Keenly aggrieved by its existence in a part of our country over which Congress possesses exclusive jurisdiction in all cases whatever—' "

There were loud cries of "Order! Order!" but Polk did not intervene.

Adams proceeded: " 'Do most earnestly petition your honorable body—' "

Now Chambers of Kentucky was on his feet calling for order. But still Polk did not intervene.

Adams went on: " 'Immediately to abolish slavery in the District of Columbia—' "

"Order! Order!" Chambers was calling, and now that the point of the petition was on record, the Speaker took action, ordering Adams to his seat.

The ex-president ignored him. "And to declare every human being free who sets foot upon its soil!" he shouted. And only then, having said what he wanted, did he yield.

The scene was repeated time and again, with Adams continuing to defy the gag rule and Polk trying to deal with him fairly. Polk seems also to have tried hard to be impartial with those at the other end of the spectrum, such as Wise and Peyton. The one instance in the First Session of the Twenty-fourth Congress when the House overturned his decision occurred when he ruled in favor of a motion made by Henry Wise on the petition issue. Wise no doubt helped convince the members to override the Speaker by using the opening, as one member described it, to get "on his tall horse and [ride] off, splashing mud all over the House."

Polk's restrained and undramatic personality enabled him to retain a certain distance from the conflict. He wrote to his brother-in-law: "It is amusing to witness the operation and see how they play into each other's hands. An opposition man from the North presents a petition, whereupon a nullifier . . . from the South, springs upon it, and makes an inflammatory speech, into which he incorporates the most inflammatory portion of the abolition publications of Tappan, Garrison and company, and these he distributes under his frank and yet cries out lustily against the dissemination of incendiary publications." It was just as well Polk was able to see a certain dark humor in the situation, because in the next Congress, the Twenty-fifth, matters grew worse. Shortly after Martin Van Buren was elected president, a financial panic struck. Administration enemies, who claimed the country was reaping what Jackson had sowed, found the House of Representatives an effective forum in which to level their charges and the Speaker a natural target for their fury. The petition controversy also broke out again, with John Quincy Adams continuing to defy the gag rule and beginning to agitate on the related matter of Texas. It was a slave state, and the old man from Massachusetts was unalterably opposed to its admission into the union.

How high the emotional tide was running can be seen from an incident that happened in June 1838. A new congressman from Tennessee, Hopkins Turney, exchanged some angry words on the floor with Polk's rival, John Bell. Bell accused Turney of acting as an agent for Polk, of being "the voluntary scavenger of all filth raked up by others . . . the tool of tools." Turney advanced on Bell, crying, "It is false! It is false!" Bell struck him, the two fell upon one another, and the House dissolved in an uproar. Polk, who had been out of the Speaker's chair, rushed back to it, and with strenuous efforts brought the House back to order. John Fairfield, a young Maine congressman, thought the whole thing "a disgraceful scene," which "will go far to destroy the dignity and character of Congress in the eyes of the Nation and the world"; but John Quincy Adams found it as exhilarating as "a bumper of pure whiskey"; and one of Polk's old foes, Bailie Peyton, thought there might be some use made of the event: maybe this would finally be the way to get the Speaker to duel. He wrote Henry Wise that Bell ought to "pull Polk's nose . . . and say . . . this is for setting on me that infamous scoundrel Hop. Turney. . . ."

Polk was not lured to the dueling grounds, but two freshman Congressmen were. It was during the Twenty-fifth Congress that Maine Democrat Jonathan Cilley and Kentucky Whig William Graves fired at one another with rifles until Cilley, the father of three young children, lay dead on a field at Bladensberg. The brutal incident led Congress to pass antidueling legislation, and that in turn led Henry Wise, who had been Graves's second and urged him on, to bemoan how unchivalrous the House of Representatives had become. Members could call one another cowards and liars now, he complained, "and, Sir, there the matter will drop. *There will be no fight.*"

Polk's job was made even more difficult because the Whigs had increased their numbers and were sometimes able to attract enough Democratic votes to defeat him. The deepening troubles of Martin Van Buren's presidency no doubt encouraged these Democrats to demonstrate their independence, and when the Whigs moved to elect a committee to investigate a sensational embezzlement in the New York custom house rather than to allow the Speaker to appoint the investigative committee, members of Polk's own party voted against him.

And so while he continued to preside with calm and dignity, behind his impassive face with its broad forehead he was making a hard decision. Should he leave the House and run for governor of

Tennessee? It would be a chancy undertaking since the Whigs were in control of Tennessee, but the potential for gain was great. If he could return the state to the Democrats, he could legitimately aspire to the vice-presidency in 1840, and then perhaps to the presidency itself. On the other side of the ledger, his congressional seat was safe, even if the speakership wasn't necessarily, and he might well be elected Speaker again, which certainly had its attractive aspects. He and Sarah ranked near the top of Washington society. They had rooms and a carriage to befit their station. James had his own private office in a corner of the Capitol as well as a personal porter. But given his ambition—and it was considerable—the Speaker's chair must have looked an increasingly dangerous place to be, positioning him where he might at any moment do damage to his long-term aspirations. If ever there were a case where different political goals might come into conflict, this seemed to be it. Every ruling he made as Speaker was potential ammunition for his opponents if he ran for higher office. Hadn't Jackson himself, when he was running for president, resigned from the Senate rather than risk that his duties there force him to make decisions that would prove embarrassing in a national campaign? And Jackson hadn't been surrounded by enemies anxious to lure him into a misstep.

In September 1838 Polk announced he would be a candidate for governor of Tennessee and began campaigning with his usual fervor. After only a week, his health gave way, but as soon as he was on his feet again, he was off on another campaign swing. Over the next months he kept to a killing schedule, crisscrossing the Cumberland plateau, meeting with supporters in East Tennessee, swinging through the Western District, speaking in the rain in Nashville. In August 1838 he was elected, but his victory brought little chance to rest, for more than he wanted to be governor, he wanted to be vice-president.

Almost all the Democratic politicians agreed that Van Buren's current vice-president, Richard Mentor Johnson of Kentucky, was impossible. A burly, sweet-natured man, he had an engaging personality and a reputation as a war hero, having supposedly killed Tecumseh in the War of 1812. But he was eccentric in dress ("There is no telling how he might look if dressed like other people," Harriet Martineau observed) and indiscreet in his personal life. His two daughters, whom he openly acknowledged, had been born to his mulatto housekeeper, and since her death, so the rumors went, he had been consorting with other black women in his household. The Whigs took gleeful delight in "Dickie" Johnson's situation. On the floor of the House, William Halstead of New Jersey delivered a speech full of complicated puns about Democrats turning *"dandies."* These "dandies had a great liking for *dickies,"* Halstead said, and *"dickies* had a close affinity to *darkies."*

Polk's victory in Tennessee increased his chances of replacing Johnson on the ticket. "Your pretensions are put on stilts after this success. . . ," a friend wrote him. His allies accelerated a letter-writing campaign that had been going on for months. Democratic newspapers came out with endorsements, public meetings called for his nomination, and only two months after he became governor, the Tennessee legislature passed resolutions proposing him as Van Buren's running mate.

But his candidacy was derailed when the Whigs nominated William Henry Harrison for president. How better to counteract a Whig ticket with a war hero on it than by having a war hero like Johnson on the Democratic ticket? There were those in the party, however, who simply couldn't abide the idea of Johnson, even if he had killed Tecumseh, and suggestions began to be made that instead of nominating a vice-president, the Democrats let different candidates run in different sections of the country where they were strong. The matter could then be settled in the electoral college, or in the Senate if no one received a majority. Polk wanted no part of such a maneuver and withdrew from the race. Perhaps he had sensed that a party unable to agree on a vice-presidential candidate had little chance of winning a national election. If so, he was right, for Van Buren went down to a humiliating defeat in 1840.

Tennessee had been as enchanted by Harrison's log cabin and hard cider campaign as the rest of the country and had voted overwhelmingly Whig. Thus Polk's reelection for governor promised to be difficult, and when the campaign skills of the Whig nominee became apparent, it began to look impossible. George C. Jones was a spindly six-foot farmer with a winning manner and a droll sense of humor. Although Polk was far more experienced, whenever he tried to make that point, Jones managed to turn it against him. During one debate, Jones listened while Polk detailed his record, which stretched over two decades by now, and when Polk had finished,

Jones unfolded his long legs, looked over the audience and declared, "Why, boys, at this rate it never will be your turn. You will never get to be constables even!"

Polk lost to Jones, but he was determined the defeat would be only a temporary setback. He set out immediately to strengthen Tennessee's Democratic party, and soon it was apparent he meant to run against Jones again in 1843. Recapturing the governorship would once more catapult him into consideration for national office, "lead on certainly to your election to the Presidency," one friend told him.

But Polk lost to Jones again, and it was now that his dogged persistence could be seen in its purest form. Almost anyone else would have decided that his political career was over. Polk decided he could still be president.

He began by campaigning for the vice-presidency once more. Losses aside, he had many assets, not the least of which was being acceptable to both the northern and southern wings of the Democratic party, and he carefully tended his relationships with both groups. When it began to look as if Van Buren would be the nominee, Polk and his friends made sure he understood the advantages of having Polk on the ticket. "Polk . . . will give you more strength than any other man. . . ," Andrew Jackson wrote to Van Buren in a shaky scrawl. "I think Gov. Polk will be your vice president—if so you will be elected by a larger majority than was ever before given to a President."

But Polk had rivals for the vice-presidency, such as the gentle, fastidious senator from Alabama, Rufus King. Despite the fact that King's enemies called him "Aunt Fancy" and gossiped maliciously about his relationship with another Senate bachelor, James Buchanan, King for a time looked as though he might capture the nomination. Then the resilient Richard Mentor Johnson surged to the fore. Still wearing red waistcoats, still amazingly popular among common folk outside the South, Johnson seemed to have convinced the Van Buren forces he would be the best vice-presidential nominee.

But even when Polk's friends suggested to him his cause was hopeless, he refused to give up. He insisted that whatever the circumstances, his name be presented to the convention in Baltimore. Polk's biographer, Charles Sellers, suggests that more than a persistent pursuit of the vice-presidency may have been at work here, that Polk may have wanted his name kept to the fore because he sensed that Van Buren's hold on the presidential nomination was slipping. Polk's friend Cave Johnson had written him that forces hostile to Van Buren intended to bring up a matter sure to operate against the New Yorker in the convention. It was the question of annexing Texas, and Polk, astute as he was politically, may well have seen how that emotionally charged issue could throw all assumptions about 1844 into disarray.

Van Buren came out against annexation, a position that his anti-slavery friends in the Northeast highly approved, since they didn't want another slave state in the union. But Van Buren's stand also united his opponents, particularly those in the South, and alienated supporters who saw Texas as a part of the nation's manifest destiny. Polk, when he was asked, promptly declared himself to be *for* annexation and, just as important, *for* Van Buren for president.

Thus he was perfectly positioned for the Baltimore convention. Once Van Buren's opponents managed to get a rule adopted that required a two-thirds majority for nomination, the New Yorker's way was blocked. After the first ballot, which gave him a majority but was thirty-one votes short of two-thirds, his strength declined steadily. It began to look as if the nomination would go to Michigan's Lewis Cass, but Cass had opposed Van Buren in the months before the convention and sought the nomination for himself. Thus the Van Buren forces considered him a traitor, and they began to rally behind Polk, who had remained faithful. On the ninth ballot, amid frenzied cheering, he was nominated for the presidency. "The [convention] is shouting," an excited friend wrote to him. "The people in the streets are shouting ... and I can't write any more for shouting."

Five days before Polk was nominated, Samuel F. B. Morse had inaugurated his new electric telegraph. The line ran between Baltimore and Washington, and at the Washington end, Morse had set up in the Supreme Court chamber in the Capitol. Congressmen gathered for word from the convention, and soon they were shouting too. The news that came over the wire brought joy to most southern Democrats, a somewhat more restrained cheer to Democrats from the North, and to the Whigs, cause for catcalls. "James K. Polk, candidate for President!" the party's official newspaper exclaimed. "When will wonders cease?" Soon Tom Corwin, a portly, witty congressman from Ohio, was regaling audiences by asking, "And *who* have they nominated? James K. Polk of Tennessee?" Then he would pause, glance about the crowd, and exclaim with mock horror, "*After that*, who is safe?" It wasn't long before a derisive refrain was echoing across the country: "Who *is* James K. Polk?" The Whigs knew who he was, of course, but they seized upon the dark-horse aspect of his candidacy to make it appear that the Democrats had nominated an unknown mediocrity to run against their great man, Henry Clay.

In the contest that followed, both Clay and Polk proved exactly who they were. Clay, a man of fire and wit, was exceedingly gifted at creating consensus within small groups. As Abraham Lincoln described his method, he habitually framed a proposal in language unlikely to offend those whose support he needed, then presented it "to the strong men whose help he must have or whose opposition he must stifle, and who were of strong wills, and either argued them into support or made modifications as they insisted on, or added palatable features to suit them, and thus got a powerful force enlisted in behalf of his measure;—then he visited the members of feeble wills and simply bullied them into its support without yielding one iota to them." Novelist William Gilmore Simms, describing Clay in action, told of him entering a caucus where most were opposed to his viewpoint: he "passed down its lines, speaking as he went, in triumphant manner, with bold fearless eloquence, breast open, and, at length, confronting Webster, he seemed to concentrate the whole weight of what he had to say upon him. And so powerful was his eloquence, so keen his shafts, so personal their aim, that Webster actually crouched under him, and slid down in his seat, so that his head was almost on a level with his belly. And Clay triumphed. There were but *two* after he was done, who voted in opposition to the measure."

Clay was so good at this kind of politicking that it was never necessary for him to learn any other, and he fell into it instinctively. Polk, an introvert who had to teach himself to be a politician, was able to approach a campaign more analytically, appraising the situation with a cold eye, deciding what action was necessary, and carrying it out. What success required in the campaign of 1844, he perceived, was not dealing with men in small groups, emphasizing this in one place or that in another, according to what the listeners wanted to hear. That might work in a caucus, but it would only confuse a nation, and so Polk issued carefully crafted statements on the day's important questions and then declined to comment further. Once he had taken a stand, such as favoring the annexation of Texas, he simply didn't waver.

Clay kept writing letters, particularly about Texas. First he wrote he was opposed to annexation; then that he wasn't personally against annexation, but feared it to be an issue that threatened the union; then that he would be happy to see Texas annexed if it could be managed "without national dishonor, without war, with the general consent of the States of the Union, and upon reasonable terms." No sooner would he appease one group, however, than another would become angered, and soon he had earned himself a reputation for equivocation. A Missouri editor composed a bit of doggerel about him:

> *He wires in and wires out,*
> *And leaves the people still in doubt,*
> *Whether the snake that made the track*
> *Was going South or coming back.*

In New York, antislavery voters who had rallied behind him when they thought him firmly opposed to annexing Texas became alarmed and started to drift toward a third-party abolitionist candidate. It was enough to swing the state—and the election.

Other factors entered into the outcome, of course, but the Texas question illustrates best why Polk beat Clay. And perhaps it also shows why Polk was able to make the transition, which history has shown to be so difficult, from the speakership to the presidency. Although Polk had spent many years in a legislative body, he was a superb enough strategist to know that pursuing the presidency requires its own kind of political behavior, and he was also a self-conscious enough politician to be able to shift from one mode to another.

Polk became president at forty-nine, an earlier age than anyone before him. He proved to be as good a chief executive as he had been a candidate and is today considered to have been one of our strongest presidents. He set himself a limited number of goals, which included acquiring California, as well as Texas, and settling the matter of Oregon. He worked with typical perseverance to achieve these aims, leaving Washington only twice in the first eighteen months he was in office, and then but for one day. He insisted on mastering the detail of government, and although this knowledge put him firmly in control, acquiring it left little time for relaxation. Halfway through his term, he wrote in his diary, "Though I occupy a very high position, I am the hardest working man in this country."

His presidency saw the country acquire vast new territory, 850,000 square miles, almost as much as had been in the Louisiana purchase. Having accomplished what he set out to, Polk remained firmly committed to a pledge to serve but a single term, and on March 5, 1849, his presidency completed, he set out for Tennessee on a journey he had made many times. This time, however, the strain of travel, added to the stress of the last four years, was more than his body could endure. He sickened, seemed to rally, then sickened again. On June 15, 1849, in his fifty-fourth year, he died. "He knew what he wanted," Arthur Schlesinger, Jr., has observed, "and got it, but it killed him."

William Marcy, who had been Polk's secretary of war, was shocked and saddened at the news of Polk's death. Grieving, he sat down with his diary and made a short entry. "What shadows we are," he wrote. "What shadows we pursue."

3

OLD THAD STEVENS

In the nineteenth century, the House was dominated by young men. Clay was elected Speaker at thirty-four, Polk at thirty-nine, and every Speaker between them was under forty when he began serving. One reason for this youthful dominance was that seniority was not thought important. Turnover in the House was high, with the average term of service at mid-century of four years. There was a philosophical basis for the rotation of House seats—the Jacksonian idea that democracy was better served by frequent change in public officials—but there was a pragmatic reason too. The rigors of congressional life were such that a man risked his health by long service. Simply getting to and from Washington could be a grueling ordeal. "I was for two days and a half drenched with rain," John Randolph of Roanoke reported, "forced to sleep in hovels and litter with beasts in the shape of men, under a burning fever all the while." The roads were bad and bridges rare so that streams had to be forded even in the coldest weather. James and Sarah Polk, neither of whom could swim, nearly drowned on one trip home to Tennessee when a stream they were crossing suddenly flooded and water began to fill their carriage.

Nor was life in the capital especially conducive to good health. Malaria was common in certain places along the Potomac. The "Tiber" canal, which cut through the city, was full of raw sewage. Water supplies in hotels and boardinghouses were often contaminated so that dysentery was common. Even the House chamber wasn't a terribly healthy place. The roof leaked badly so the floor was often damp, and the hot-air furnaces gave off so much heat that "the effect produced by them," in the words of one representative, "is that upon an oyster baked in a Dutch oven." Small wonder that much "switchell"—a rum drink—was consumed while the House was in session. And small wonder that so many people were sick so much of the time: William Lowndes with "constiveness" (constipation), Clay with bronchial problems, Polk with diarrhea, John Randolph of Roanoke with everything. During one call of the House in the Thirty-eighth Congress, so many were reported sick that someone proposed a sanitary commission. Someone else suggested moving the capital to a healthier spot. John Fairfield, a congressman from Maine, went to two funerals for members during the first two weeks he was in Washington; he himself died years later when a Washington physician decided to cure his leg trouble by injecting vitriol into the knee joint. As late as 1889 it was considered a death sentence for Speaker Samuel Randall, who was ill, to have to spend the summer in Washington's hot, humid climate.

Thus youth was important simply for its resilience, and when it came to picking someone to fill what James G. Blaine called "the arduous duties of the chair," representatives in the nineteenth-century Congress turned to the younger members among them. There were, however, two members of advanced years, who, though not Speakers, managed to impose their wills on the House. One was the rigorously moral, often self-righteous John Quincy Adams, who after he had served one term as president, entered the House at age sixty-three, began the petition fight with Polk at sixty-nine, and finally got the gag rule overturned in 1844, when he was seventy-seven. The other patriarch was Thaddeus Stevens, a grim and tough-willed man, who first entered the United States Congress at age fifty-seven. He served two terms without much distinction, but later, as the country was plunging into civil war, he returned to the House, this time at age sixty-seven. Over the next eight years, he led the fight both for equality for former slaves and for harsh punishment for leaders of the Confederacy, leaving behind a record that confounds with its mixture of altruism and vengefulness. And the power he gathered unto himself in the course of his struggles is equally discomforting, for it permitted him to bring against the presidency a challenge that came very close to altering our form of government.

* * *

A crusade in which Adams became involved while he was president first brought Thaddeus Stevens into politics. It began with William Morgan, an itinerant bricklayer in Batavia, New York, who had quarreled with the fraternal order of Masons and decided to reveal their secrets in a book; but a group of Masons who did not take kindly to the idea abducted him, and he was never heard from again. His disappearance caused some public indignation, but when efforts to bring his abductors to justice were frustrated by Masonic sheriffs, judges, and jurors, the anti-Masonic movement really gained momentum. Andrew Jackson, who was working to replace Adams in the White House, happened to be a Mason (as were George Washington, Benjamin Franklin, Patrick Henry, Lafayette, and Henry Clay), and Jackson's connection caused many anti-Masonic voters in New York to turn to Adams, who was not a member of the order. In a year when Adams received few votes from anybody, the anti-Masonic support must have been gratifying, and by 1831 the former president was attending anti-Masonic rallies and writing in his diary: "In the conflict between Freemasonry and its adversaries, I apprehend the time is approaching when my duty to my country will require a free and open avowal of my opinions; and, whatever may be the consequences, I should not flinch from it. The danger is not imaginary, nor, I hope, underrated by me." Adams's chief contribution to the anti-Masonic movement was a series of highly literate and logical commentaries attacking the order. He also led a movement to remove the veil of secrecy from another fraternity, Phi Beta Kappa, of which he had long been a member.

Thaddeus Stevens was a Pennsylvania lawyer in his mid-thirties when Morgan was kidnapped, and the event aroused his indignation as much as it had Adams's, though for very different reasons. Although Stevens was successful in his profession and had accumulated a fair amount of wealth, he had never been accepted by the political and social elite to which Adams belonged as a matter of birthright. Phi Beta Kappa, for example, had rejected Stevens, and this, a Dartmouth roommate of his reported, "was a source of great vexation to him, though he was careful not to express his vexation." But if Stevens tried to hide his feelings in front of his roommate, he made no effort to disguise them in a letter to a friend about a mutual acquaintance. He wrote: "Charles Leverett has entered into the service of the aristocracy, in the capacity of scullion, and it is expected as a reward for his services, he will be Knighted, i.e., elected Phi Betian. Those fawning parasites, who are grasping at unmerited honors, seem for once to have blundered into the truth. That they must flatter the nobility, or remain in obscurity; that they must degrade themselves by sychophancy, or others will not exalt them."

Stevens was born a poor boy, painfully poor, and even worse he was crippled. His clubfoot not only brought teasing and ridicule from his childhood playmates, it caused him to be regarded by many in the small, superstitious New England towns where he grew up as somehow accursed. "You have heard that I was one of the devil's children," he once said to a young companion, "and that even this poor clubfoot of mine was a proof of my parentage." Throughout his life, Stevens had to fight the idea that he was somehow unclean and undeserving, and he usually conducted his battle against this stereotype with such bitterness and resentment that he managed to renew the charge. And that in turn hardened his own heart further against those for whom life was easy, the elect whom birth and beauty and luck had elevated and among whose ranks he would never be included. Thus the idea of fighting an elite conspiracy, such as Masonry was purported to be, naturally appealed to him. He mobilized citizens opposed to secret societies, started an anti-Masonic newspaper, and became a political power. He rode about the countryside on horseback making anti-Masonic speeches, including one in Hagerstown, Maryland, where he called the Masons, among other things, a "feeble band of lowly reptiles," the "base-born issue of a foreign sire," and a "prostituted harlot."

This was too much for one Masonic newspaper editor, who promptly published a letter that revived certain rumors about Stevens. Several years before, the body of a pregnant black woman had been found in a pond. Foul play was suspected, and gossip in the small town of Gettysburg hinted that Thaddeus Stevens might have had good reason for wanting the woman dead. The whisperers asked: wasn't the child that the woman was carrying white? And hadn't Stevens attended the inquest and been overly insistent in urging a verdict of suicide?

Stevens brought charges of criminal libel against the newspaper and won, an action that effectively quashed the rumors. Yet the same kind of thing continued to happen to him throughout his life. Even in an age when calumny was common, the charges brought against Stevens were spectacular. There was murder, as we have seen. He was also accused of being a bastard in a bizarre but persistent rumor that claimed he was the natural son of Talleyrand. A friend whose unmarried daughter became pregnant brought charges of fornication against Stevens, which were later dropped. And for the last twenty years of his life, he was pursued by rumors that his mulatto housekeeper, Lydia Smith, was really his mistress. Shortly before Stevens died, the abolitionist Jonathan Blanchard wrote to him, "At present, in every part of the United States, people believe that your personal life has been *one prolonged sin*; that your lips are defiled with blasphemy! your hands with gambling!! and your body with women!!!"

In his public life, Stevens was sometimes as careless with his reputation as he was in his personal life. In Pennsylvania's "buckshot war," he was involved in the most flagrant use of patronage for political gain, and then when his party still failed to win a clear victory, he used tactics so offensive in order to gain advantage that a mob formed and chased him and his cohorts out of the statehouse. He could be tough and mean, a real streetfighter, but even his enemies had to admit that he often fought on behalf of others rather than himself. He was a believer in free public schools, for example, and during his first term in the Pennsylvania legislature, a bill was passed to institute free schooling throughout the state. A taxpayers' revolt resulted, and in the next election most legislators either promised to overturn the school bill or they were voted out of office. As the legislature gathered in Harrisburg, a repeal seemed inevitable— until Thaddeus Stevens took to the floor. He was forty-three years old now and totally bald. He had lost all his hair more than a decade before in a bout of "brain fever," and he wore a reddish-brown wig. Still, he was not unattractive; he stood six feet tall and had a full, strong-featured face. He spoke with only a few notes, but he had much conviction, and within minutes it was clear that an extraordinary oratorical event was taking place. Word spread, and soon there was not even any standing room left. "This law is often objected to because its benefits are shared by the children of the profligate spendthrift equally with those of most industrious and economical habits," Stevens told the crowd. "It ought to be remembered that the benefit is bestowed, not upon the erring parents, but the innocent children. Carry out this objection, and you punish the children for the crimes and misfortunes of their parents. You virtually establish castes and grades, founded on no merit of the particular generation, but on the demerits of their ancestors; an aristocracy of the most odious and insolent kind—the aristocracy of wealth and pride." When he finished there were cheers and applause. "Those who were almost ready to take the life of Thaddeus Stevens a few weeks before, were instantly converted to his admirers and friends," one newspaper reported, and instead of repealing the free school act, the Pennsylvania house voted to strengthen and enlarge the measure. It was an achievement that gave Stevens pride to the end of his days. "After all," he said to a friend a few weeks before his death, "I may say that my life has not been entirely vain. When I remember that I gave free schools to Pennsylvania, my adopted state, I think my life may have been worth living."

Given Stevens's hatred of castes and grades, it seems almost inevitable he should have taken up the antislavery cause. Surprisingly for him, he edged into it, first joining a colonization society, then contributing money to abolitionists, then fighting for suffrage for free blacks. By 1837, he was a true abolitionist, proclaiming in the Pennsylvania Constitutional Convention of that year, "I wish I were the owner of every Southern slave, that I might cast off the shackles from their limbs and witness the rapture which would excite them in the first dance of their freedom." As Fawn Brodie has pointed out, Stevens's metaphor is revealing. It seems to show that, at least subconsciously, he saw a similarity between the slaves' fate and his own. They, like him, suffered from an inequity for which they were in no way responsible. They too had shackled limbs and a longing to be free.

The sudden expansion the United States underwent while Polk was president greatly aggravated the conflict over slavery by forcing a decision about whether the new territories would be free or slave. In 1848, Stevens ran successfully for the United States House of Representatives on a platform that Congress should exclude slavery from all the new territories. "He is," a Lancaster newspaper reported, *the sworn foe of the South.*" This reputation preceded him to Washington, where he received a number of votes from antislavery congressmen in an acrimonious three-week contest for the speakership. But once the contest was over and a southerner elected, Stevens's influence waned. He was assigned a low-ranking seat on the Judiciary

Committee, and over the next four years his role was mainly that of gadfly. He sat at his desk and made caustic comments, which the House reporter couldn't quite catch. He took to the floor now and again to make speeches that enraged not just southerners, but moderate northerners as well. "You have more than once frightened the tame North from its propriety, and found 'doughfaces' enough to be your tools," he declared to the southern members. These "doughfaces"—northerners who did not oppose slavery—were "unmanly," Stevens went on, "an unvirile race, incapable according to the laws of nature, of reproduction."

Stung by Stevens's words, Thomas Ross, a Democrat from Pennsylvania, declared in a speech that "language so offensive, and impudence so unblushing have never before been seen or heard, in any respectable assemblage of men." Stevens replied that he would ignore such insults: "There is in the natural world, a little spotted, contemptible animal, which is armed by nature with a foetid, volatile, penetrating *virus* which so pollutes whoever attacks it, as to make him offensive to himself and all around him for a long time. Indeed, he is almost incapable of purification. Nothing, sir, no insult shall provoke me to crush so filthy a beast."

But skilled as it was, such vituperation was not affecting the course of events. Henry Clay masterminded the Compromise of 1850 to deal with the new western lands, and although Stevens found its provisions odious, he was helpless to prevent its passage. He watched his moderate northern colleagues unite with southerners to turn it into law, even the measure that made rules regarding fugitive slaves much harsher. Some northern congressmen who couldn't quite bring themselves to vote for the fugitive slave measure absented themselves from the chamber when it came time for a vote, but their action did not escape Stevens's watchful eye. When the result was announced, he sarcastically suggested that the Speaker send a page to the Congressional Library to inform the members they could return with safety "as the slavery question has been disposed of."

Thus he was fairly well isolated in his political life, and probably in his personal life as well. He was never a man who made many friends, never a sociable creature, and the southerners who dominated Washington society were unlikely to coax him out. He did love his cards, however, and no doubt found recreation at the gambling houses sprouting up on the north side of Pennsylvania Avenue. He also began finding more and more excuses to spend time away from the capital city.

The Christiana riot trial in Philadelphia gave him the chance to make the kind of impact it was impossible for him to have in Washington. A Maryland slaveholder who had cornered four runaway slaves in a Christiana, Pennsylvania, farmhouse had been killed and his companions wounded. A white man riding by had refused to help capture the slaves, as had two Quakers, and they were all three put on trial along with thirty-eight black men and women said to have taken part in the violence. It was the first high-court trial in Pennsylvania under the new fugitive slave law; Stevens organized the defense, and the jury brought in a verdict of not guilty. None of this impressed his foes in Congress. "What service did the gentleman from Pennsylvania render this House or this country," one demanded to know, "while he was away for several weeks of the present session, in defending those who were engaged in a mob which destroyed the lives of our citizens?"

Nor were Stevens's constituents enthusiastic about his involvement in the Christiana trial. For many of them the riot had been terrifying, and fearing that strong antislavery policies such as Stevens's would result in further racial atrocities, they refused to nominate him for a third term in Congress. He accepted what looked like retirement with unusually good grace. "It is more than probable," he said on the floor of the House, "that hereafter I shall never meet any member here or elsewhere officially, and I desire to part with no unfriendly feeling toward any of them."

Back in Lancaster, Stevens continued to dabble in politics and briefly joined the Know-Nothing party. But the real vehicle of his political future was created in 1854 when Congress passed the Kansas-Nebraska Act. It aroused so much indignation in the North, where it was viewed as one more triumph for the forces of slavery, that a new political party, the Republican, was formed. Thaddeus Stevens was one of the first in Pennsylvania to join it, and he attended its national convention in 1856. Although he did not think the party's nominee, John C. Fremont, could win, he campaigned hard for him, spurred on by the fact that the Democrats had nominated James Buchanan. Stevens's acquaintance with Buchanan went back a long way, since they were both residents of Lancaster,

Pennsylvania, and had frequently locked horns on the slavery issue. But Buchanan won despite Stevens's efforts, and Stevens subsequently decided to run for office again. In the six years since he had left the House, public opinion had changed sufficiently so that his antislavery views were not now a hindrance. He won a congressional seat with 75 percent of the vote and took particular satisfaction in having turned President Buchanan's home district to the Republicans.

Between the time Stevens was elected and the time he was sworn in, John Brown conducted his raid on Harpers Ferry and was tried and hanged. (Polk's old nemesis, Henry Wise, now governor of Virginia, had signed the death warrant.) Thus the atmosphere of the Thirty-sixth Congress was explosive, with many members actually appearing on the floor with weapons. "The House was more like a powder magazine than a deliberative assembly," one member observed. Southerners were convinced that Republicans were bent on inciting further insurrections such as John Brown's, and they had as proof a scheme the Republican party had devised to condense and distribute a book by Hinton Rowan Helper called *The Impending Crisis of the South—How to Meet It*. The book was ill-conceived, poorly written, and incendiary, suggesting among other things that slaveholders wear sackcloth for a season and then hang themselves. A proposal was put in by a Missouri member that no representative who had recommended the book was fit to be Speaker, and that threw the House into chaos. The Republicans had a plurality, but sixty-eight of them—which included every logical candidate for Speaker—had endorsed Helper's book. Day after day passed with the House unable to elect a Speaker, scarcely able to maintain a semblance of order since the presiding officer was a hesitant clerk who was uncertain of his duties. It was a setting well suited to the aggressive parliamentary style that Stevens had honed in Pennsylvania's political wars, and he scored many points. His sharp, sardonic manner was also a sure catalyst for violence, and before the session was a week old, one southern member had brandished fists at him and another a bowie knife.

It was two months before the House could calm itself enough to elect a Speaker, two months of stalemate and then exhaustion before the members finally settled on William Pennington of New Jersey, a sixty-three-year-old freshman who was new enough to Republican politics that he hadn't had a chance to endorse the Helper book. The interim gave Stevens frequent opportunity to display the kind of wit for which he was by now famous. It wasn't a storytelling wit such as Lincoln's, nor did it produce comfortable laughter. Stevens's humor sprang from the occasion, was Swiftian, shocking, the kind that makes one wince. During the protracted contest for the speakership, he said he would never vote for anyone but Galusha Grow, and when he later cast his ballot for someone else, a colleague reminded him of his promise to support Grow "until the crack of doom." Stevens replied, "I thought I heard it cracking." When a Virginia congressman named Pryor, for whom Stevens had little respect, challenged another member to a duel, Stevens suggested the appropriate weapon would be dungforks. Later that evening, he told a gathering that he had just introduced a bill to "change the name of Pryor to Posterior."

Abraham Lincoln's election provided more occasion for such wit. Stevens took a look at the new cabinet and declared it to be "an assortment of rivals whom the President appointed from courtesy, one stump speaker from Indiana, and two representatives of the Blair family." He was sufficiently upset about the appointment of the smooth-faced Simon Cameron to the War Department for him to go to the president and share his opinion that Cameron was dishonest.

"You don't mean to say that Cameron would steal?" Lincoln is said to have asked.

"No," said Stevens. "I don't think he would steal a red-hot stove."

Word of Stevens's witticism reached Cameron, and in his next interview with Lincoln Stevens asked the president-elect why he had repeated the story.

"I thought that it was a good joke, and I didn't think it would make him mad."

"Well," replied Stevens, "he is very mad and made me promise to retract. I will do so now. I believe I told you that I didn't think he would steal a red-hot stove. I now take that back."

Later, when Cameron had become such an embarrassment to the administration that Lincoln decided to send him off to Russia as ambassador, Stevens was heard to say, "Send word to the Czar to bring in his things of nights."

The same biting quality that characterized Stevens's wit was present in his speeches. As the Thirty-sixth Congress struggled to an end, he took to the floor to condemn compromise efforts being made to keep the South from seceding. A circle of members began to gather round him, to protect him, some said, from southern representatives who would do him harm. But more likely they drew near because they wanted to hear what he had to say. This seventy-year-old man, once merely a gadfly, was beginning to assume a very significant role, and members who sat at their desks couldn't hear him. The new chamber, which the House had occupied since late in 1857, had acoustics almost as bad as the old one. In addition, Stevens was hoarse from a recent illness; but if his voice was weak, his words were most assuredly not. No compromise was possible, he declared to those gathered near him. His own state, Pennsylvania, would never sacrifice principle in order to conciliate armed insurgents: "If I thought such was her character, I would expatriate myself. I would leave the land where I have spent my life from early manhood to declining age, and would seek some spot untainted by the coward breath of servility and meanness."

When the next Congress, the Thirty-seventh, met in special session, none of the Confederate states except Virginia had any representation. In their absence, Galusha Grow, a strong antislavery man who had become a hero for besting a southerner in a fist fight on the floor, was easily elected Speaker, but it was Stevens who led the House, "by common consent," as James G. Blaine put it. His main qualification was his absolute commitment to destroying slavery, but he'd also shown himself skilled at parliamentary maneuvering; he was unafraid to face down his enemies and, in Blaine's words, "never overmatched in intellectual conflict." Grow appointed him Ways and Means Committee chairman, thus giving him the power to rise any time to discuss committee matters and granting him precedence in discussions of other business as well. With these powers, Stevens became a kind of one-man Rules Committee, able to determine the circumstances under which bills would be considered. When the president needed money to conduct the war, Stevens was able to get a debt bill passed quickly by limiting debate on it to a single hour. When Lincoln sent a message to the Congress explaining his controversial decision to suspend the writ of habeas corpus, Stevens managed to get a bill expressly granting him that right introduced and passed in a single day.

But Stevens was not often to be Lincoln's helpmate, and their paths first diverged over the issue of emancipation. Lincoln waited, unsure that he had the constitutional authority to act and concerned with maintaining the loyalty of the slaveholding areas that had not seceded. Stevens was certain the president had the authority to free the slaves, and as for the border states, he agreed with James Russell Lowell, who asked, "*How* many times are we to save Kentucky and lose our self respect?" In addition to that, there was no doubt in Stevens's mind that freeing the slaves would hasten the end of the war.

Along with Massachusetts Senator Henry Wilson and his handsome, pompous colleague, Charles Sumner, Stevens repeatedly went to the White House to put pressure on the president. One Sunday afternoon, Lincoln was telling Senator John Henderson of Missouri about the three men. "They are coming and urging me, sometimes alone, sometimes in couples, sometimes all three together, but *constantly* pressing me." As he spoke, he stepped to a window, and looking out, he saw Wilson, Sumner, and Stevens. He remarked to Henderson that watching them approach the White House reminded him of a story from his school days in Indiana: "One day we were standing up reading the account of the three Hebrew children in the fiery furnace. A little towheaded fellow who stood beside me had the verse with the unpronounceable names. He mangled up Shadrach and Meshach woefully and finally went all to pieces on Abednego." This earned the boy a cuff on the ear, Lincoln said, and hardly had the little fellow wiped away his tears when it was his turn again. He took one look at the passage he was to read, set up a loud wailing, and when the schoolmaster asked what was wrong, pointed to the passage: "Look there! look! there comes them same damn three fellers again!"

Meanwhile the Congress itself began to pass measures that provided for limited emancipation. Just a few days after his seventieth birthday, Stevens rose on the floor to bring to completion the antislavery fight John Quincy Adams had waged for so long. Stevens moved consideration of a bill to abolish slavery in the District of Columbia, and when there was an objection that other bills were due for consideration first, Stevens made clear who was really in charge. Let the Speaker call up the other bills. "I shall move to lay them aside until I get to the bill I have indicated," Stevens declared. And so he did, one bill after another, until the slavery measure came up. It was subsequently threatened by amendment, but Stevens managed to get debate on his opponents' proposal limited to one minute. Nor was this the only kind of force he brought to bear. Attorney Alexander McClure happened to be sitting with him in the House one morning before the session had begun, and he heard a Pennsylvania congressman come up to Stevens and voice doubt about abolishing slavery in the District. "Stevens' grim face and cold gray eye gave answer to the man before his bitter words were uttered," McClure wrote. "He waved his hand to the trembling suppliant and bade him to go to his seat and vote for the measure or confess himself a coward to the world." Stevens had developed intimidation into a fine art and much of his success as leader was owing to it. To confront him was to risk his verbal blows, "sudden, unexpected flashes and bolts that blasted and destroyed," and his slightly unsavory reputation added to his fearsomeness. One could not depend upon his behaving like a gentleman; in fact, it seemed safer to assume the contrary. Nor did the members think for a minute they could slip anything past him. He was regarded as the smartest among them, an acknowledgment they sometimes made humorously. "The House begins to weary," one member wrote. "Thaddeus Stevens leaves; a motion is made for a burial service, as when the brains are out, the body dies. 'We have lost our head,' said one, as Stevens departs."

In addition to the District of Columbia abolition bill, Congress also passed a measure prohibiting slavery in the territories. In July 1862 they went even farther with the Second Confiscation Act, which not only freed rebel slaves, but provided for confiscating rebel property. "I would seize every foot of land," Stevens declared, "and every dollar of their property as our armies go along, and put it to the uses of war and to the pay of our debts. I would plant the South with a military colony if I could not make them submit otherwise. I would sell their lands to the soldiers of independence; I would send those soldiers there with arms in their hands to occupy the heritage of traitors, and build up there a land of free men and of freedom, which, fifty years hence, would swarm with its hundreds of millions without a slave upon its soil." Lincoln was troubled by the confiscation provisions and determined to keep the waging of war in presidential hands. But instead of provoking a confrontation with Congress by vetoing the bill, he let it be known that he *intended* to veto, and that was sufficient to get the bill's most noxious features removed.

Even amended as it was, the Second Confiscation Act went beyond the Emancipation Proclamation, which Lincoln issued in preliminary form on September 22, 1862. Stevens, who was out campaigning for reelection, nevertheless took Lincoln's action as a sign that the president was moving in the right direction, and he was positive and enthusiastic in commending him. If he were sent back to Congress, he told an audience, he would give full support to the "patriotic President."

Stevens was reelected, but many of his Republican colleagues were not so fortunate. The war was not going well for the North: McClellan's peninsular campaign had been a failure; Pope had been defeated at the very gates of Washington; and for the second time, defeated Union troops had fallen back on the city from Bull Run. Turning against the party in power, many voters cast their ballots for the Democrats, and among the casualties was Galusha Grow. A new Speaker would have to be elected, but because congressional elections in those days were held almost a year before members began to serve, there was time in the interim for another change in the mood of the North. Union victories at Vicksburg and Gettysburg helped restore citizens' faith in the administration, and as state and local elections progressed, a groundswell of Republican support was evident. From New Hampshire and Michigan and Iowa, from Massachusetts and Maine and Vermont, the news was good for Lincoln. By December 1863, he might well have been pardoned for feeling a moment or two of elation, and perhaps it was in such a mood that he decided it was time for him to get some control over the unruly House of Representatives. He set out to get his own man elected Speaker, and he chose as his candidate Frank Blair, Jr., the Missouri scion of the Maryland Blairs and a man who it was guaranteed would never appoint Thaddeus Stevens to the chairmanship of the Ways and Means Committee.

The Blairs were moderate Republicans—sufficient in itself to make them antagonists of a radical such as Stevens—but that was only the beginning. The hollow-cheeked senior Blair had once been a Democrat, an intimate of Presidents Jackson and Van Buren; and a few weeks before the 1863 elections, the oldest Blair son, Montgomery, who was Lincoln's postmaster general, had rekindled animosities by declaring in a speech that the "radical party" was "as despotic in its tendencies" as "the Slavocrats of the South." He went on to bring against them the worst charge that could be made against the black man's friend. He said they favored miscegenation, sought "to make a caste of another color by amalgamating the black element with the free white labor of our land, and . . . would make the manumission of slaves the means of infusing their blood into our whole system. . . ."

Stevens, who had brought his pleasant, attractive black housekeeper, Lydia Smith, to live with him on Capitol Hill, thus occasioning much gossip, may well have taken these charges personally. He wrote that the postmaster general's speech was "much more infamous than any speech made by a Copperhead orator. I know of no rebel sympathizer who has charged such disgusting principles and designs on the republican party as this apostate."

One can easily imagine Stevens's rage as he began to pick up rumors that the president was promoting Montgomery's brother, Frank Blair, Jr., for Speaker. The tall, redheaded junior Blair had been a member of the Thirty-seventh Congress, but had been off fighting since it adjourned. He was currently a major-general with Sherman in Tennessee, and he was trying to decide whether to stay there or return to Congress. Lincoln's advice was sought, and the president wrote: "My wish, then, is compounded of what I believe will be best for the country and best for him, and it is that he will come here, put his military commission in my hands, take his seat, go into caucus with our friends, abide the nominations, help elect the nominees, and thus aid to organize a House of Representatives which will really support the government in the war. If the result shall be the election of himself as Speaker, let him serve in that position; if not, let him retake his commission and return to the army."

Lincoln's attempt to interfere in the affairs of the House motivated Stevens to patch up damaged relationships so that the radicals could elect one of their own. These efforts were aided immeasurably when Blair was unable to extricate himself from the army quickly enough to attend the opening days of the session. Schuyler Colfax was elected Speaker, and Stevens retained his Ways and Means chairmanship.

The audacious Blair was nevertheless a thorn in Stevens's side. As soon as he arrived in Washington and took his seat, he began to speak out against the measures radicals were advocating for the South, and he did so in condescending tones that implied he was the administration's spokesman. The radicals soon got their chance for revenge, however. An embarrassing invoice was published in the newspapers; it showed that Blair, who had a reputation for heavy drinking, had ordered an extraordinary amount of liquor while at Vicksburg. Lincoln's letter recommending that he run for Speaker also reached the press. An investigating committee was set up to look into the liquor order, and Stevens brought in a resolution demanding to know how Blair could be a civil and a military officer simultaneously. Ultimately, the House declared that his military commission disqualified him from being a congressman, and his seat was declared vacant.

The Blair episode is important because it helped define the terms in which the power struggle between the executive and the legislative branches would be conducted during the war and Reconstruction. Just as Lincoln had tried to determine the officers of the House, so would Congress attempt to determine the cabinet, the officers of the executive branch. It was on this issue that Andrew Johnson would ultimately be impeached. More immediately, the Blair episode spurred Stevens on in his effort to bring down Montgomery Blair, the postmaster general. In August 1864, sensing that the upcoming presidential elections gave him leverage, Stevens went to see the president. "In order that we may be able in our state to go to work with a good will," he said to Lincoln, "I want you to make us one promise, that you will reorganize your cabinet and leave Montgomery Blair out of it." The threat was clear. Just a few months before, a group of radicals had nominated John C. Fremont for president, and if Lincoln wanted those radicals brought back home to the Republican party, he had better get rid of Blair.

The president was highly agitated, and despite the heat and humidity, he paced up and down in his White House office. "Has it come to this," he demanded of Stevens, "that the voters of this country are asked to elect a man to be President—to be Executive—to administer the Government, and yet that man is to have no will or discretion of his own? Am I to be the mere puppet of power? To have my consitutional advisers selected beforehand, to be told I must do this, or leave that undone? It would be degrading to my

Beyond that, who had given the president the right to determine the terms of Reconstruction? Stevens wasn't alone in thinking the matter belonged to Congress and in resenting executive incursion. The congressional counterproposal on Reconstruction was none of his doing—he didn't think it stringent enough—but even without his support, a bill passed both Houses that required a majority of citizens to take loyalty oaths before a state could be readmitted. The measure also effectively disenfranchised Confederate civil and military leaders.

Lincoln thought the plan too harsh, and in the last hours before Congress adjourned he refused to sign it. One of the bill's sponsors subsequently issued a fiery manifesto condemning the president and asserting that *"the authority of Congress is paramount."* Stevens too was upset at the way Lincoln handled the matter, but he didn't give up on the president. When Congress was in session once again, he went to the White House to urge Lincoln to use a firmer hand with the South. The president responded with a characteristically earthy metaphor: "Stevens, this is a pretty big hog we are trying to catch, and to hold when we do catch him. We must take care that he doesn't slip away from us."

It was the last meeting between the two men. A bullet from an assassin's gun intervened, and Stevens found himself facing a new president. Although he had often been angry and impatient with Lincoln, he had believed in his patriotism and integrity. "There is no danger that the highest praise that the most devoted friends could bestow on him would ever be reversed by posterity," he said of him two years later. "So solid was the material of which his whole character was formed that the more it is rubbed, the brighter it will shine." But the new man, Andrew Johnson, he liked not at all. That Johnson was a Democrat certainly didn't help; nor did it aid matters that he had appeared drunk to take the oath for the vice-presidency. Stevens, an avowed teetotaler, did not feel very charitably inclined when he heard reports of how the former Tennessee governor embarrassed himself and everyone around him by prating about his humble origins: "I'm a-going for to tell you—here today—yes, I am a-going for to tell you all that I am a plebian. I glory in it. I am a plebian. The people—yes, the people of the United States, the great people—have made me what I am."

Actually Stevens and Johnson had many things in common. Both were handicapped in a sense, Stevens by his clubfoot and Johnson by his lack of education (he had not known how to write until his wife taught him). Johnson also suffered from the fact that he had worked as a tailor, an occupation considered feminine and therefore demeaning. But like Stevens, he had succeeded despite obstacles. His rise to the governorship of Tennessee was remarkable since few men of humble origin ever made it to high political office in the South. And neither Johnson nor Stevens had any use for well-born members of the gentry who looked down on self-made men like themselves. But Stevens, with his stiff-backed pride, would have sooner perished than brag about his humble origins in a way sure to indicate sensitivity about them. As for Johnson, he had, in Jefferson Davis's words, "the pride of having no pride," and this transparent behavior was probably doubly hateful to Stevens since it revealed emotions with which he was painfully familiar.

Many of Stevens's radical allies assumed Johnson would champion their cause. He was given to using words such as *treason* and *traitor* and had often spoken of the necessity of inflicting harsh punishment on the South. But he soon proved himself to be the opposite of what they had imagined. Congress was out of session when he assumed office, and he began reorganizing Confederate states by executive order. By July 1865, all but Texas had been reconstructed. Stevens wrote to warn him about acting without Congress: "Reconstruction is a very delicate question. The last Congress (and I expect the present) looked upon it as a question for the Legislative power exclusively. . . . My only object is to suggest the propriety of suspending further 'reconstruction' until the meeting of Congress. Better call an extra session than to allow many to think the Executive was approaching usurpation." When Johnson didn't answer this letter, Stevens wrote again, this time adding a word about the thousands of pardons Johnson was granting: "Profuse pardoning also will greatly embarrass Congress if they should wish to make the enemy pay the expense of war or a part of it."

Again there was no answer. Johnson chose to ignore the most powerful man in Congress, something Lincoln, with his greater political skill, would never have done, and Stevens wasn't long in taking up the challenge. Although he had been so ill for the past eighteen months that his face looked like a "death mask," he began to gird for battle. He could no longer walk more than a few steps at a time, but he became animated at the idea of the upcoming conflict, and his wit was as biting as ever. "What shall I do when you are dead and gone?" he asked the two young men who carried him everywhere in a special chair.

On an unexpectedly springlike day in December 1865, Stevens had his young men carry him into the House chamber. A new Brussels carpet had been laid and the galleries handsomely refurbished, but the crowds who jammed the Capitol had not come to see the decorations. They expected that on this opening day of Congress Stevens would challenge the president, and he did not disappoint them. His first move was to deny representatives from Tennessee and Virginia, states reorganized by Johnson, seats in the House. When the clerk of the House, an old ally of Stevens's who owed his job to him, read the roll, he simply omitted Tennessee and Virginia. Horace Maynard, the Tennessee representative, protested strenuously, but the clerk refused to recognize him, and there was a motion to proceed to the election of a Speaker. When Maynard continued his protestation, Stevens moved the previous question. Still Maynard would not be silent: "I appeal to the gentleman from Pennsylvania to listen to me for a moment."

"I cannot yield to any gentleman who does not belong to this body—who is an outsider," Stevens replied.

The clerk hammered for order, Stevens's motion was carried, and the matter was settled.

When Schuyler Colfax had once again been elected Speaker, Stevens pulled from his pocket a paper that outlined the most powerful committee Congress had ever formed. His plan provided for a joint House-Senate Committee of Fifteen to "inquire into the condition of the States which formed the so-called Confederate States of America, and report whether they or any of them are entitled to be represented in either House of Congress." Since Stevens had already obtained unanimous support in the Republican caucus, the matter passed handily. There was one brief parliamentary flare-up, but he put it out by getting the rules suspended and moving the previous question. He was named to head up the House side of the committee, and although William Pitt Fessenden of Maine, who headed the Senate side, was technically the chairman, Stevens was, in fact, the leader. From this position, he could not only control whom the House would admit, but also the Senate, and thus he was in the extraordinary position of being able to influence both houses. To free him for these responsibilities his former duties were divided. The appropriations function of Ways and Means was given to a new committee, and Stevens moved from the chairmanship of Ways and Means to the chairmanship of the Appropriations Committee.

Even before the Committee of Fifteen began its inquiries, there were reports of gross injustices in the South. The northern press published Mississippi's "black code," which imposed such harsh restrictions on blacks that many of them found their new-won freedom meaningless. Carl Schurz, after touring the South at President Johnson's request, spoke of "reports of bloody outrages inflicted upon colored people": "I had occasion to examine personally into several of these cases, and I saw in various hospitals negroes, women as well as men, whose ears had been cut off or whose bodies were slashed with knives or bruised with whips, or bludgeons, or punctured with shot wounds. Dead negroes were found in considerable number in the country roads or on the fields, shot to death, or strung upon the limbs of trees. In many districts, the colored people were in a panic of fright, and the whites in a state of almost insane irritation against them." Thus one of Stevens's first efforts involved the Freedman's Bureau, an agency set up in early 1865 to help in the transition from slavery to freedom. Stevens wanted to continue the bureau and expand its authority to include judicial procedures, but Johnson, appalled by the cost and seeing it as an encroachment on states' rights, vetoed the bill. Although there were enough votes in the House to override, there were not in the Senate, and so Stevens found another way to respond to what he considered executive hostility. He obtained a resolution from the Committee of Fifteen that put a halt to plans to admit the president's state of Tennessee, then pushed the resolution through the House without debate. He and his allies also began working to build radical strength, particularly in the Senate, where they succeeded in unseating a Democratic supporter of the president. Within a month, they had a coalition large enough to override Johnson, and when he rejected the Civil Rights Bill, it was promptly passed over his veto. The same thing happened somewhat later with a second Freedman's bill.

The battle was joined, and it was all too seldom conducted on an elevated level. At a Washington's birthday speech, Johnson let himself be drawn into some intemperate remarks about those who were thwarting him. Stevens and those like him, the president declared, were rebels. Just like Jefferson Davis, they were trying to destroy the Union. Stevens responded in what seemed at first an astonishingly mild fashion. The president couldn't have made such an inflammatory statement, he said on the floor of the House. Obviously someone was going around giving speeches under Johnson's name. "That . . . speech was one of the grandest hoaxes ever perpetrated. . . . It is part of the cunning contrivance of the copperhead party, who have been persecuting our President since the fourth of March last." He then had the clerk read into the record the "slander" that had marked the start of the "persecution." It was a newspaper account of Johnson's drunkenness at the March fourth inauguration. As representatives guffawed, the clerk read aloud: "The drunken and beastly Caligula, the most profligate of the Roman emperors, raised his horse to the dignity of consul. . . . The consulship was scarcely more disgraced by the scandalous transaction than is our Vice Presidency by the late election of Andrew Johnson . . . *this insolent drunken brute, in comparison with whom even Caligula's horse was respectable.*"

Johnson and Stevens also crossed swords when Stevens introduced legislation for Negro suffrage in the District of Columbia and shepherded it through the House. The president called Stevens's bill "ill-timed, uncalled for and calculated to do great harm" and implied that Congress should not deal with matters of political equality. When Stevens heard what the president had said, he accused him of violating the privileges of the House and growled ominously, "Centuries ago, had [such remarks] been made to Parliament by a British king, it would have cost him his head."

During the efforts to put together the Fourteenth Amendment, Stevens's ideas on suffrage made even some of his radical colleagues nervous. He proposed that universal black suffrage should come in "four or five years," but the majority of the Committee of Fifteen worried about the effects of such a proposition on the upcoming elections. Black suffrage did not exist in most northern states, and the prospect of it might anger white voters there. And so as it was finally presented to the House, the amendment approached black voting by trying the *denial* of suffrage to reduced representation: if blacks could not vote, they could not be counted in determining the number of representatives a state should have—a requirement that was important chiefly in southern states, where there were significant numbers of blacks. To further insure that southerners and copperheads would not win control in the next national election, the amendment disenfranchised until 1870 all who had participated in the rebellion.

This last clause generated opposition. Those who thought it too harsh, however, had their case undercut by riots in Memphis. Led by the police, rampaging crowds had burned Negro cabins and schoolhouses and killed forty-six blacks. In the House, Stevens declared that southern rebels should not be restored to citizenship until they had worn "sackcloth and ashes. . . . I hear several gentlemen say that these men should be admitted as equal brethren. Let not these friends of secession sing to me their siren song of peace and good will until they can stop my ears to the screams and groans of the dying victims at Memphis." After his speech, the Fourteenth Amendment passed the House easily, but when it reached the Senate, the clause disenfranchising southern whites was softened. Stevens continued to support the bill nonetheless, explaining his position in a remarkable statement that had less to do with race relations than with his vision of life:

> In my youth, in my manhood, in my old age, I had fondly dreamed that when any fortunate chance should have broken up for awhile the foundation of our institutions, and released us from obligations the most tyrannical that ever man imposed in the name of freedom, that the intelligent, pure and just men of this Republic, true to their professions and their conscience, would have so remodeled all our institutions as to have freed them from every vestige of human oppression, of inequality of rights, of the recognized degradation of the poor, and the superior caste of the rich. In short, that no distinction would be tolerated in their purified Republic but that arose from merit and conduct. This bright dream has vanished "like the baseless fabric of a vision." I find that we shall be obliged to be content with patching up the worst portions of the ancient edifice, and leaving it, in many of its parts, to be swept through by the tempests, the frosts, and the storms of despotism.
>
> Do you inquire why, holding these views and possessing some will of my own, I accept so imperfect a proposition? I answer because I live among men and not among angels. . . .

As the Fourteenth Amendment was sent to the states for ratification, the congressional elections of 1866 were beginning. Johnson, determined to break the radicals' hold on Congress, set out on the campaign trail, and at stop after stop he flailed away, shouting, "Hang Thad Stevens!" and blaming the radicals in Congress for a recent and bloody race riot in New Orleans. Stevens, sick in Pennsylvania, said little, giving all the more significance to the words he did utter. "The great issue to be met at the election is the question of Negro rights," he declared. "This doctrine may be unpopular with bespotted ignorance. But popular or unpopular, I shall stand by it until I am relieved of the unprofitable labors of earth."

Aided by Johnson's graceless campaigning, the Republicans swept the election. (No orator, observed a caustic *Nation*, ever accomplished so much by a fortnight's speaking.) At the same time, the South, with the active encouragement of the president, was rejecting the Fourteenth Amendment. Thus the stage was set for a historic confrontation.

But before events rushed to their sad conclusion, there was a curious interlude. Stevens, so ill now he could not sit up and had to ride to Washington lying on the floor of a railroad coach, began an intense lobbying effort to get himself appointed to the Senate. His friend Alexander McClure pointed out the obvious to him: "For a man who was the confessed Commoner of the nation during the greatest period of its history, . . . who was undisputed and absolute leader, to accept a seat in the Senate, would be to give up the highest honors the nation can accord to any one, and descend to the position of a Senator, where he would be no greater than most of his fellows." But Stevens persisted. Perhaps he knew how near the end was, knew that he wouldn't have long to serve in either House, and so wanted to add the prestige of being a senator to his record. Or perhaps he sensed the ugliness that lay ahead, sensed that he was finally losing control of the hatred he felt for Johnson and the southern white aristocracy. Perhaps he had an intimation of the extremes to which he would be driven and wanted to avoid them. When one considers his good qualities—his indomitable spirit, his lifelong pursuit of justice for the downtrodden—one would like to think it was so.

But the Senate seat went to someone else, and the final battle was joined. The catalyst was a Supreme Court decision on the Milligan case, which, in Stevens's eyes, nullified both Freedman's Bureau legislation and the Civil Rights Bill, thus robbing blacks and loyal whites in the South of the protection that Congress had thus far provided them. If the Court was going to hand down such decisions, he concluded, then it was necessary to establish the sovereignty of the Congress over the Court. If the president was determined to encourage a willful South in its wrongful ways, then it was essential to insure congressional dominance of the executive. And if such actions overrode the Constitution, then so be it.

The Reconstruction Act was one of the first steps in undercutting Johnson's authority. It did away with the civil governments in the South to which he had given his blessing and instituted military rule. Stevens guided the bill through Congress and then worked to get it passed over presidential veto, even though his colleagues in the House and Senate had insisted on softening what he thought were key provisions. He wanted the term of military rule left indefinite, while they insisted on a formulation that would end it when a state established universal male suffrage and ratified the Fourteenth Amendment. Stevens's fellow representatives also rejected his new efforts at a confiscation measure. He had been promoting such legislation for five years, and it seemed to have its origins in the darkest part of his character, in a place where the pain imposed on the landholders was at least as important to him as the benefit intended for blacks. "I have never desired bloody punishments to any extent," he explained once, "not even for the sake of example. But there are punishments quite as appalling, and longer remembered than death. They are more advisable, because they would reach a greater number. Strip a proud nobility of their bloated estates; reduce them to a level with plain republicans; send them forth to labor, and teach their children to enter the workshops or handle the plow, and you will thus humble the proud traitors." A bill he introduced now—which the House turned down—would have seized all estates worth more than five thousand dollars and divided them into forty-acre farms for black families.

A second step in diminishing the president's authority was the Command of the Army Act, which Stevens got passed and signed by attaching it to an appropriations bill. It took the army out of the president's control by requiring that he issue all military orders through the General of the Army, whom he could not remove from office. A third step was the Tenure of Office Act, which Stevens introduced in the House. It took from the president the right to remove officeholders, including members of his own cabinet, except with the consent of the Senate. Like the other two measures, this one became law on March 2, 1867. Thus, on a single day, much was accomplished toward making the president a mere figurehead and establishing a form of parliamentary government in the United States.

The crippled old man with wasted body and feverish gaze who was chiefly responsible knew how revolutionary these steps were. Instead of trying to construct a constitutional rationale, he frankly admitted these actions were outside the Constitution. "Some members of the Senate," he wrote, "seemed to doubt their power under the Constitution which they had just repudiated, and wholly outside of which all agreed we were acting; else our whole work of Reconstruction was usurpation." Stevens also had plentiful evidence in the elections of 1867 that as far as the country was concerned he had gone too far. The Democrats carried New York, New Jersey, Maryland, and Ohio, and were strong even in states where the Republicans won. Beyond that, Minnesota, Kansas, and Ohio rejected Negro suffrage. But Stevens was locked on a final course now, and he reacted to this repudiation of Republican policy by ignoring it. When it looked as though the Supreme Court might rule on the constitutionality of Reconstruction legislation, he got a bill through the House that would require a two-thirds ruling of the justices to declare laws unconstitutional. When that measure failed in the Senate, he introduced another one even more to the point, which forbade the Supreme Court from taking jurisdiction on any case arising out of the Reconstruction acts. But even the House wouldn't pass that measure, and it was left to another of the radicals, Congressman Robert Schenck, to slip through a more indirect piece of legislation, which nonetheless had the effect of taking Reconstruction legislation out of the Supreme Court's jurisdiction. Johnson vetoed it, arguing that it would set a precedent that, "if followed, may eventually sweep aside every check on arbitrary and unconstitutional legislation." It was passed over his veto.

Stevens did not let the court controversy distract him from the matter of the president. Johnson was impotent now, but that wasn't enough; Stevens wanted to see him driven from office. Agitation for impeaching him had begun as early as his disastrous campaign swing in 1866, and a resolution introduced by an Ohio congressman early in 1867 had started hearings in the Judiciary Committee. Many accusations were made, including one that had Johnson a party to Lincoln's assassination; but nothing was proved, and the House Impeachment Committee decided there was no ground for action.

And then Johnson provided the necessary cause. For months he had delayed firing his secretary of war, Edwin Stanton, even though it was clear that Stanton's loyalties lay with the radicals in Congress. Then after the Tenure of Office Act had been passed, Johnson decided to remove Stanton from his cabinet, and it is hard to conceive how he could have done it more clumsily. He managed in the process to alienate Ulysses S. Grant, possibly the most popular man in the nation, and he set abroad rumors of renewed civil war, which were so convincing that two members of Congress actually gathered a company of a hundred men and went to guard the War Department.

It was all Thaddeus Stevens needed. On a snowy Saturday afternoon in February 1868, he rose in the House and directed the clerk to read a resolution from the Committee on Reconstruction: "*Resolved*, That Andrew Johnson, President of the United States, be impeached of high crimes and misdemeanors in office." Debate on the resolution went on until late the following Monday afternoon and left Stevens exhausted, but he insisted on delivering the final speech. Haggard and trembling, he began. To all who watched and listened, it was clear he was a very sick man. He had rheumatism, jaundice, and dropsy. His legs, heart, and liver were all failing, and on this dark and snowy afternoon his voice failed too. By flickering gaslight, the clerk finished his speech for him, and when he was through, the roll was called. The House of Representatives voted to impeach Andrew Johnson.

But at the very moment it seemed the old man would triumph, the Republican coalition in the Senate, where Johnson would be tried, began to crumble. Senator Fessenden wrote to a friend, "Whatever may have been Johnson's misdemeanors, it would have been better to tolerate him to the end of his term, rather than to expose our party and our country to so great a hazard." Senator Grimes declared on the floor of the Senate that Johnson was not a fit person for the presidency; but that was not the issue at hand, he went on, and he would have to vote for acquittal. When the roll was called on May 16, 1868, seven Republicans voted with the Democrats, and the president was acquitted by a single vote.

Stevens did not give up immediately. He prepared another set of impeachment articles, but his colleagues in the House voted them down. This final defeat was enough to make him wonder if his whole life had been a failure and to cause him to have doubts about the future of the country. "With all this great struggle of years in Washington," he told a friend, "and the fearful sacrifice of life and treasure, I see little hope for the Republic."

But as if to make sure that no historian would ever find the task of reading his heart an easy one, in his last formal speech in the House he painted a hopeful vision. The nation would flourish and prosper, he said to the Speaker, if only the equality of man to man were recognized:

> My sands are nearly run, and I can only see with the eye of faith. I am fast descending the downhill of life, at the foot of which stands an open grave. But you, sir, are promised length of days and a brilliant career. If you and your compeers can fling away ambition and realize that every human being, however lowly-born or degraded, by fortune is your equal, and that every inalienable right which belongs to you belongs also to him, truth and righteousness will spread over the land, and you will look down from the top of the Rocky mountains upon an empire of one hundred millions of happy people.

When he had finished, he was carried back to his modest brick house on B Street, where on August 12, 1868, he died. With him in his last hours were two black nuns, Sisters of Charity, and his housekeeper, Lydia.

4

BLAINE AT BAY

After Thaddeus Stevens's body had been embalmed, it was taken to the Capitol, where it lay in state in the Rotunda. Thousands filed by to pay tribute, and among them was a tall, bearded representative from Maine. His sharp eye would not have missed the symbolism of the Negro Zouaves who had been chosen from a black Massachusetts regiment to stand honor guard around the catafalque, and as the word *emancipation* floated through the representative's mind and connected with the memory of the heavy-handed way Stevens had dominated the House, he leaned over to a companion. "The death of Stevens," he whispered, "is an emancipation for the Republican party."

The whisperer was a young man, just thirty-nine, and within a year he would be elected Speaker of the House, thus taking command of the institution where Stevens had reigned. He would be a strong ruler, but with a manner very different from Stevens's, for he was a very different kind of man: handsome, genial, with a loving wife and family. Indeed, one can hardly imagine a life more dissimilar to Stevens's than this young congressman's as he gathered his wife and children around a family hearth that, according to one description, "he believed, and pronounced, and made the happiest fireside in the world." It is Clay whom the young congressman seemed very like, Clay of the great charm and the long political career, which curved up and up without ever reaching the peak he had set for himself. Like the Kentuckian, the magnetic young man from Maine rose to national prominence as Speaker, but was frustrated again and again in his attempts to reach the presidency. In his case, the failure had much to do with money and the whole perplexing matter of the financial lives of public officials.

Although salaries for senators and representatives usually seem exorbitant to the public, compensation has always been less than the brightest and most capable lawmakers could earn outside of government. In the nineteenth century, the problem became more pronounced as the congressman gained importance in the Senate or House. There were long breaks between sessions, and while junior members could work at their professions during these months, senior members found politics absorbing more and more time until it was impossible for them to earn much practicing law or teaching or farming. An official with independent wealth—Polk, for example—wouldn't find the low salary constraining; but for others, financial pressures almost inevitably increased, fueled by comparisons with peers not in government service or with wealthy officials who may have had less power but considerably more income. Sooner or later, the important senator or representative would be offered a way to "supplement" his salary, nothing illegal necessarily (at least not according to the laws of those times), but a "favor" or special "arrangement." Many refused, but some went along, and they were not always the thoroughgoing reprobates one might suppose. In other areas of life, they might have a discerning moral sense—but they proved blind in this one. One such was Daniel Webster, who could demand his "usual" retainer from the National Bank at the very moment the Senate was debating the bank's charter. Another was James G. Blaine, the young congressman from Maine. A man of wide-ranging gifts and a multiplicity of talents, he would hold many high offices, but never the presidency. The main reason was that he was suspected of financial dishonor.

Blaine had come to Washington with warm recommendations. "I want you to know Mr. Blaine," the governor of Maine wrote to Justin Morill, a prominent congressman. "You will find him one of the most able and brilliant men in the House and altogether worth knowing." It was that way most of his life; people would be so taken with him that they would go out of their way to help. Indeed, his career in Maine as a newspaperman was not one he had sought. He was a young teacher in Pennsylvania reading law in his spare time when the owners of a Maine newspaper, who had met him and been impressed, approached him with the offer of an editorship. He accepted, the newspaper was chosen as the official state printer, and he found himself, as he remembered it later, "making $4000 a year and spending $600, a ratio between outlay and income which I have never since been able to establish and maintain."

Within four years, he had been elected to the Maine legislature; two years after that, he became Speaker of the Maine house. He moved his wife and three children—eventually there would be six—into an old-fashioned, wood-sided mansion near the state Capitol, which no doubt helped take care of the discrepancy between dollars earned and spent. Friends began to urge him to run for the national Congress, and in 1862 he finally agreed. He was elected representative and arrived in Washington in 1863, clearly a man on the fast track.

He didn't make the mistake of advertising it among his new colleagues, but neither was he overly reticent. Several times he stood up to Thaddeus Stevens, and by presenting his case cogently and self-confidently, he was even able to prevail. This led Stevens to refer sarcastically to the "magnetic manner" of the representative from Maine, a description that stuck, though it soon lost the ironic twist Stevens gave it because it was so utterly fitting. Blaine had a way with people that drew them to him, a seemingly effortless and candid geniality that won him warm friends and ardent admirers. Wrote one congressman who came into the House when Blaine was at the height of his power: "It is my deliberate judgment that James G. Blaine was the most brilliant man of his day. His personal charm and magnetism were irresistable, and his hold on the young men of his party and of the country was almost unbelievable. I was no exception, and the Plumed Knight was frankly my ideal."

But in addition to his charm, Blaine had a quick tongue, a product perhaps of his innate self-assurance. He did not always weigh his words in the way a man who felt his position to be more precarious might have, and this carelessness made him a very important enemy: Roscoe Conkling, congressman from New York. Conkling was a huge, handsome rooster of a man, who kept his vanity on full display. He wore cream-colored pantaloons, moon-colored vests, and used mauve ink for his personal correspondence. He liked to comb his wavy auburn hair so that a single curl drooped dramatically over his forehead, and his swaggering walk could be spotted from blocks away. He was a powerful political boss as well as a dandy and was very much used to having his way. When a certain General Fry crossed him, Conkling did as political bosses do and took the first opportunity to get even. When legislation came before the House creating a permanent Provost Marshal's Bureau, which it was understood Fry would head, Conkling attacked the proposal, saying it "creates an unnecessary office for an undeserving public servant."

Blaine immediately came to Fry's defense, and in the bitter quarrel that followed, not only suggested that Conkling was seeking personal revenge, but also charged the New Yorker with unethical conduct. Conkling replied, "If General Fry is reduced to depending for vindication upon the gentleman from Maine, he is to be commiserated certainly. If I have fallen to the necessity of taking lessons from that gentleman in the rules of propriety, or of right or wrong, God help me."

This was hitting low, but before it was over, Blaine went one better. "As to the gentleman's cruel sarcasm," he said, "I hope he will not be too severe. The contempt of that large-minded gentleman is so wilting: his haughty disdain, his grandiloquent swell, his majestic, supereminent, turkey-gobbler strut has been so crushing to myself and all members of the House that I know it was an act of the greatest temerity for me to venture upon a controversy with him."

Once the exchange was finished, Blaine was ready to forgive and forget; but not Conkling. Blaine's remarks about his personal mannerisms never ceased to rankle. Almost twenty years later, when he was asked to campaign for Blaine, he replied, "No, thank you. I don't engage in criminal practice."

But at the time, the quarrel with Conkling was probably an advantage, winning points for Blaine among other members who found the New Yorker's untamed ego infuriating. When Ulysses Grant's choice of Schuyler Colfax as his running mate necessitated the election of a new Speaker, Blaine was one of the first mentioned as a possible successor. Another was Henry Dawes, a respected member from Massachusetts; but he was somewhat reticent about campaigning for himself among his fellow congressmen. Blaine, on the other hand, began to seek support as soon as Grant and Colfax were elected. He wrote to James Garfield, set forth reasons why

Garfield would not be a strong candidate for Speaker himself, and concluded, "I infer from this series of facts that you will probably not allow your name to be used. *If not*, I desire your most active sympathy and support for myself." He gave a dinner party at Welker's, an elegant Washington restaurant, and invited a number of influential congressmen, including Allison of Iowa and "Pig Iron" Kelley of Pennsylvania. His biggest coup, however, was enlisting the stout, domineering Benjamin Butler in his cause. Butler, a former Union general, now a Massachusetts congressman, controlled the bloc of southern Republicans, and as soon as Blaine had him in his camp, Dawes saw the writing on the wall. He wanted to be chairman of the Appropriations Committee, and with that in mind rose in caucus and nominated Blaine for Speaker himself, thus ensuring Blaine's election.

But Butler felt he deserved the Appropriations chairmanship and was not at all shy about pressing his claim. According to George Frisbee Hoar, who was in the House at the time, Blaine finally found a way to avoid Butler's importunities. As the hour approached for Blaine to go to the floor and announce committee assignments, Butler stationed himself outside the Speaker's room, intent on reminding Blaine at the last moment of the debt he owed. But Blaine had already decided on Dawes, and having no desire to confront Butler, he slipped out the window of the Speaker's room, went around the portico, and entered the House chamber from the other side. When Butler figured out Blaine was no longer in the Speaker's room, he rushed to the floor—and got there just in time to hear Blaine announce Dawes's appointment.

These committee assignments were one of the chief sources of the considerable power Blaine had as Speaker, and he made them with great care. "Your father sits here at the table toiling away over his committees," Mrs. Blaine wrote to her oldest son. "Hard, hard work! As fast as he gets them arranged, just so fast some after consideration comes up which disarranges not one but many, and over tumbles the whole row of bricks." As Clay had discovered half a century earlier, committee appointments were a useful legislative tool. But in 1812 Clay's task had been relatively simple. He had one overriding concern—to bring the country to war. Blaine had a whole agenda he wanted to accomplish and had to include as a factor in his considerations each representative's stand on a range of issues. A computer would have been handy. With only pen and paper, it was a difficult task. "Alas," Mrs. Blaine wrote of the committees, "if final touches are not soon put to them, I am afraid your Father will give out entirely. For the first time in his life he says he feels a strain upon him which affects his brain. His head aches badly every day, and at night his circulation is feeble and he is very languid." The appointment process was not made any easier by the lobbying that went on inside and outside the Congress to secure particular appointments for certain representatives.

Finally, however, the best possible lists would be constructed and the announcements made. Then Blaine's attention would shift to other ways of achieving the legislative program he had in mind. Chief among these was an artful use of the power of recognition. Whereas previous Speakers had sometimes acted on what they suspected a member's intentions to be, Blaine wanted definite information. He would ask to be informed beforehand of the precise reason for which the member sought the floor, and it was even said that he sometimes demanded certain amendments before he would allow a resolution to be offered. There began to be comments about his "despotic" power, and certainly Blaine had no hesitancy about using the speakership to work his legislative will. Benjamin Butler found that out when he wanted to introduce a bill that gave the president increased power for dealing with southern disorders. Because Blaine disapproved of the measure, Butler had difficulty getting recognized so he could present it. When he finally did succeed, it did him little good. As soon as the clerk, at Butler's request, began reading the bill, Speaker Blaine recognized another member, who moved to suspend the rules in order to pass a joint resolution dealing with coal duties. Butler's bill was thereby killed for the Forty-first Congress, a bit of homicide Blaine later explained by saying that while the clerk is reading no one, technically speaking, has the floor.

With similar tactics, Butler was kept from presenting the bill in the next Congress, and meanwhile Blaine appointed his own committee on the matter. When they came forth with legislation he approved, it was introduced and passed without debate. Angered, Butler wrote a letter denouncing Blaine's actions, and that in turn so provoked Blaine that he stepped down from the chair and chastised Butler from the well of the House. "It was thunder and lightning altogether," an observer in the gallery commented. The next day, however, Butler and Blaine were chatting as if nothing had happened.

That was the way it usually went when Blaine butted heads with one of his colleagues. Except for Roscoe Conkling, they found it hard to hold a grudge against him. He was too likable, too little given to holding a grudge himself, and his adored and adoring family added to his appeal. The visitor to his home was likely to find him lying on the floor helping a child with a lesson, and even if the visitor had come on business, the children might well stay to listen. One acquaintance who came to see Blaine found him writing an important paper while the children played around him. "How *can* you write with these children here?" asked the friend. Blaine replied, "It is because they *are* here that I can write."

As soon as he had become Speaker, Blaine had bought a home in Washington so his family could be with him while Congress was in session. Although the house was a large one on Fifteenth Street— next door to Senator Buckingham on the one side, Congressman Swann on the other, with Secretary of State Hamilton Fish living across the street—the Blaines did not affect a particularly elegant or sophisticated style. The atmosphere in their home was comfortable, expansive, often a bit confused, but unfailingly attractive. Mrs. Blaine sketched a word picture of their Washington life for an absent son: "So now at 9:15 we are all at liberty to go our several ways: Father to the parlor crowded full of gentlemen; Shermy to his writing-table; A. to the baby, the petted darling of upstairs, downstairs, and my lady's chamber; M. and Q. with spade and shovel to the yard, and the mamma to her dearest and best of boys. . . . Indeed, Walker, we are a most happy family. So much of life and so much love do not often go together."

But even though their life wasn't showy, to the newspapers it looked quite grand. Two large houses, servants, children traveling in Europe—how did Blaine manage on his congressional salary? His official biographer, who was a cousin of Mrs. Blaine's, emphasized that he invested early and profitably in Pennsylvania coal fields; but still the family felt pinched. "A great family we are," Mrs. Blaine commented, "so far as the circulation of money is concerned." Blaine himself was sometimes close to despair. "I do not really know which way to turn for relief," he wrote, "I am so pressed and hampered. . . . Personally and pecuniarily, I am laboring under the most fearful embarrassments." As Mrs. Blaine saw it, the problem was that Blaine had so little time for financial matters. "My dearer self," she wrote, ". . . is looking up his sadly neglected stocks. . . . All that fine Fortunatus's purse which we once held the strings of, and in which we had only to insert the finger to pay therewith for the house, has melted from the grasp which too carelessly held it."

A raise in congressional salary would have been of some help, but nineteenth-century voters didn't look any more kindly on that idea than twentieth-century ones do. In 1816, when Congress had voted to raise its pay from six dollars a day to fifteen hundred dollars a year, the electorate was so outraged that two states set up grand juries to look into the matter. The entire delegations of Ohio, Delaware, and Vermont were subsequently defeated, as were most of the members from Georgia, South Carolina, Maryland, and Connecticut; in the next Congress, the raise was rolled back. While Blaine was Speaker, there was another attempt at a pay raise—this one to seventy-five hundred dollars a year for members and ten thousand for the Speaker. Like the 1816 effort, this one had a retroactive feature sure to outrage the voters, and no matter how straitened his financial circumstances, Blaine had no intention of doing that. He got into the bill a phrase exempting the Speaker from this "bonus" and so received no blame when the bill was passed. His colleagues who voted for the bill felt their constituents' ire, and in the next Congress, the salary increase was repealed.

Given Blaine's financial circumstances, it is not surprising that a friend of his, Congressman Oakes Ames, thought he might be interested in some Credit Mobilier stock. It paid such handsome dividends that the buyer not only recovered the purchase price almost immediately, he showed a profit as well. When the *New York Sun* broke the story that a number of public officials had been bribed with the stock in order to secure legislation favorable to the Union Pacific Railroad, Blaine, whose name headed the list of those alleged to have taken stock, stepped down from the chair and moved to appoint an investigating committee. Subsequent testimony by Blaine and Ames confirmed that Blaine had been offered Credit Mobilier stock—and that he had refused it. His record was clear, but other officials, like Vice-President Schuyler Colfax, whose denials Ames contradicted, came out of the investigation with their reputations tarnished, and the Republicans paid the price in the next election. Government scandals and the panic of 1873 caused voters to reject the party in power, and for the first time since southerners had left the House of Representatives to join the Confederacy, the Democrats were in control.

Thus when the House adjourned in March 1875, Blaine stepped down as Speaker. Since he was the most partisan man who had yet sat in the chair, one might have expected that not all the members would regret his departure. When Polk, also a strong party man, had left the speakership, for example, there had been an effort to deny him the customary vote of thanks, and when it did come, it was far from unanimous. But with Blaine, it was quite different. The *Boston Daily Advertiser* described the scene that followed his farewell speech: "The House rose in unison and every man joined with equal heartiness in a round of applause such as never was heard before in the Capitol. It had hardly died away when it swelled again into a perfect storm, accompanied by cheers, and soon for the third time, the applause swept through the hall as the Speaker stood at the clerk's desk, bowing his thanks and shaking the hands of members who thronged about him." "No such ovation," wrote Emma James in the *Cleveland Daily Herald*, "was ever before given to a retiring Speaker. No other since Henry Clay has been so popular."

The outpouring of affection from Democrats as well as Republicans moved Blaine deeply, but did nothing to dull his partisan edge. Before the next Congress was more than a few hours old, he was demonstrating that it was possible to command the House from the minority leader's position. At issue was the seating of representatives from Louisiana. After elections there had resulted in two rival governments, a compromise had been agreed to that gave the governorship to a Republican and the legislature to the Democrats. Now, however, there were two individuals claiming the same congressional seat. One had his election papers signed by Republican Governor Kellogg, the other by Democratic gubernatorial aspirant McEnery. Fernando Wood, a Democrat from New York, moved to send the matter to the Democrat-controlled Committee on Elections, to which Blaine immediately objected, saying that McEnery was no more governor of Louisiana than Mr. Wood was governor of New York. There were attempts made to counter Blaine's objection, but the new Speaker, Michael Kerr of Indiana, could see that Blaine was carrying the day, and he sent word down to Wood to withdraw his motion. The representative whose election papers the Republican governor had signed was seated.

Blaine's next foray created a national stir. It began when the Democrats introduced a bill declaring a general amnesty: all persons would be relieved of the disabilities imposed by the Fourteenth Amendment. Blaine announced that he had an amendment, one that would except from the amnesty Jefferson Davis, "late President of the so-called Confederate States." Although the amendment was not admitted to either vote or debate, it cast enough of a shadow to keep the amnesty resolution from gaining the two-thirds vote it needed. Blaine immediately moved reconsideration, and the speech with which he reopened debate was one of the most controversial ever delivered in the House.

It began quietly enough:

> Every time the question of amnesty has been brought before the House by a gentleman on that side for the last two Congresses, it has been done with a certain flourish of magnanimity which is an imputation on this side of the House, as though the Republican party which has been in charge of the government for the last twelve or fourteen years has been bigoted, narrow, and illiberal, and as though certain very worthy and deserving gentlemen in the Southern States were ground down today under a great tyranny and oppression, from which the hard-heartedness of this side of the House cannot possibly be prevailed upon to relieve them.

He went on to point out that under Republican rule, citizenship after citizenship had been restored, until now only 750 men remained unpardoned. He was willing to restore their rights—with the exception of Jefferson Davis: "It is not because of any particular and special damage that he above others did to the Union, or because he was personally or especially of consequence. . . . But I except him on this ground: that he was the author, knowingly, deliberately, guiltily, and willfully, of the gigantic murders and crimes at Andersonville." Blaine went on to recount in awful and bloody detail the horrors of that southern prison camp, to tell of starving, vermin-eaten soldiers burrowing holes in the ground for shelter. "I hear it said," he concluded, that "We will lift Mr. Davis again into great consequence by refusing him amnesty." That is not for me to consider. I only see before me when his name is presented, a man who by a wink of his eye, by a wave of his hand, by a nod of his head, could have stopped the atrocity at Andersonville. Some of us had kinsmen there, most of us had friends there, all of us had countrymen there, and in the name of those kinsmen, friends, and countrymen I here protest, and shall with my vote protest, against their calling back and crowning with honors of full American citizenship the man who organized that murder.

The Democrats who had so recently given Blaine a standing ovation now attacked him furiously, calling him a ghoul and a "howling hyena." This was the nation's centennial year, they pointed out, and Blaine was like a "magician of the black art, with devilish incantation, calling up grim and gory spectres from the political inferno to mar the fair form of the festal cheer of the Republic." Others impugned Blaine's motives: he had "waved the bloody shirt" to distract from a corrupt Republican administration; he had done it to advance his own presidential prospects. Blaine always maintained that righteous indignation had been his sole motivation, but that was too simple an analysis for his rivals. They saw a complex maneuver to obtain the presidency, too complex for Blaine's own good, some judged. Carl Schurz wrote, "It seems almost as if Blaine had virtually killed himself as a candidate, as I always thought he would. He may seemingly revive, but I am sure he will die of too much smartness at last."

But for the short run, at least, Schurz was wrong, and Blaine had mastered the situation yet once more. There were thousands of northerners in whom Blaine's speech struck a responsive chord, and they flooded the newspapers with letters praising him. Jefferson Davis helped matters along by writing a letter himself. He didn't want a pardon from the North, he wrote, because the North had no right being in the pardon business in the first place. It was the south that had much to forgive, the South that had suffered so grievously at the hands of "invaders." Commented the *New York Tribune*, "When Mr. Blaine proposed to distinguish Jefferson Davis by refusing to include him in a general amnesty, a majority of the Republicans of the North believed he had made a great mistake. More than half of Davis' letter, however, is taken up showing that Mr. Blaine was right."

The Blaine-for-president movement took fire. A Chicago supporter wrote to Blaine about a Republican conference in Illinois: "The presidential expression was generally in your favor." Word came in that Washington Territory had elected Blaine delegates to the national convention. But along with the enthusiastic letters pouring in, there was one that hinted at difficulties ahead. A friend wrote that a director of the Union Pacific Railroad was claiming that the road had purchased worthless Little Rock and Fort Smith bonds from Blaine for sixty-four thousand dollars. Two months before the Republican convention, the charges became public, and as he had done so many times before, Blaine went on the offensive. On April 24, 1876, he took the House floor on a question of personal privilege and denied the charge. He produced statements from Union Pacific officials and from bankers denying he had been paid any money. It was true he had owned Little Rock and Fort Smith stock, he said, but that was surely an irreproachable investment since the railroad received both its charter and public land grants from the state of Arkansas rather than from the federal government. And he certainly hadn't been granted any special privilege in his stock purchases. "Instead of receiving the bonds of the Little Rock and Fort Smith Railroad as a gratuity," he said, "I never had one except at the regular market price . . . instead of making a large fortune out of that company, I have incurred a severe pecuniary loss. . . ."

Closing with a declaration that "my whole connection with this railroad has been as open as the day," Blaine seemed once more master of the situation. The speech squelched the scandal stories and his candidacy picked up momentum again. Even though the Democrats appointed a House committee to look into the matter, Blaine's progress wasn't slowed much, because none of the testimony supported the accusation of his having received sixty-four thousand dollars for worthless stock.

Then on May 31, 1876, a new witness was sworn in. His name was James Mulligan and he had been a clerk for Blaine's brother-in-law, Jacob Stanwood. After he had left Stanwood's employ, there had been a quarrel in which Blaine took Stanwood's side, leaving Mulligan with a grudge he now had the means to satisfy. He had in his possession a number of letters Blaine had written to a builder of the Little Rock and Fort Smith Railroad, one Warren Fisher.

At the first mention of the letters, Blaine asked the Republican member of the investigating committee to seek an adjournment. That afternoon he confronted Mulligan and demanded the letters. When Mulligan refused, he asked simply to look at them—and then when they were given to him to examine, he refused to return them. He left the hotel where Mulligan was staying with the letters in his pocket. He refused to turn them over to the committee, saying they were "strictly private" and had no more connection to the investigation than "the man in the moon." To strengthen his assertion, he offered a signed opinion from two respected lawyers who had examined the letters and found them to have "no relevancy whatever to the matter under enquiry."

But it became clear almost immediately that stonewalling was not going to work. Why, Blaine would be asked again and again, why was he refusing to release the letters? If they were so innocent, why not let the public see them? The accusations and denials would go on and on, and the Republican convention was less than two weeks away. Blaine could not hope to be the nominee unless he could put the matter behind him quickly. Word spread throughout Washington that Blaine meant to take to the floor once more to defend himself against his accusers.

On Monday, June 5, the galleries were packed. The doorkeepers were unable to cope and dozens of unauthorized persons crowded onto the floor. The crowd jostled and whispered until Blaine rose to speak, and then there was a tense, expectant hush. All eyes focused on the gray-haired, gray-bearded man, tall and dignified in a buttoned-up black frock suit. He looked like a president, and his next words might well determine whether he would ever be one.

Standing at the top of the aisle on the Republican side, he began with a full account of all the investigative machinery arrayed against him and described how far afield it had gone. Now there was even a demand that he exhibit private memoranda that had "no more to do with that investigation than with the North Pole." Because this was an extraordinary violation of his rights, Blaine said, he had refused, and he was ready to go to any lengths to defend such rights. "And while I am so," he said, knowing he was about to produce a sensation, "I am not afraid to show the letters. Thank God Almighty, I am not ashamed to show them. There they are (holding up a package of letters). There is the very original package. And with some sense of humiliation, with a mortification that I do not pretend to conceal, with a sense of outrage which I think any man in my position would feel, I invite the confidence of forty-four million of my countrymen while I read those letters from this desk." A cheer went up. There was wild applause, and when it had died down, Blaine started reading, offering brief explanations as he went along. He did not present the letters chronologically, and since they gave but one side of the correspondence it must have been difficult to make much out of all the facts and figures they contained. But for the moment, that was beside the point. Blaine was reading the letters, making them public. Only a man who knew he was innocent would dare do that. And if there were any doubters left, he converted them with the way he concluded his presentation. There had been effort after effort to make him out a guilty man, he said, yet not a single bit of proof had been turned up.

"There is one piece of evidence wanting," he declared, turning to Proctor Knott, chairman of the Judiciary Committee, and demanding to know if a dispatch had been sent to Josiah Caldwell, the chief promoter of the Little Rock and Fort Smith Railroad. Knott answered, "I will reply to the gentleman that Judge Hunton and myself have both endeavored to get Mr. Caldwell's address and have not yet got it."

"Has the gentleman received a dispatch from Mr. Caldwell?" Blaine asked.

"I will explain that directly," said Knott.

"I want a categorical answer."

"I have received a dispatch purporting to be from Mr. Caldwell."

"You did?" Blaine said.

"How did you know I got it?"

"When did you get it?" Blaine asked. "I want the gentleman from Kentucky to answer when he got it."

"Answer my question first."

"I never heard of it till yesterday."

"How did you hear it?" Knott asked.

"I heard you got a dispatch last Thursday morning at eight o'clock from Josiah Caldwell completely and absolutely exonerating me from this charge, and you have suppressed it."

The audience erupted into cheers. The Speaker pounded his gavel and demanded order, but no one paid him the least attention, and so he ordered the floor to be cleared of intruders. He would empty the galleries too, he threatened, unless order were restored. But the doorkeepers were unable to manage even the floor, and the crowds remained and kept on cheering.

Knott didn't get a chance to press Blaine on how he knew about the Caldwell cable (in fact, Blaine's friends had solicited it). Nor did he get much of a hearing when he tried to explain that he had kept the Caldwell telegram secret for fear that it was not genuine. Blaine partisans were too busy celebrating what seemed a sure victory. "The cheering . . . seemed to come from all over the House," one wrote. "It was wild and long and deep. It was a perfect roar of triumph." But over the next few days, more objective observers would consider the letters Blaine had read and understand why he had tried to suppress them. It was true that they contained no evidence he had sold worthless Little Rock and Fort Smith stock to the Union Pacific, but they did reveal embarrassing aspects of his Little Rock and Fort Smith connection. Blaine had, for one thing, boasted of his power as Speaker to the promoters of the enterprise, and he had done so by pointing out that he was the one who had secured in the House the renewal of the land grant to Arkansas upon which the railroad depended. He had no interest in the railroad when the grant was renewed. "At that time I had never seen Mr. Caldwell," he wrote in one of the Mulligan letters, "but you can tell him that, without knowing it, I did him a great favor." But no favors, witting or unwitting, could have been managed if what Blaine had said earlier had been true. He had told his colleagues in April that the Little Rock and Fort Smith Railroad "derived all it had from the State of Arkansas and not from Congress."

He had also told the House that he had acquired his Little Rock and Fort Smith stock at regular market price. But the letters showed he had received it as a commission for selling stock to others. Furthermore, he had assured the promoters with the statement: "I do not feel that I shall prove a dead-head in the enterprise, if I once embark on it." His enemies would trumpet this about as a promise to use official influence, but the real message Blaine was sending was much subtler. I will be a first-rate salesman, he was saying, for who could turn down a chance to buy bonds from the Speaker of the House? To someone who suggested this was unethical, Blaine might have responded, "You mean just because I am Speaker, I should be prohibited from selling bonds? Why shouldn't I have the same opportunities a private citizen enjoys?" And because he was a devoted family man, he might have added, "And why shouldn't I be able to give my children the advantages my neighbors give theirs?"

If Blaine had seen the private correspondence of men whom he approached in his salesman's role, he might better have understood the problem. Financier Jay Cooke, one of the men to whom Blaine tried to sell the Little Rock bonds, turned him down, but wrote his brother, "Try and do everything that is right and kind and generous by him at the right time." Shortly thereafter, Blaine, who was in the process of moving his family to Washington, secured a mortgage for thirty-three thousand dollars on his new home from Jay Cooke and Company. Blaine might have fooled himself into believing that this was a straightforward financial transaction, but Cooke, whose Northern Pacific Railway depended absolutely on congressional action, knew it was a "special" arrangement and described the loan as "too much on such a property" in a note to the manager of his Washington office. When Blaine approached Cooke and Company on another matter, Cooke's brother Henry wrote to the financier that Blaine "is a formidable power for good or evil, and he has a wide future before him. However unreasonable in his demands he may appear to you to be, my conviction is irresistable that he should in some manner be appeased."

When a powerful public official offers someone an investment, that person is very likely to react differently than he would if he were approached by a private individual. Blaine chose not to recognize an impropriety in this. He had understood that taking Credit Mobilier stock was wrong, but he did not perceive that it was unethical for him to sell on commission to people whose lives and fortunes he could greatly affect in his political role. Nor did he perceive a problem in receiving lucrative commissions from men to whom his political decisions could mean millions. Quite the contrary, he saw himself as a man of honor, for the Mulligan letters also showed that when the bonds he sold his friends and acquaintances went bad, he undertook personally to pay the interest due on them. The idea that his hopes for the presidency could be destroyed by what he saw as undeserved attacks gnawed at him and began to take a toll. He paced distractedly, took to bed with a slight fever. "Once, lying on a sofa," a female relative reported, ". . . he suddenly raised his clenched hand high and exclaimed in a voice thick with emotion, 'When I think—when I think—that there lives in this broad land one single human being who doubts my integrity, I would rather have stayed'—but instantly controlled himself and did not finish the sentence."

On Sunday, June 11, three days before the Republican convention was to meet in Cincinnati, he seemed to be feeling better. He came to breakfast with a child perched on each shoulder and insisted he would walk the half-mile to church despite the heat. As he and his family approached the door of the First Congregational Church at Tenth and G Streets, Blaine fainted. He was taken home and for hours was insensible. Outside his house an anxious crowd gathered and grew to such proportions that the street had to be barricaded. In Cincinnati, his delegates were buffeted by rumors, even one that he had died. Finally he was able to send them word by wire. He was recovering—and they were ecstatic. Enthusiasts before, they were now transported with joy, animated by what they saw as their hero's brush with martyrdom. The Democrats, particularly those from the South, had tried to destroy him and had failed. Blaine, their Blaine, had come through and was sure to triumph.

Robert Ingersoll had been chosen to place Blaine's name in nomination. He was not yet a man of national reputation, and when delegates who had never heard of him began to find out about him, they must have wondered at Blaine's choice. A round-faced, kindly seeming man, Ingersoll was a Democrat turned Republican who had lately been making speeches notable not only for their striking oratory, but also for their startling point of view: they advocated agnosticism. But as Ingersoll, smiling and self-possessed, strode to the podium of Exposition Hall and began speaking, it became apparent that Blaine had made a brilliant choice. "He had not spoken five minutes," an eyewitness observed, "until he had the convention wrought up to the wildest enthusiasm, and he was halted time and again in his impressive sentences by the cheers which arose and echoed through the large auditorium. . . ."

Ingersoll made no attempt to ignore the events of the last few months. To the contrary, he made capital of them. "This is a grand year...," he told the crowd, "a year in which [the people] call for the man who has torn from the throat of treason the tongue of slander—for the man who has snatched the mask of Democracy from the hideous face of rebellion; for the man who, like an intellectual athlete, has stood in the arena of debate and challenged all comers, and who is still a total stranger to defeat." The crowd burst into applause, and when it had died down, Ingersoll delivered the passage that generations of schoolboys would memorize: "Like an armed warrior, like a plumed knight, James G. Blaine marched down the halls of the American Congress and threw his shining lance full and fair against the brazen foreheads of the defamers of his country and the maligners of his honor. For the Republican party to desert this gallant leader now is as though an army should desert their general upon the field of battle." Once more there was applause, and then Ingersoll worked to his climax: "Gentleman of the Convention, in the name of the great Republic, the only Republic that ever existed upon this earth; in the name of all her defenders and of all her supporters; in the name of all her soldiers living; in the name of all her soldiers dead upon the field of battle, and in the name of those who perished in the skeleton clutch of famine at Andersonville and Libby, whose sufferings he so vividly remembers, Illinois—Illinois nominates for the next President of this country that prince of parliamentarians, that leader of leaders—James G. Blaine." The hall went mad. Hats were thrown into the air and handkerchieves waved. "Blaine, Blaine, James G. Blaine!" the crowd began to chant. "There was not a friend or foe of Blaine in the convention," one delegate observed, "who did not feel that Blaine must win an easy triumph."

But then something happened that some felt was fatal to Blaine's chances. Evening had come—and the lights could not be turned on. All day Blaine's friends had been struggling to make sure that a ballot was taken before the convention adjourned for the day, and they were even more anxious for balloting to begin when they saw the reaction to Ingersoll's speech. But without lights, the convention had to adjourn. The faulty lighting worked so much to the advantage of Blaine's opponents, that some suspected they had cut off the gas to the building.

By the next day, Blaine's momentum had slowed. The first ballot showed him leading, but almost a hundred votes short of the necessary number. His total rose and fell, rose and fell, but not substantially until the sixth ballot. Then there was a break, and his total went up to 308, just 61 short of victory. His lieutenants scrambled frantically, picking up a vote here and a vote there until it looked as if Kentucky would do it. But Benjamin Bristow, Kentucky's favorite son, was not inclined to help. He had been serious about securing the nomination for himself, and during the spring a certain tension had developed between him and Blaine. Then on June 11, when Blaine had fainted, Bristow had rushed to his home to see how he was. Mrs. Blaine, who probably regarded Bristow's behavior as a bit ghoulish, did not receive him graciously, and he was still nursing hurt feelings.

Meanwhile Roscoe Conkling had been actively organizing an anybody-but-Blaine movement, and when he approached Kentucky he got their promise to vote for Rutherford B. Hayes. When the voting began and Kentucky announced for Hayes, she was joined by other states that had formerly been scattered among a number of Blaine's opponents. The final balloting was Hayes, 384; Blaine, 351.

And so there were many "what ifs" for Blaine to consider. He might have been nominated *if* the convention hadn't adjourned on Wednesday; *if* Mrs. Blaine had not alienated Benjamin Bristow; *if* he hadn't made an enemy of Conkling years before. But most important was the fact that he had been vulnerable to scandal. The Republican newspapers in Cincinnati, which the delegates would have been reading daily, were hostile to him, almost as suspicious of his Mulligan explanations as the Democratic papers were, and that had to have had an effect. George Frisbee Hoar, a delegate and a congressman who had been on the investigating committee, believed Blaine entirely innocent of criminal wrongdoing, but concluded it was unwise to nominate him. The Republicans needed to run against scandal, as Hoar saw it, not put at the top of the ticket a man who must continually protest his innocence.

Blaine took the loss well. After he had sent a congratulatory telegram to Hayes, he ordered an open carriage and went riding through Publisher's Row on Fourteenth Street in Washington to show that he was neither ill nor despondent. Everywhere he went, he was cheered, both on that day and for most of the next two decades. He was appointed to the Senate (thus ending the House investigation), he would serve as secretary of state for two presidents, and he would be a serious candidate for president twice more. In 1884, he would win the Republican nomination for the presidency, and in the subsequent campaign against Grover Cleveland, all of the old scandals would be unearthed. Mulligan released new letters, which like the previous ones showed no criminal activity but much that was questionable. Political cartoonists injected vitality into the old charges with some fiendishly skillful drawings. One by Bernard Gillam for *Puck* showed Blaine in his underwear sporting as body tattoos certain damning phrases such as "Mulligan letters" and "Little Rock Railroad." The caricature, said one contemporary, aroused "a certain irresistible thrill of loathing."

During the hot July days before the election, it became clear that Cleveland had his own scandalous troubles, namely an illegitimate child. The capital that Republicans were able to make of this led Democrats to turn a spotlight on Blaine's past. How long, they began to ask, had he and Mrs. Blaine been married before their first-born (who died in infancy) arrived on the scene? Not long enough, they concluded, and as if to get proof, someone entered the graveyard where the child was buried and chiseled his birthdate from the tombstone.

This act was so outrageous that it shamed scandalmongers on both sides into silence. The election turned out to be close, heartbreakingly close for Blaine. Cleveland won—and a six-hundred-vote turnaround in New York State could have made the difference. Blaine's loss was partly the fault of a certain Reverend Burchard, a Blaine supporter who in the last days of the campaign used the phrase, "Rum, Romanism and Rebellion" to describe the Democrats, thereby alienating Catholics who might have otherwise voted for Blaine. But in an election as close as 1884, many things could have made a difference, and one was the question of Blaine's financial dealings. Reform Republicans such as Carl Schurz bolted the party. "I am indeed of the opinion . . . that the author of the Mulligan letters can never be, and ought not to be President of the United States," Schurz wrote, and he and his fellow "Mugwumps" worked for Cleveland.

Had Blaine's record been spotless, he might well have been president. That it was not makes him quite typical of his time. Few men had spotless records and many had much worse ones than Blaine's. General Grant saw nothing wrong with accepting a Philadelphia mansion from a dry-goods magnate who wanted to reward his Civil War service, or with letting the New York financial community pay off the hundred-thousand-dollar mortgage on his Washington home. Benjamin Butler had requisitioned eighty thousand dollars from a New Orleans bank when he was military governor there, and when a lawyer who was suing him to recover the money suggested his neighbors wouldn't think much of him for living off stolen funds, he replied, "The people would think I was a fool for not having taken twice as much." Such attitudes led Henry Adams, who watched it all through world-weary eyes, to conclude, "The moral law had expired, like the Constitution."

But not for everyone. There were some, such as George Frisbee Hoar, who could see through the gilding of the age, and although he admired Blaine in many ways, he thought he had been wrong to get involved in railroad speculation. "Members of legislative bodies," wrote Hoar, "especially great political leaders of large influence, ought to be careful to keep a thousand miles off from relations which may give rise to even a suspicion of wrong." But Blaine was not careful, and so, like Clay, he did not reach the goal toward which his whole career had been leading. He was loved, however, adored by his family and friends, idolized by thousands upon thousands of Americans—just as the Kentuckian had been. "No public man in the country," one of Blaine's contemporaries observed, "except perhaps Henry Clay, had such a devoted following." In his later years especially, he was received wherever he went with what John Hay called "a fury of affection."

Blaine was only too aware of the resemblance to Clay. Shortly after he had been nominated in 1884, he had pointed out the similarities to a young reporter. Walking along the Kennebec River, he noted: "Clay was defeated in two conventions when he could have been elected President, and he was nominated for President when his competitor was elected, and that competitor was one who had not been publicly discussed as a Presidential candidate before the meeting of the Baltimore convention of 1844. I was defeated in two conventions when I could have been elected. I am nominated now with a competitor alike obscure with the competitor of Clay." Blaine concluded his soliloquy by holding up his hand and repeating two numbers: "1844-1884." Clay had been defeated in 1844, and Blaine apparently had a premonition that the Kentuckian's defeat foreshadowed his own.

There was a final, tragic similarity between Blaine and Clay: both learned that there are far worse things fate can do to a man than deny him the presidency. All six of Clay's daughters, including his beloved Anne, died before him. He was also predeceased by two of his sons, one of whom was killed in the Mexican War. Still another son went mad. For Blaine the shattering blow was the death of both his eldest son and eldest daughter within two weeks in 1890. Within two years, his next son, Emmons, died, and shortly thereafter Blaine took to his bed. His home now was on Lafayette Square, right across from the White House, and there in view of the mansion he had wanted so much to occupy, he grew weaker and weaker. As it became clear he was dying, even his foes were sorrowful, and some of them joined the sympathetic crowds that gathered outside his door. On January 27, 1893, the doctors came out on the front steps and announced that Blaine was dead.

5

REED AND THE RULES

Many Republican political pros had been convinced it was a mistake for their party to nominate James G. Blaine in 1884. Financial scandal had tainted him fatally, they believed, but they were overwhelmed by popular sentiment. At a frenzied convention dominated by his followers ("a mass meeting of maniacs," one journalist called it), Blaine was chosen the party standard-bearer.

Not long after, a scholarly young man named Henry Cabot Lodge happened to meet a rotund Republican representative on the street.

"What did you think of the nomination?" Lodge asked.

"Well," came the answer in a sarcastic Yankee drawl. "It is a great comfort to think that the wicked politicians were not allowed to pick the candidate and that the nomination was made by the people. The politicians would have been guided only by a base desire to win."

The congressman was Thomas Brackett Reed, and though he, like Blaine, was from the state of Maine, that didn't stop him from skewering the Republican nominee. Indeed, no one was truly safe when Reed was around, not his fellow members of the House ("They never open their mouths without subtracting from the sum total of human knowledge," he said of two of them), not Democrats ("We live in a world of sin and sorrow," he declared. "Otherwise there would not be any Democratic Party"), and particularly not the United States Senate, which he called the "little" House as opposed to the "large" one in which he himself served. The Senate, he once said, was "a place where good Representatives go when they die." Another time he called it "a close communion of old grannies and tabby cats." Still another time, he wrote an account of a futuristic United States in which the president was to be chosen by secret vote in the Senate. But when the ballots were counted, lo and behold, each and every senator had received exactly one vote.

Reed was unabashedly a man of the House, and he made himself more expert in its rules and proceedings than any representative had ever been. The knowledge he acquired gave him great power even before he became Speaker, and once he sat in the chair he used what he knew to bring about the most revolutionary changes ever accomplished in the institution's way of doing business. "He was easily," Henry Cabot Lodge testified, "the greatest parliamentary leader I ever saw."

Reed was a huge man, standing over six feet tall and weighing somewhere close to three hundred pounds. ("No gentleman weighs more than two hundred," he once admonished a colleague who pressed him on the point.) His quick wit was oddly at home in his massive, slow-moving body, but that was only one of many seeming contradictions about him. He was a politician, but never went out of his way to curry favor with his constituents. ("I am not in the old junk business," he told one who urged him to obtain a Civil War cannon for a local park.) He was successful in an age when moral corners were frequently cut, but was scrupulously honest himself. ("I do not expect by acting thus strictly to escape public slander," he said. "I only expect not to deserve it.") He acknowledged himself to be wary of change, declaring, "Most new things are not good," but he was a strong advocate of female suffrage three decades before women finally got the vote. He was caught up in a fast-paced world where few found time to do more than react, but he managed to read widely, contemplate philosophy, and even, when he was forty, to teach himself French. It was he who saw to it that a national library was built.

And though he had one of the wickedest tongues in the House or anywhere else, he could be a warm and valued friend. "No more agreeable companion ever lived," Henry Cabot Lodge declared. Mark Twain, to whom Reed was extremely close in his last years, wrote, "His ways were frank and open and the road to his large sympathies was straight and unobstructed. His was a nature which invited affection—compelled it, in fact—and met it halfway."

He had been born in Portland, Maine, to a family of Mayflower ancestry and modest means. He went off to Bowdoin College, teaching school during the long winter vacations to help pay his way, and after graduation he studied law. Like many a young man of the time, he sought his fortune in California, but he found the West uncongenial. "Nature never intended any man to live there," he declared, "only to dig gold and get himself out of it." He served a short stint in the navy, an experience he refused to take very seriously. "You just say to them that I kept a grocery on a gunboat down in Louisiana," he declared to a supporter who wanted to use his Civil War record in a campaign. After the war, he returned to Maine, began practicing law, and was elected to the state legislature. In 1870 he married the daughter of a prominent clergyman and was appointed state attorney general. In 1876 the same year Blaine moved to the Senate, Reed was elected to Congress.

He began his career in the House ordinarily enough, quietly accepting a rather dull assignment to the Committee on Territories. "I pledge you my word," he commented later, "that I would not have known a territory if I had met one on the avenue." But when the chance came to him, as it did with the Potter investigation of the 1876 presidential election, he distinguished himself. By audaciously questioning witnesses, he showed that Republicans had not been alone in the use of doubtful tactics and thereby defused the Democrats' charges of fraud. He also began to establish for himself the reputation of having "a tongue that at one stroke sliced the whiskers off his opponents' faces." Once when a questioner interrupted him in the middle of an explanation, he made a stinging retort, paused, looked about him, and said, "Now, having embalmed that fly in the liquid amber of my discourse, I wish to proceed."

At the beginning of Reed's third term, Republicans took over control of the House. In their caucus, Reed's name was put in nomination for Speaker, and though he trailed far behind the winner, Kiefer of Ohio, the fact that he was in the race at all spoke highly of the way he was viewed. He had devoted much of his time in the Congress to studying the rules of the House, a body of knowledge "full of intricacies and secrets," as one member expressed it, and Reed's command of this esoterica won him much respect. He was made chairman of the Judiciary Committee and was the obvious choice to move onto the Rules Committee when a vacancy occurred.

The rules of the House had been revised and codified in 1880, but they still did not constitute an efficient mechanism for enacting legislation. A determined minority could keep any action at all from being taken, as an election case in 1882 illustrated. The Democrats, intent on keeping a Republican from being seated, began to filibuster by moving to adjourn and making other dilatory motions. After seven days, Reed had had enough. As a member of the Rules Committee, he secured the floor to submit a privileged report.* It provided that in election cases there could be no obstructive motions until the matter had been decided, but hardly had the proposal been made when it was beset by a host of obstructive motions, whereupon Reed offered the further view that such tactics could not be used when the matter under consideration was whether they were to be in order. "There is no such thing as suicide in any provision of the Constitution of the United States," he declared. The Speaker upheld him, the Republicans upheld the Speaker, and Reed had succeeded in his first major effort to improve the procedures of the House. "From that hour," wrote Congressman DeAlva Alexander, "Reed became the real leader of his party. Ever after, so long as he remained in Congress, his voice gave the word of command."

Reed's next victory was a truly astonishing feat of legerdemain. The Democrats had won enough seats in the fall elections that it was clear they would be in control of the next Congress, and they were determined that no tariff legislation would be passed until then. The Republicans were equally anxious to enact legislation before they lost control, and Reed saw that a Senate tax bill, which had amendments relating to the tariff, might provide a way. The Senate bill lay on the Speaker's table, however, and getting it to the floor would require suspension of the rules. That meant a two-thirds vote, which the Republicans could not muster. Reed got around this with a maneuver the Whigs had used once, some forty years before. He presented a privileged report from the Rules Committee, which provided for suspending the rules. A report could be adopted by a mere majority, which the Republicans could manage, and after bitter denunciation by the Democrats ("a monstrous proposition," Representative Carlisle called it), this one was adopted.

Besides suspending the rules, the report declared the House's dis-

---

* The ability to intervene and present such a report—which had to be taken up immediately—was a recent innovation and a considerable source of power for the Rules Committee.

agreement with the tariff amendments on the Senate bill and required that a conference committee resolve the differences. Since Reed was a protectionist and the Senate amendments reduced tariffs, many members must have wondered why Reed wanted to bother with them at all; but when they saw the makeup of the conference committee, they understood. It was overwhelmingly protectionist, and the bill that emerged from it reflected that viewpoint. Reed, by using a bill that lowered tariffs, managed to achieve a law that actually raised many of them.

At the beginning of the Forty-ninth Congress, Reed was the Republican candidate for Speaker. Nominated in the caucus by a likable young Ohio congressman named William McKinley, he defeated his nearest Republican rival by a substantial margin. Because the Democrats controlled the House, he did not win the balloting on the floor, but he was now his party's leader in title as well as in fact.

He looked the part. With his huge bulk he seemed "to fill the room with his presence," Henry Cabot Lodge reported; he had "a commanding figure and . . . the sense of power and force which went with it." Another contemporary described him as "a slow-moving giant hulk of a barge moving down the ways into the water, a form dressed completely in black, out of whose collar rose an enormous, round, clean-shaven baby face. A Cassaba melon flowering from a fat, black stalk. A sprawling, shuffling being, a subject for Frans Hals, with long white fingers that would have enraptured a Memling." His size not only gave him commanding presence, it provided others with something to joke about, and that was important considering how caustic his own wit was. Those who had been hurt by it could relieve their resentment by laughing at the source of their pain, a release without which his leadership might have been intolerable. No doubt there were more than a few satisfied smiles in the Republican as well as the Democratic cloakroom where the *Washington Post* reported that Reed's linen summer suit had *finally* been pressed, but that somehow the creases ran down the sides of the trousers rather than up the front. "Mr. Reed's capacious legs looked as if they had wings on them," the *Post* reporter wrote, "for the creases stood out conspicuously and with generous expansion." Laughter would also have risen on both sides of the aisle when one member remarked how fortunate it was for Reed that dueling was no longer the vogue.

His tongue would surely have got him in trouble, noted the wag, and his huge figure would have been an impossible target to miss.

In the more important ways, however, Reed was invulnerable. He never left anyone in doubt about his intelligence or his integrity. He kept himself so far from the appearance of wrongdoing that he even refused the free service the telegraph companies provided congressmen for the conduct of their official business. Although he was in Congress for more than twenty years, he never bought a house in Washington and stayed with his wife and daughter in boardinghouses and hotels. His reputation for honesty was important to him, and when another member of Congress, Richard Townshend of Illinois, suggested there was some doubt about it, Reed delivered one of his most devastating put-downs. He took to the floor and declared there were only two sets of people whose opinions he cared about: his constituency, which knew him, and the House, which knew Townshend. "It is hardly necessary to say," he concluded, "that I shall stand vindicated before both."

As a debater, Reed was formidable. He didn't go in for flamboyant gestures, but planted himself in the Republican aisle, his hands resting on desks on each side. With no trace of expression on his face, he would fill the chamber with his peculiar, rasping voice (a "dry, saw-like, cooing, matter-of-fact drawl," one listener called it), and well before his five minutes were up, he would have stated his argument so lucidly it seemed unanswerable. He was the "best short-speech maker I ever saw or heard," wrote Champ Clark. Said Joe Cannon, "I have never heard my distinguished friend from Maine take the floor upon any subject but that I did not feel sometimes regretful that I could not crystalize an idea . . . as he does, roll it up with my hands into proper shape and hurl it at the head of my opponent."

He was magnificent at repartee, particularly when his opponents offered him the target of exaggerated virtue or self-importance. When William Springer of Illinois took a line from Henry Clay and announced he "would rather be right than President," Reed shot back instantly, "The gentleman need not worry. He will never be either." The same unstudied wit made Reed a delight at the card game or the dinner table. In one gathering of friends, Joseph Choate was moved to remark, "I think I can say that I have lived a clean

and decent life. I have none of the vices and a good many of the virtues, and I think I average up pretty well."

"I wish I could say that," another of the dinner guests lamented.
"Well, why don't you say it?" Reed asked. "Choate did."

But the most important source of Reed's influence in the House
was his knowledge of the rules, and he persisted in trying to improve
them. One problem, as he saw it, was the vast power of the Appropriations Committee. The House had long passed the stage where it
was able to deal with all the bills introduced in each Congress; fewer
than 10 percent were acted upon. Because of the precedence given
appropriations matters, the Appropriations Committee could control the floor, and often the only way a measure could be enacted
was by getting it attached as an amendment to an appropriations
bill. It was a process, Reed noted, akin to running "Niagara through
a quill." It also gave great power to the chairman of the Appropriations Committee, the hard-working and forceful former Democratic
Speaker, Sam Randall. It was a standing joke in Washington that
Congress "consisted of the Senate and Sam Randall."

Reed had spoken out against the power of the Appropriations
Committee in the Forty-eighth Congress, but it wasn't until the
Forty-ninth, when he had become minority leader, that he was able
to do something about it. By capitalizing on a long-standing feud
between Chairman Randall and another senior Democrat, William
Morrison of Illinois, he was able to get to the floor a Rules Committee report that gave appropriations authority to five committees besides Randall's. The fact that Randall had long been out of harmony with his party on the tariff issue made him vulnerable, but the
high personal regard his colleagues had for him meant he would not
be beaten easily. In the more than two decades he had been in the
House, Randall had never had any source of income besides his
five-thousand-dollar-a-year salary. Unlike most of his colleagues, he
had only one profession, being a congressman, and although the result was severely straitened financial circumstances for him and his
family, he consistently refused all offers of financial assistance. As
Speaker, he had presided over the Hayes-Tilden election dispute in
bold and unselfish fashion, and on other issues as well, when he believed he was right, he held firmly to his course, so that he had a reputation for courage, albeit of a somewhat stubborn brand. These
were virtues Reed admired, and when he addressed the House on

the matter of the Appropriations Committee, his speech, though tough, was not without a note of compliment. "For the last three Congresses," he declared, "the representatives of the people of the United States have been in irons. They have been allowed to transact no public business except at the dictation of a small coterie of gentlemen who, while they possessed individually more wisdom than any of the rest of us, did not possess all the wisdom of this world." Reed struck exactly the right tone, and the House voted overwhelmingly to break the Appropriations Committee's stranglehold.

For a time, matters seemed to improve, but in the Fiftieth Congress it became glaringly apparent that deep-seated problems remained. The *Washington Post* said the House was "slowly doing nothing," and the *New York Tribune* dubbed its members "the incapables." In January 1889 one member, James Weaver of Iowa, dramatically illustrated why the House was paralyzed. Under the rules as they existed, a minority—even a minority of one, in Weaver's case—could bring business to a halt. For eight days, Weaver, who wanted to force consideration of a bill organizing the territory of Oklahoma, proposed two or three separate motions in alternating succession and thus blocked all legislation. Not until party leaders promised to take up his bill did he stop his obstructive tactics.

As soon as it became clear that the Republicans would control the House of Representatives in the Fifty-first Congress, a contest for the speakership began. The affable and handsome William McKinley, prodded on by his new mentor, Mark Hanna, challenged Reed for the leadership position. But Hanna, who would later prove himself an astute politician, was still honing his skills, and Reed had high-powered help of his own. Henry Cabot Lodge, in Congress now, was working for Reed, as was a young civil service commissioner named Theodore Roosevelt. "Theodore," said Reed to him on one occasion, "if there is one thing more than another for which I admire you, it is your original discovery of the ten commandments." But for the moment, he probably appreciated Roosevelt's zeal. On one of his hunting trips west, the New Yorker stopped off to lobby the Minnesota congressional delegation, in which Hanna was making some inroads. He spoke out in Reed's favor at the Federal Club and set up a Reed-for-Speaker headquarters in a back room of the Wormley Hotel. To the frustration of his backers, Reed would not promise committee assignments or make commitments on legislation in order to obtain votes; but that did not mean he was inactive on his own behalf. He wrote two long articles for national magazines describing the sorry state of affairs in the House. "There is only one way to remedy the situation," he wrote, "and that is to return to the first principles of democracy and republicanism alike. Our government is founded on the doctrine that if one hundred citizens think one way and one hundred one think the other, the one hundred one are right."

To his fellow Republicans in the House—the ones who would decide if he would be Speaker—this was an important declaration, for they held a very slim majority, only a few more than the number constituting a quorum. Under current conditions, the Democrats could block all legislation, but Reed was promising to change the conditions and insure majority—which for the moment meant Republican—rule. On that platform he was elected.

He began his career in the chair by delaying a procedure that had become standard. In its opening days, a new House typically adopted the rules of the one preceding it, but Reed saw to it that the Fifty-first proceeded under general parliamentary law instead. This meant that, as long as he was sustained by a majority, *he* could decide what was parliamentary, a prospect that made the Democrats exceedingly apprehensive. As it turned out, their fears were well founded.

On January 29, 1890, a resolution was offered that settled a disputed election in favor of the Republican claimant. After demanding a roll call on whether the resolution would be considered, the Democrats sat silently at their desks, refusing to vote. To a visitor in the gallery, their behavior must have seemed peculiar. Why would they call a vote and then refuse to participate in it? But those on the floor were well aware that this was a time-honored method of filibustering known as the "disappearing quorum." As early as John Quincy Adams's time, members had realized that on a matter where the sides were closely divided (as they would be on any partisan issue in the Fifty-first Congress), if the minority simply refused to vote, it would usually mean there would be no quorum for conducting business. The majority was almost certain to have a few absentees, and so the votes cast would number fewer than half the members of the House.

Which is exactly what happened. There were 161 yeas, 2 nays, 165 not voting. "No quorum," Mr. Crisp of Georgia shouted.

But Reed ignored him. "The Chair directs the Clerk to record the following names of members present and refusing to vote," he said, and instantly a dozen Democrats were on their feet shouting objection. Never before had a Speaker taken a quorum to mean those present rather than those voting. Even when directly requested, Blaine had refused to do it. "The moment you clothe your Speaker with power to go behind your roll-call and assume that there is a quorum," he told the House, "why, gentlemen, you stand on the very brink of a volcano." The accuracy of his prediction was proved now. As Reed called out names for the clerk to record, more Democrats rose to their feet to protest, and when that had no effect, they began to rush frantically about the floor, shouting denunciations at the Speaker. Seeming unperturbed by it all, Reed continued with the roll: "Mr. Blount, Mr. Breckinridge of Arkansas, Mr. Breckinridge of Kentucky."

"I deny the power of the Speaker," the silver-haired Breckinridge of Kentucky roared, "and denounce it as revolutionary."

Ignoring the applause on the Democratic side of the House, Reed continued: "Mr. Lee, Mr. McAdoo, Mr. McCreary."

"I deny your right, Mr. Speaker, to count me as present," shouted McCreary.

"The Chair is making a statement of the fact that the gentleman from Kentucky is present," Reed replied. "Does he wish to deny it?" When another member whose name he called shouted, "I am not here!" Reed smiled at him benevolently, "as one looks at a pet lunatic," and continued on through the alphabet. "Mr. Montgomery, Mr. Moore of Texas, Mr. Morgan." By the time he called the last name, the floor was in complete uproar. Reed pounded the gavel and patiently called for order until the chamber was quiet enough for him to make a statement. His pale face impassive, he cited state precedents as well as the logic of the Constitution and declared, "The Chair thereupon rules that there is a quorum present within the meaning of the Constitution." Now the whole House was on its feet, Republicans cheering, Democrats screaming in protest. As the *Washington Post* described it, "Bedlam matched against pandemonium in a contest for supremacy would have been but the ripple on a mill pond by comparison."

Charles Crisp of Georgia elbowed his way to the Speaker's desk to enter an appeal. "The gentleman from Georgia appeals the decision," Reed boomed above the uproar, "and the question before the House now is shall the decision of the Chair stand as the judgment of the House?"

Instantly, Lewis Payson of Illinois moved to lay the appeal on the table, a motion that would have cut off debate. A roar of defiance rose from the Democrats, and even a few Republicans voiced sympathy with them. Reed was persuaded that debate should be allowed, and Payson's motion was withdrawn.

When the tumult had subsided sufficiently for debate to proceed, the Democrats pointed out that nine years before Reed himself had argued against the idea of a Speaker doing what he had just done. Crisp quoted Reed's own words to him: "It is not the visible presence of members, but their judgment and their votes the Constitution calls for." It was a telling point, which Reed would later answer by drawling, "It was Napoleon who said, 'the Bourbons never learned anything.'" Meanwhile, his trusted lieutenant, Joe Cannon, made a more parliamentary response. "I say that a majority under the Constitution is entitled to legislate, and that, if a contrary practice has grown up, such practice is unrepublican, undemocratic, against sound policy and contrary to the Constitution." Added William McKinley, "It is about time, Mr. Speaker, to stop these legal fictions."

The Democrats, convinced Reed's action was unjust, continued their frantic struggles, but were unable to do anything about it. They made one obstructive motion after another, but Reed either ignored them or declared them not in order. They called him "tyrant," "usurper," and—the name that stuck—"czar." At times they would become so angry they would rise in unison to denounce him, and on one such occasion tiny Joe Wheeler, a former Confederate cavalry officer, was so determined to make himself heard that he climbed on a desk and began jumping toward the front, "leaping from desk to desk as an ibex leaps from crag to crag." The only Democrat not on his feet was "Howdy" Martin, a six-foot-six Texan who sat at his desk whetting his bowie knife on his cowboy boot. Even the press got caught up in the frenzy, and those who sympathized with the Democrats leaned over the press gallery railing, shook their fists at the Speaker, and added their imprecations to the uproar. "It is to be doubted," wrote one observer, "whether there was ever such wild excitement, burning indignation, scathing denunciation, and really dangerous conditions as existed in the House ... while quorum counting was being established."

Through it all, Reed sat calmly, "cool and determined as a high-wayman," said the *New York Times*. "A hundred Democrats were on their feet howling for recognition," another reporter wrote, "yet the moon-faced despot sat silent and gazed vacantly over their heads." Part of this was simply Reed's habitually serene and tran-quil demeanor. While his close friends knew he was quite capable of anger, to an acquaintance it seemed "the ordinary worries and anxi-eties of life did not ... disturb him in the least." But as he sat in the chair, he also had the advantage of believing he was right and of knowing exactly what he would do if he should lose the battle: he would resign the speakership and his seat in Congress. "I had made up my mind," he said, "that if political life consisted in sitting help-lessly in the Speaker's chair and seeing the majority powerless to pass legislation, I had had enough of it and was ready to step down and out."

At the end of the second day, the motion appealing Reed's ruling was voted on. There were 162 yeas, 0 nays, 167 not voting, and Reed once again counted a quorum, thus tabling the appeal. The Demo-crats continued to fight, demanding votes on such matters as ap-proving the journal and then disputing Reed's right to count a quo-rum when they did not vote. William Bynum of Indiana promised the Democrats would "dispute every inch of ground, burn every blade of grass," and declared "the last intrenchment of liberty shall be our graves." But Reed ignored such fulminations, ruled the Dem-ocrats' protests out of order, and declined their appeals. For all practical purposes, the revolution had been accomplished, and the majority was firmly in control.

When the election case that had originally precipitated the uproar was voted on, the Republican claimant won, and when rules came forth from the Rules Committee formalizing the decisions Reed had made, they were approved. Besides giving the chair the power to count a quorum and to refuse to entertain motions it regarded as dil-atory, the rules provided that the Rules Committee should write for each bill a special rule that would determine the conditions under which the bill would be considered. Since Reed was the dominant member of the Rules Committee, this last measure increased his power still further. The Democrats had warned darkly that "the Speaker, instead of being as for the past one hundred years the servant of the House, shall be its master," but their protests were in vain. Reed had his rules.

Now that they were in control, the Republicans acted to increase their numbers. Wyoming and Idaho, which were likely to send Republican representatives, were admitted as states, and a total of nine contested seats were given over to the Republicans. In an effort to halt the slaughter, the Democrats tried absenting themselves from the floor, hoping in that way to prevent a quorum. On at least one occasion Reed locked the doors, and a bearded Texas Congressman, C. Buckley Kilgore, earned everlasting fame (and the sobriquet "Kicking Buck") by applying his size-thirteen boots to one of the doors until it crashed open and he could make his escape.

As "czar" of the House, Reed was becoming a national figure. Cartoonists delighted in draping his rotund form with ermine and giving him a crown labeled "dictator." Speaking invitations came in from Pennsylvania, Connecticut, Illlinois, and Iowa, and wherever he appeared, large crowds turned out. John Singer Sargent painted his portrait, but the result was not entirely successful. The painting was supposed to show Reed counting a quorum, but newsman suggested it looked more as if he had just bitten into a green persimmon. ("His exterior does not somehow correspond with his spirit," Sargent wrote to Henry Cabot Lodge. "What's a painter to do?")

Reed lost the speakership when the elections of 1890 decimated Republican ranks, and some thought he was partly responsible for the reversal in Republican fortunes. His "high-handed conduct" contributed to Republican losses, Champ Clark believed, and Henry Adams suggested that perhaps the country didn't want an efficient Congress. "If the elections settled anything," he wrote, "I imagine they settled this. The more efficient you make Congress, the more dangerous you make it, and the more unpopular." Nevertheless, Reed was still very much a national leader. Reporters flocked to interview him, and they were almost certain to come away with a good quote. When one newsman, obviously new to Washington, momentarily mistook him for President Cleveland, Reed responded, "For heaven's sake, never let Grover know that. He is too vain of his beauty now." Another who asked him to define the word *statesman* received an unexpected reply, but one so incisive it soon became a commonplace. "A statesman," Reed declared, "is a successful politician who is dead." It was inevitable that the press would begin to speculate about him for the presidency. "Was his party likely to nominate him?" one reporter asked. "They might do worse," Reed declared, "and I think they will." Certainly that was how he felt in 1892 when the Republicans renominated Benjamin Harrison, a dour, standoffish man whom Reed called a "Siberian solitude." The president had deeply offended the speaker by naming one of his political foes to an important patronage position. As Reed liked to tell it, "I had but two enemies in Maine, and one of them Harrison pardoned out of the penitentiary and the other he appointed Collector of Portland."

But the elections of 1892 did give Reed a chance to shine in the House again. After 1890 he had had only eighty-seven Republicans with him, hardly enough to protest when the Democrats wiped out his rule changes, but now his party had forty more seats, and he decided to convince the Democrats they would be better off with Reed's rules. He gave them a little hint of coming events on November 2, 1893. Because the House was to adjourn the next day, many members had left town—enough, Reed realized, so that if the Republicans did not vote, there would be no quorum. Thus his followers sat silently through roll call after roll call. As the day dragged on, Reed took particular delight in pointing out to the chair the advantages of counting a quorum, because the Speaker now was the gray-eyed, round-faced Crisp of Georgia, and he had been elected largely as a result of his spirited opposition to Reed's quorum counting. "We are quite ready to have the Chair count us," Reed suggested sweetly before he finally allowed the House to proceed with its business.

In February he tightened the screw several turns, blocking all business for a month. "Downright filibustering," one of his opponents huffed. "Downright? You mean upright," Reed rejoined. He held up business again in March, and finally Crisp gave in. Reed was astonishingly restrained in his victory remarks. "I congratulate [the House] on the wise decision it is about to make," he said, and on April 17 his rule for counting a quorum was adopted by the Democrats. Champ Clark believed that for all Reed's impassivity, he had been deeply hurt by the abuse heaped upon him in the quorum fight, and if that was so, the vindication he experienced now would have been sweet. Previously upheld by the Supreme Court, his quorum counting was now blessed by his opponents.

For Republicans 1894 was a banner year. Reed became speaker again in the Fifty-fourth Congress and an active presidential candidate. But now a foe arose whom he himself had helped create: William McKinley. After he had defeated him for the speakership in 1889, Reed had appointed McKinley to the Ways and Means Committee chairmanship, a position that identified McKinley with the highly protectionist bill the Fifty-first Congress passed. Being the father of the McKinley Tariff was not an immediate political asset. Many blamed the bill and the rising prices that resulted from it for the Republican debacle in the 1890 elections, and McKinley himself had lost his seat that year. But the economy grew worse under a Democratic House, worse still under Cleveland, the Democratic president elected in 1892. By 1894 McKinley was beginning to look like a hero—and possibly a president.

In the contest for the Republican nomination, he had two distinct advantages over Reed. The first was his personality. McKinley was an exceedingly likable fellow, kind and gentlemanly, in contrast to Reed, whose tongue could create enemies instantly. McKinley recognized his opponent's weakness. "Everybody enjoys Reed's sarcastic comments and keen wit," he commented, "except the fellow who is the subject of his satire." Reed himself was well aware that people often responded negatively to him. "My opponents in Congress go at me tooth and nail," he said once, "but they always apologize to William when they are going to call him names." Reed's appearance and voice—both quite singular—also counted against him. Members of the House had long grown used to them, even come to view them with a certain warm regard; but for audiences who had never seen Reed before, it must have been difficult to imagine this strange-looking man with his screeching nasal voice as president. After Mark Hanna saw a midwestern audience's reaction to Reed, he was certain the speaker could easily be beaten.

And it was Hanna who was McKinley's second big advantage. The Cleveland businessman was so determined to get his Ohio friend into the White House that almost four years before the 1896 elections, he was at work on a McKinley organization. Reed had Henry Cabot Lodge and Theodore Roosevelt working for him, but they had their own political careers to worry about, and managing Reed was more than a full-time occupation. He had his own notions of what a presidential campaign should be like and they did not include deal making, fund raising, or even tact. When railroad magnate Colis Huntington offered to contribute to his campaign (as he had to McKinley's), Reed turned him down. When the governor of Michigan, who controlled that state's delegation, asked to see him, Reed could barely be persuaded to come to a meeting, and when he did appear, he proceeded to lambaste the governor's economic views. The governor soon signed on with McKinley, as did a California newspaper publisher who made the mistake of asking Reed for certain assurances about cabinet appointments. As Cabot Lodge described Reed's campaign, "He kept his honor pure and his high conception of public duty unstained and unimpaired." He also suffered a crushing defeat. When the balloting was completed at the convention, he had 84½ votes to McKinley's 661½.

Reed did not lose gracefully. Once he perceived McKinley's victory was certain, he wrote to Theodore Roosevelt, "I am tired of this thing. . . . Moreover the receding grapes seem to ooze with acid and the whole thing is a farce." Bitter at the outcome, he chose to blame Hanna and McKinley for his loss, maintaining that Hanna's tactics were dishonorable and that any candidate who would let himself be manipulated as Reed thought McKinley had was a weakling. He was reported to say that McKinley had "all the backbone of a chocolate eclair," and once the Ohioan became president, Reed felt he had proof of his opinion.

Since 1895 a war had been going on in Cuba, where rebels wanted to break away from Spain. Initially Reed and McKinley agreed that the United States should not get involved in the fighting. Although sympathy for Cuban insurgents was growing in this country, fueled by sensational newspaper stories of Spanish atrocities, McKinley resisted the pressure for war and worked to negotiate a settlement. Reed supported him by keeping the subject of Cuba off the floor of the House, sometimes quite arbitrarily. Once, when the war party found an opportune moment to present a resolution recognizing Cuban belligerency, Reed ignored them entirely and called on his friend Nelson Dingley of Maine instead. As it happened, Dingley had been paying little attention to the proceedings and had no idea why he had been recognized, but Reed helped him out: "The gentleman from Maine moves that the House do now adjourn. Do I hear a second? The motion is seconded. The question is now on the motion to adjourn. All in favor will say 'aye.' Those opposed 'no.' The 'ayes' have it. The-House-stands-adjourned!" Such tactics led Senator William Allen of Nebraska to issue a harsh condemnation of the Speaker: "We have a horrid example before us constantly, like a nightmare, in another end of the Capitol building, where one man transacts the business of 357, which absolutely paralyzes one branch of Congress, a thing which, to my way of thinking is an absolute, positive, inexcusable, bold, and open disgrace to the American people. . . . Forty-five States of this Union, with their Representatives numbering 356, all held, metaphorically speaking, by the throat as a highwayman would treat you when he wanted you to deliver your money."

An attack by a populist senator wasn't likely to disturb Reed much, but on February 15, 1898, there occurred an event he couldn't ignore. The battleship *Maine*, which had been sent to Cuba to look after American interests, was blown up at her moorings in Havana harbor. Since most of the nation assumed the Spanish were responsible, war debate was inevitable. Reed kept it restrained in the House by placing severe limits on the time allotted for general debate, and he was bitterly indignant when the Republican Senate became a forum for war advocates. On March 17, Redfield Proctor of Vermont read a report on the Senate floor that Reed considered irresponsibly inflammatory, and the Speaker lashed out by reminding a reporter that the senator owned large marble quarries. "Proctor's position might have been expected," he said. "A war will make a large market for gravestones."

Under pressure from both the national press and his colleagues in the House, Reed continued to stand firm. But not so McKinley. Convinced he was about to lose control of his party, he yielded and sent a war message to Congress. At that point, there was nothing Reed could do. Governor Morton of New York urged him to step down from the chair and make a speech that would dissuade the members from war, but Reed knew that was futile. "Dissuade them!" he exploded in front of a group of reporters. "The Governor . . . might as well ask me to stand out in the middle of a Kansas waste and dissuade a cyclone." Since it was not traditional for a

Speaker to vote (unless his vote would be the deciding one), Reed could not even cast a ballot against the resolution. After a riotous session in which he had to send the sergeant-at-arms onto the floor with the great silver mace, the House's symbol of authority, to quell disorders, the war measure passed the House overwhelmingly. There was another vote after differences with the Senate had been resolved, and on this one there were only six nays. Later, Reed called one of the dissenting members to take the chair, and as he passed him the gavel, said, "I envy you the luxury of your vote. I was where I could not do it."

As the country rushed into war with Spain, Reed supported the measures necessary for a fighting force, but he would go no farther. After Dewey's victory in Manila Bay, many politicans became enthusiastic about annexing Hawaii. The islands were necessary to our security in the Pacific, advocates claimed, but Reed thought this was simply the old expansionist wolf, which he had always considered a threat to our national interests, decked out in a new set of clothing. A joint resolution to annex Hawaii appeared in the House on May 4, but Reed managed for weeks to keep it from coming to the floor. Lodge described him as "straining every nerve to beat Hawaii," and in pursuing this course, Reed was acting not only against administration policy, but against the wishes of his fellow Republicans in the House. They began to petition for a caucus to consider the annexation resolution, and Reed was too long schooled in the emotions of the House not to understand their indignation. They were overwhelmingly for annexation; they were a majority—and hadn't he predicated his career on the idea that their will should prevail? A note from Nelson Dingley helped decide him. Dingley was an old friend, a small frail man whose morals were as upright as his posture was stooped, and when he wrote to Reed that he ought to give up his fight, the Speaker gave in. He called his parliamentary assistant, Asher Hinds, aside and suggested that the annexation forces should make a motion to "proceed to the public business." It was an obscure motion, which hadn't been used in the House for fifteen years, but Hinds passed the word along, as Reed meant him to, and when the motion was made, Reed ruled it in order. The annexation measure came to the floor, and after three days' debate passed by a vote of 209 to 91. Reed was absent—ill, he said—but he took the extraordinary step of having it announced to the House that, had he been present, he would have voted no. Only three of his fellow Republicans had voted that way.

Thus it happened that majority rule, which Reed had insisted upon as a political and moral necessity, brought the triumph of a cause he thoroughly despised. The irony was neat, and all the more so because Reed, that most ironical of men, could not appreciate it. He was no more able to detach himself emotionally from the annexationists' victory than he had been able to from McKinley's, and his mood grew steadily darker. "Reed is terribly bitter," wrote Lodge to Roosevelt, "saying all sorts of ugly things about the Administration and its policy in private talks, so I keep out of his way, for I am fond of him, and I confess that his attitude is painful and disappointing to me beyond words."

Having given up in the fight against Hawaiian annexation, he refused to become engaged in any others. He thought the final settlement with Spain, which transferred sovereignty of the Philippines to the United States, a travesty of American ideals. How could a country that had entered a war in order to help throw off a colonial power end that war by becoming a colonial power herself? Reed was not the only one thinking this way, and it was suggested that he lead a movement to pass a House resolution denouncing the treaty. By doing so he might well affect the outcome, for the treaty vote in the Senate would be so close that a strong statement by the House could make the difference.

But he no longer had any heart for the battle. He was isolated from former friends: Lodge, in the Senate now, was leading the fight for ratification, and Roosevelt, the hero of San Juan Hill, had just been elected governor of New York. His closest friend in the House, Nelson Dingley, had recently died, and he was alienated from most of the others in his party, who favored the treaty. "The Speaker of the House," observed the Washington Post, "looms up colossal above all other figures. He has no intimate associate. On pleasant days he lumbers along the Avenue on his way to the Capitol, silent and alone. . . . He lives upon a column far more lofty than that of Simon Stylites, enwrapped in his own personality, placidly surveying the political herd below him; and no earthquake has as yet overthrown the column."

Although Reed refused to get publicly involved in the treaty fight, his off-the-cuff comments no doubt provided some aid to the anti-imperialist cause. Of the twenty million dollars the United States was paying Spain for the Philippines, he observed, "We have bought ten million Malays at two dollars a head unpicked, and nobody knows what it will cost to pick them." As it turned out the expense was great, for even before the treaty was voted on Filipino insurgents began to fight for their independence. By the time the treaty was ratified on February 6, 1899, there were already more than three hundred American casualties and five hundred Filipino. In private conversation Reed made no pretense of his feelings. The very mention of the situation, wrote one journalist, was like "touching a match" and resulted in most "sulphurous language."

Congress adjourned in March, and in April it was announced that Reed would be joining a New York law firm. To many it seemed impossible that he should retire, and there were discussions about how he could remain in the Congress and the speakership even though living in New York. But he soon made it clear that his political career had come to an end. If he were to stay in the House, he would either have to be an obstructionist, standing in the way of majority rule, or a hypocrite, supporting a policy he detested. He could do neither. Telling his parliamentarian, Asher Hinds, "I have tried, perhaps not always successfully, to make the acts of my public life accord with my conscience, and I cannot now do this thing," he formally resigned from the House of Representatives. "Congress without Tom Reed!" exclaimed the *New York Tribune.* "Who can imagine it?"

One of those who must have found it difficult was Reed himself, who was turning his back on a career he loved. As a lawyer, he was soon earning many times what he had made in the House, and he quickly formed a congenial group of New York friends. Among them was Mark Twain, even more a legend than Reed when it came to sardonic wit—or bad poker. At one legendary session, Reed, whose friends reported he was totally inept at cards, actually won twenty-three hands in a row. But neither the generous salary nor the newfound friends could take away all the sting. One acquaintance noticed "a change coming over him both in weight of body and seriousness of mind. He was like an actor who had spent the best of a lifetime in the glare of the footlights and the din of popular comment, and, after passing the age of highest elasticity, was trying to accommodate himself to the less colorful conditions of private society."

In 1902, on a visit to Washington, Reed collapsed in the Capitol. Although he was hospitalized, he quickly grew worse and soon fell into a delirium in which he imagined himself in the Speaker's chair again or debating on the House floor.

His Washington friends had been looking forward to having him at the Gridiron dinner scheduled for that Saturday night, but instead came word that he was ill, and then at the end of the evening, the sad news that he had died. As the entire company rose in tribute, there was scarcely a dry eye among them. They sang one of Reed's favorite songs, then dispersed into the night, each of them feeling, as one of them put it, "that the life of one of our greatest Americans had closed."

1

Henry Clay, a man of fire and wit, made the office of Speaker of the House powerful and used it to propel the country into the War of 1812.

2

The determined and hard-working James K. Polk saw to it that the House of Representatives carried out Andrew Jackson's policies. Polk subsequently became president himself—the only Speaker of the House ever to do so.

3

Polk defeated Clay for the presidency in 1844, an outcome this cartoonist hadn't been counting on.

4

Although never Speaker, the grim and tough-willed Thaddeus Stevens dominated the House and nearly brought down a president.

5

James G. Blaine, the magnetic man from Maine, was a devoted family man and a strong and effective Speaker of the House, but he failed to keep his financial dealings above reproach.

6

This cartoon, showing Blaine tattooed with various scandals, cost him votes when he ran for president.

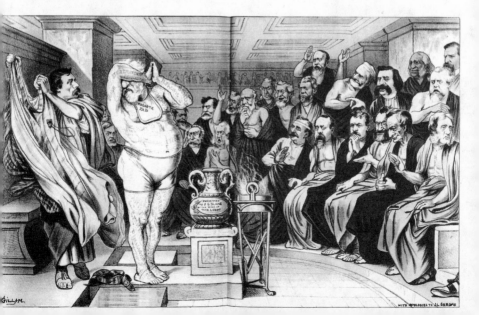

7

Sharp-tongued Tom Reed was, said Henry Cabot Lodge, "the greatest parliamentary leader I ever saw."

Reed ruled that the minority party in the House of Representatives could not obstruct the will of the majority, an action that led this cartoonist to picture him as a none-too-benevolent despot.

8

9

Crafty Joe Cannon was the most powerful Speaker the House ever had, until his colleagues ran a coup on him.

10

The polished and suave Nicholas Longworth restored to the speakership much of the power Joe Cannon had lost.

11

Marrying President Theodore Roosevelt's daughter Alice hurt Longworth's political career as much as it helped it.

12

Sam Rayburn was one of the Kings of the Hill, despite the fact that for most of his career he tolerated a recalcitrant Rules Committee.

"I Said I Had Him Trained — Notice How He Sits Up?"

A German illustrator portrayed the House in session in the semi-circular chamber where the representatives met for nearly fifty years.

15

Sam Rayburn swears in freshman representatives in the chamber where the House has met since 1857.

16

House Minority Whip Newt Gingrich of Georgia addresses Republican congressional candidates on Capitol Hill during a 1994 rally in which all signed the "Contract with America." The GOP won control of both houses of Congress in the November elections, assuring that Gingrich would become House Speaker.

6

ATTACK ON UNCLE JOE

William Howard Taft had made a campaign promise to lower tariffs. He knew that Joe Cannon, the wiry, cigar-chewing Speaker of the House didn't much like the idea, but the big, slow-moving president was determined to prevail. "I don't care how he feels or how they feel in the House," he wrote to Theodore Roosevelt shortly after he had been elected to replace him. "I am not going to be made the mouthpiece of a lie to the people."

The tariff bill that the House Ways and Means Committee first drafted seemed reasonable enough. Lumber, petroleum, and hides were all placed on the free list; but after the bill was shown to the Speaker, the lumber tariff was put back in place and the petroleum duty actually raised. When the Senate Finance Committee went into action, the duty on hides was restored.

Taft began to worry, but Speaker Cannon persuaded him that the proper place for him to make his influence felt was in the Conference Committee. Then Cannon saw to it that by the time the conferees met, the issue was fairly well decided. He appointed only the most dependable protectionist congressmen to the committee, as did Nelson Aldrich, the leader of the Republican majority in the Senate. Taft felt cheated. "I don't think that Cannon played square," he grumbled, but he waded into the fray nonetheless, staying in Washington through most of the muggy summer to lobby congressmen at breakfast meetings and White House dinners. Although he refused to use his most potent weapon, the threat to withhold patronage, he did manage to get hides and petroleum back on the free list and to obtain reductions for lumber. The bill was to be signed in the president's room of the Capitol, and as Taft, rather snappily attired in a cutaway suit and straw hat, rode to the Hill in his touring car, he felt quite satisfied with the ways things had turned out. As he wrote to his brother a few days later, "I did defeat . . . Cannon."

The trouble was, nobody else thought so. When the hundreds of provisions in the new law were scrutinized, it became clear that, although the president had got reductions on the few items on which he had concentrated, many other rates went up, and overall there had been no significant lowering of the tariff. Headlines across the country were soon proclaiming that the real victor in the tariff fight was not Taft, who had promised reduction, but the ruddy-faced, silver-bearded Joe Cannon, the most powerful Speaker the House had ever known. A self-described "stand-patter" who liked things just fine the way they were, Cannon saw no reason to change the country's protectionist ways, and so, like Henry Clay before him, though with considerably more indirection, he made his will prevail over the president's.

But as often happens in politics, there were wheels within wheels, mirrors reflected in mirrors, and Taft's was not the only illusory victory. Although Cannon's triumph, like Clay's over Madison almost a century before, had important consequences for the House, they ran in the opposite direction. Clay's victory had established the speakership as a power center, whereas Cannon's brought it a step closer to being stripped of its influence. In winning the tariff battle, Cannon provided the final catalyst to the forces that would bring him down.

But that lay ahead. For now he was the seasoned politician who had shown the new boy on the block a thing or two. He had been in the House thirty-four years when Taft came along. He had first been elected when Ulysses S. Grant was in the White House, and he had seen six other presidents come and go. By the time the portly fellow who thought he could lower the tariff arrived on the scene, Cannon had become, in Mark Sullivan's words, "the most familiar [of all public men] with every subterranean channel of politics, the most cunning in its devious ways, the most artful in the craft."

He was also a character, though no one could say for sure how much that was because he carefully cultivated an unsophisticated rural image and how much because he had given up trying to be anything but himself. On the one hand, it seemed certain that a man so crafty and discerning would control the image he presented, but on the other, some wondered if anyone with an option would choose to be the way Cannon was. The tales about his language were legion. "I can yet . . . hear the roar of his Niagara-like profanity," one of his colleagues wrote, and his barnyard humor could be equally startling. Remarks he made in the House about the "wind" of one of his fellow representatives became known as the "foul-mouthed speech" and caused such public indignation they helped keep him out of Congress for a term. Almost as offensive to the ladies was his cigar. A contemporary described the way he smoked: "[Cannon's] restless teeth bit off large untidy sections from the near end of a maltreated cigar, until his wet lips from one side of his long mouth to the other were strewn with sodden, shredded tobacco leaves, and the neglected, fitful smoulder at the cigar's far end seemed to be in greater danger from flood than from fire." He also chewed tobacco, which meant a spittoon had to be kept close. Alice Roosevelt Longworth had heard about Uncle Joe's ways—President Taft warned her never to get between Cannon and his spittoon—but she thought it was all a joke until she spent an evening playing poker with Cannon. When their hostess didn't have a spittoon, Cannon allowed as how the umbrella stand would do just fine and used it "freely and frequently."

Cannon's attitudes were regarded by some to be as unenlightened as his manners. When it was first suggested that congressmen needed private offices, he proposed erecting two skyscrapers on the ends of the Capitol. Further testimony to his philistinism was offered by Roosevelt's and Taft's military aide, Archie Butt. At a White House dinner for visiting Chinese dignitaries, Butt reported, he approached the Speaker and asked if he wanted to meet the guest of honor. In a voice loud enough for the foreign visitors to hear, Cannon demanded, "You mean for me to go over there and meet that Chink?"

"Not unless you desire to," said Butt, "but he is the guest of honor."

"Oh, all right," Cannon agreed. "I will do as you say, but it goes against my pride for an American free-born citizen to cross a room to meet a heathen Chinee." As the evening progressed, however, Cannon warmed to the Chinese. "Later in the library," Butt records, "while the men were smoking, . . . Uncle Joe, a little the worse for dinner, amused the entire room by keeping one arm around the shoulder of the Prince and the other around the neck of Lord Li, with a cigar stuck at seventy degrees out of the corner of his mouth, telling them all about the Constitution and government in general and airing his ignorance of Eastern affairs."

But many of Cannon's contemporaries would have found Butt's reaction overdelicate. They realized the Speaker had his foibles, but regarded them as harmless enough, and they would have pointed out that his honesty and common sense could be relied upon. Behind Cannon's rough exterior was a shrewd mind that never dropped a detail when it came to appropriations and a genial soul that inspired great affection. Even his enemies understood that it could be counterproductive to attack Cannon himself, and as they revolted against the power of his speakership, they felt obliged to emphasize that nothing personal was meant by it. Many of those who worked against him would participate in one of the most sentimental moments in the history of the House, the celebration of Cannon's eightieth birthday. Claude Kitchin, who had once thrown his all into the fight against "Cannonism," rose to praise him. "I am going to say in public now what I have a hundred times said in private, that of all the public men whom I have ever met the gentleman from Illinois is the most remarkable and possesses the strongest, most practical common-sense intellect."

Cannon came to the House thirty years before he assumed the speakership. He was from a rural district in Illinois and such renown as he had in his early terms came from his pride in being a son of the prairie. "I have oats in my pocket and hayseed in my hair," he declared in his maiden speech, and it was an unusual enough introduction to draw newspaper attention. "I soon learned that an introduction with a laugh is better than no introduction or a mere mention as 'also spoke,'" Cannon wrote in his later years, but his role as "member from the wild and wooly West" was not entirely disingenuous. He had come from rural, independent-minded forebears and been forced into self-reliance at a young age. His father, a country doctor, died when Joe was fourteen, and the youth had to begin clerking in an Illinois country store. Parsimonious and farsighted, in six years he had saved five hundred dollars, enough to quit his job and study law. In a few years, he was ready to hang out his shingle, but he found clients hard to come by around Shelbyville and Tuscola. He moved to Danville, where his brother Bill, an albino whom Cannon had always assumed he would have to care for, had proved to be a spectacularly successful businessman. Bill and Joe entered into a financial partnership, an arrangement that permitted Joe to marry and embark on a political career.

He was successful in his second try for a congressional seat, and the voters of Danville returned him to the next eight Congresses in a row. Although the publicity he received during these years came largely because of the "hayseed" image, he was, among his colleagues, slowly building a reputation as a hard-working, dependable legislator. In his fourth term, he was appointed to the Appropriations Committee by Speaker Randall; in his eighth term, he was appointed to the Rules Committee by Speaker Carlisle. At the beginning of his ninth term, when the Republicans took over the House, Cannon ran for Speaker, but he finished a poor third behind the principal contenders, Reed and McKinley. Reed subsequently assigned him two very important positions: membership on the Rules Committee and the chairmanship of Appropriations. He was Reed's lieutenant during the great quorum-counting battle of the Fifty-first Congress, and one of his duties was to speak in favor of Reed's position. The record shows he was short and to the point—what it couldn't show was the whole encyclopedia of body language with which he embellished his speeches. "As he warms to a subject," one correspondent reported, "he limbers up one organ after another until the whole of the man gets in motion—legs, arms, fingers, face, even the lapels and back of his coat—reminding one of a gas engine working with a defective valve gear and on a wobbling foundation." Speaker Champ Clark swore he once saw Cannon make a complete circle on his heel in the heat of debate, and Speaker Gillett liked to remember how Cannon would rise on his toes and prance up and down the aisle as he spoke. During one such performance, Tom Reed brought down the House by asking, "Joe, are you making this speech on mileage?"

Cannon's championing of Reed's rules helped cost him his seat. All the publicity accorded the battle insured that the voters were aware the Republicans controlled the House—and weren't they, therefore, responsible for the sour economy? If Cannon's constituents had any doubts about replacing him with a Democrat, he helped them decide with the "foul-mouthed" speech, and in 1891, he found himself out of office. Losing was traumatic, as Cannon would acknowledge to friends. Encountering McKinley, who had also been defeated, and an out-of-work Republican senator in Chicago one day, Cannon listened while they explained how it was all for the best. "That is what I am saying to everyone," he finally interrupted, "but, boys, don't let's lie to one another."

In the next election, he was returned to the House, and in the Congress after that, when the Republicans were once more in control, Reed again appointed him to the chairmanship of Appropriations. One of the advantages of having the Speaker make committee appointments was that he, unlike a seniority system, recalled where a member had been when he left and could restore him to his place. Thus, two years after the voters of Danville decided to return Joe Cannon to the House, he was again at the head of one of its most powerful committees.

Chairman Cannon did not believe in spending the taxpayers' money foolishly, and he had a very short list of wise expenditures. "You think my business is to make appropriations," he said once, "but it is not. It is to prevent their being made." One of those who came with his hand out was a fast-talking civil service commissioner named Theodore Roosevelt. He wanted more clerks and more money, and when his requests weren't granted, he became so convinced that Cannon was trying to destroy the merit system that he urged his friend Henry Cabot Lodge to make public attacks on the chairman. To the Cannon forces, Roosevelt seemed to be "careless about money matters" and to look upon the government "as holding a bottomless purse." Consequently, he fared little better when he came before the Appropriations Committee as assistant secretary of the navy. Wrote Cannon's private secretary, "No matter how large the Navy was, it would never have been quite large enough for him."

Occasionally, however, Cannon would shock everyone by saying yes. One of these rare moments came when the head of the Smithsonian Institution made a request for ten thousand dollars to experiment with a manned flying machine. After listening to Dr. Langley's explanation of how the aerodrome would be launched from a catapult that was located on a houseboat anchored in the Potomac, Cannon authorized the expenditure—and he soon regretted it. Langley's device flipped over on its back as soon as it was launched and crashed into the Potomac. Cannon's instinct that the time for manned flight was near was correct. Before the year was out, the Wright brothers would fly at Kitty Hawk. But that didn't save the chairman from a merciless ribbing by his colleagues. The cartoonists were after him too, one picturing him as a witch sailing through the air on his flying broomstick.

Cannon also rather unexpectedly came up with money just before the outbreak of the Spanish-American War. A distraught McKinley called him to the White House and explained that, although he did not want war, it looked inevitable, and the country needed money to prepare. According to a plan worked out with the president, Cannon introduced a bill appropriating fifty million dollars for national defense, and when he reported it to the floor, it passed almost unanimously. Leaving the House that day, Cannon encountered Speaker Reed, who adamantly opposed the war and whom Cannon had not consulted. As they walked to the streetcar together, Reed asked, "Joe, why did you do it?"

"Because it was necessary," Cannon replied. "I suppose I should have consulted you, but you had left the Appropriations Committee to my direction, and after considering the whole situation I felt this was the only way to get ready for the war that is sure to come. We can't prevent it. If I had consulted you and you did not approve I would have introduced the bill anyway without your approval, and that would have given you cause for feeling that I had not been quite sincere in seeking your advice."

"Perhaps you are right," said Reed. "Perhaps you are right." And the two men never discussed the matter again.

When Reed retired, Cannon ran for Speaker a second time. Unfortunately for him, Albert Hopkins, another member from Illinois, also decided to have a run at the speakership, and somehow the red-haired Hopkins managed to get the delegation's endorsement. Cannon knew Hopkins couldn't win—he was too unabashedly aggressive for the taste of most members—but he also knew Hopkins had doomed his own chances. Furious, he watched as the caucus settled on David Henderson of Iowa, a genial fellow who had lost a leg at the siege of Corinth. Henderson was elected Speaker, and Cannon sat back in his chairman's seat to wait. After two terms, Henderson abruptly announced his retirement. There were rumors that he had a drinking problem, caused, some thought, by the pain of his Civil War wound. It had never healed properly, and the doctors had to keep amputating more and more of his leg. Others said Henderson's mind was slipping. Whatever the reason, in 1903 Cannon once more had a chance to become Speaker—but would the House, which had twice rejected him, be willing to accept him now?

He received aid from an unlikely source, the United States Senate. By acting irresponsibly, one of its members gave Cannon a chance to indulge in a favorite sport of the House: Senate baiting. Congress was in its closing hours when Senator Tillman made it clear that he would hold up the Sundry Appropriations Bill unless a "nice dish of pork" was included in it for South Carolina. Midnight came. Then 1:00 A.M., then 2:00. Members grew more irate with each passing hour, and they reacted enthusiastically when Cannon rose at three o'clock in the morning to castigate "the other body," a circumlocution he had to use because of a House rule that forbids direct criticism of the Senate. "I have made my protest," he shouted, waving his left fist in the air, stretching up on tiptoe. "In my opinion, another body . . . must change its method of procedure, or our body, backed by the people, will compel that change." The cheers and applause that greeted his outburst did not prevent Tillman's raid on the Treasury, but they did tell Congress-watchers that Cannon's chances for the speakership were excellent.

Among those interested was Theodore Roosevelt, president since McKinley's assassination some eighteen months before. Realizing how important Cannon's goodwill could be, Roosevelt began cultivating him, writing him chatty letters soliciting his advice. Once Cannon became Speaker, Roosevelt had him to the White House frequently. Two or three times a week, Roosevelt would write a note or have his secretary telephone and invite the Speaker to drop by. The two men would sit late into the night, discussing policy usually, but also telling one another tales from their earlier days. Roosevelt further courted Cannon by seeing to it he was named permanent chairman of the 1904 Republican convention. He also tended to the Speaker's feelings when Cannon took offense at being invited to a White House dinner where he would be seated below the Supreme Court justices. Roosevelt arranged for a special banquet in Cannon's honor, thus starting the tradition of the Speaker's dinner.

But if Roosevelt thought that all this presidential attention would make Cannon march to his drumbeat, he was much mistaken. In the

Fifty-eighth Congress, Cannon did press forward with administration plans for the Panama Canal, but that was a project he had always favored. He did see to it that the president got the battleships he wanted, but he had always been reasonably supportive of national defense. An interstate commerce measure the president wanted also got through the House during Cannon's first term as Speaker—but only after it was too late for Senate action. When it came to tariff revision, Cannon was firmly opposed, and that, apparently, was enough for Roosevelt. As the Fifty-eighth Congress was winding down, the president invited the Republican leadership of the House and Senate to the White House. He had been urged to say something about the tariff in his upcoming inaugural address, he told them. What did they think of his recommending that the next Congress take up revision? Senator Aldrich supported the idea, as did Senators Allison and Hale and Congressmen Payne, Tawney, and Grosvenor. Only one, Senator Platt, had so far opposed the idea when Roosevelt asked Cannon for his opinion. As Cannon told it, his response was short and pointed: "I said Platt expressed it. Mr. Roosevelt had been sitting on the table swinging his legs, listening, asking a short question now and then, but for him, remarkably quiet. When I finished he got up, and with a grin said: 'It is evidently the consensus of opinion that the tariff should not be revised until after the next presidential election.'"

Once when he was told by a supporter that he must "lay down on Uncle Joe," Roosevelt replied, "It will be a good deal like laying down on a hedgehog." But in Cannon's second term as Speaker, Roosevelt decided to try. No longer an "accidental" president, he had been elected now in his own right—and overwhelmingly too. The pressures for reforms that would regulate business were growing stronger every day, and though Roosevelt was not necessarily in sympathy with the reformers, he felt that their complaints had been inspired by real problems. "I do not at all like social conditions at present," he wrote his secretary of war, William Howard Taft. "The dull, purblind folly of the very rich men; their greed and arrogance . . . the corruption in business and politics, have tended to produce a very unhealthy condition of excitement and irritation in the popular mind, which shows itself in part in the enormous increase in socialistic propaganda."

Roosevelt began to push harder. When the House was slow to

consider pure food and meat inspection bills, he released a report that told of tubercular workers in the packing houses and bits of garbage ground up in canned meat. The report had at least some of the effect the president hoped for: both bills were passed, and though the meat inspection bill was weakened considerably, the president got the pure food act he wanted. As politicians will, Cannon put the best face on things, letting it be known that he had been in favor of pure food all along, but in his heart of hearts he did not believe that government's proper role was to insure it. He was becoming increasingly restive at the direction of Roosevelt's policy and by the end of the Fifty-ninth Congress was digging in his heels. The panic of 1907, which was devastating the business community, seemed to him the logical outcome of Roosevelt's "radical" economic notions. The final wedge in the relationship between the two men was not a money matter, however, but a conservation issue: in defiance of the Congress, Theodore Roosevelt decided to preempt seventeen million acres of western territory.

Roosevelt's conservation policies had become unpopular in the West, partly because of the autocratic way they were administered by the chief of the Forest Service, Gifford Pinchot. In the last days of the Fifty-ninth Congress, the appropriations bill that funded the Forest Service was amended so that no further forest reserves could be created without a specific act of Congress. When the bill was forwarded to the president, he let it lie on his desk, signing it only after he had created twenty-one new reserves by executive order. Cannon had never been particularly fond of conservation ("Not one cent for scenery," was the way Pinchot described the Speaker's attitude), but the seventeen million acres probably didn't bother him as much as Roosevelt's haughty defiance of the Congress. When the House reconvened, Cannon took his revenge by seeing to it that bills creating forest reserves in the White Mountains and southern Appalachians died a lingering death in the Judiciary Committee.

Roosevelt seemed increasingly bent on confrontation. The man Henry Adams called "pure act" could bring himself to cajole and persuade only so long, particularly since he was so often unsuccessful. In December 1907 he presented the Congress with a two-and-one-half-hour message that proposed everything from an income tax to tariff-free wood pulp. When no action was taken, he sent a special message framed in pointed language, denouncing "predatory wealth" and calling opposition to his policies "brazen protests against moral regeneration." When still nothing happened, he sent another message, then another, each more emotional in tone than the last. In March 1908 he told the Congress he wanted to curb the abuses of "that particular kind of multi-millionaire . . . of whom it has been well said that his face has grown hard and cruel while his body has grown soft; whose son is a fool and his daughter a foreign princess; whose nominal pleasures are at best a tasteless extravagant luxury, and whose real delight, whose real life-work, is the accumulation and use of power in its most sordid and least elevating form." In total, the president sent twenty messages to the Sixtieth Congress, most of them futile. Cannon saw to that. By delaying, by assigning bills to hostile committees (particularly Judiciary, which became known as "the morgue"), by selectively using his power of recognition, he made sure that the majority of the president's proposals never saw the light of legislative day. "Everything is all right out West and around Danville," the Speaker liked to say. "The country don't need any legislation."

One result was to make Roosevelt so angry with the Congress that as his presidency neared an end, he abandoned discretion altogether. He had been in the habit of allowing various departments, especially the Interior Department, to use the Secret Service to conduct investigations, and when the Congress passed legislation limiting the service to detecting counterfeiting and protecting the president, Roosevelt flew into a rage. In his annual message of 1908, he declared that "the chief argument for Congress's having restricted the activities of the Secret Service was that Congressmen did not wish themselves to be investigated by the Secret Service men." The accusation stung the House into activity. After a meeting of congressional leaders in Cannon's office, a committee was formed and a demand made that the president present evidence for such accusations. The message Roosevelt sent in reply did little to ease the situation, for though he denied having accused the Congress of corruption, he could not restrain himself from noting that the restriction of the Secret Service "was emphatically an action of benefit only to lawbreakers." The House promptly voted to lay his message on the table. It was the first time since Andrew Jackson's day that the representatives had refused to accept a message from the president.

A second result of the rupture with Roosevelt was in the way Cannon himself was perceived. He became the symbol of reaction, and those who believed economic and social changes were necessary attacked him again and again. Almost every issue of *Collier's* magazine pounded away at how he held the House in thrall. The American Federation of Labor distributed a pamphlet called "How Speaker Cannon Has Abused Labor," which declared him "a vindictive man of power." An Anti-Saloon League publication declared he was "a living offense to the right-minded people of this country." There had been talk of Cannon for president in 1908, talk he had liked, but opposition to him became so vocal and vehement that he spent most of the campaign making sure he won reelection in his own district. William Howard Taft, who had received the Republican presidential nomination, was glad to see him tied down at home. "The burden I have to carry in this campaign is largely Cannonism," he complained to Theodore Roosevelt.

Opposition to Cannon was growing even within the ranks of House Republicans. Those who opposed him were mostly from the Midwest, where the desire for progressive reforms was catching fire like prairie grass. But the Speaker's foes were not entirely motivated by progressive ideals. Many of them were angry at the spectacular way he had used committee assignments to reward and punish. In 1905 he had made the faithful James Tawney of Minnesota chairman of the Appropriations Committee even though Tawney had not served on that committee before. In 1907 he removed Edward Henry of Connecticut, the ranking member on Agriculture, from that committee and put in as chairman a member whose ideas about pure food and meat inspection were more in line with his own. Less spectacular, but also important, were the small humiliations a man not in favor with the Speaker had to endure. These were proud men who found it difficult to submit to his will time after time. Hadn't they been elected by as many voters as he? Why should their voices go unheard?

One of the loudest complaints of the insurgent Republicans was that they couldn't get bills to the floor. To do so required Rules Committee approval, and since the committee was appointed by the Speaker and consisted of himself, two Republicans, and two Democrats ("three very distinguished Republicans and two ornamental Democrats" was how Champ Clark described it), "Rules Committee approval" meant Cannon's approval. Trying to come up with a way to circumvent him, some of the insurgents hit on the idea of "Calendar Tuesday," a day in which committees could call up reported bills without Rules Committee approval. As the Sixtieth Congress met in lame-duck session, Cannon responded to their complaints by preempting their solution. One of his lieutenants, John Dalzell, introduced a measure calling for "Calendar Wednesday," and it passed, although hard-core insurgents, sputtering mightily that the change was purely cosmetic, voted against it.

Setting their hopes on defeating Cannon for the speakership when the Sixty-first Congress convened, the insurgents sought the aid of President-elect Taft. But much as Taft wanted to see Cannon defeated, he realized it would be the height of foolishness to campaign against him unless it was certain he could be beaten. "To attempt to defeat Uncle Joe and not succeed," he wrote, "would be worse than to let him get in and deal with him as best I can." When it looked likely Cannon would be reelected Speaker, Taft told one of the insurgents, "I must abide the election and then do the best I can afterwards."

In the spring of 1909, when the Sixty-first Congress gathered in special session to consider the tariff, Cannon was elected to a third term as Speaker by a comfortable margin. But Champ Clark, the new Democratic leader, suspected there were a number of Republicans who, though unwilling to join the Democrats in electing a Speaker, would be happy to vote with them to reform procedures. He gave them their chance by demanding a roll call when the customary motion was made to adopt the rules of the previous House. Clark's instincts were right; the motion was defeated by four votes, and the way was open to amend the rules. He promptly offered a resolution that would enlarge the Rules Committee, remove the Speaker from it, and drastically curtail his power to make committee appointments. Clark listened intently as the clerk called the roll. The insurgent Republicans were holding with him, but what was happening to the Democrats? A block of them voted with the regular Republicans, and his resolution lost. Hardly believing what had happened, Clark, a huge, muscular man, had tears streaming down his face as he thanked John Nelson, the leader of the insurgents, for standing firm. Why had his Democratic ranks crumbled?

As it turned out, Cannon and his lieutenants had not been waiting idly by to see power stripped from the speakership. They had been on the telephones doing some horse-trading, and the fact that the tariff would be revised gave them the wherewithal to trade. Those who were interested in seeing the principles of high protection prevail were urged to contact congressmen about keeping the priest of protectionism, Joe Cannon, in full power. And many believed more specific commitments were also made, certain duties promised in return for bringing influence to bear on the Speaker's behalf.

Having turned back the threat to his speakership, Cannon worked to make sure the revised tariff was as protectionist as the previous one had been. On the day of the bill's final passage, he also made certain that the penalties for opposing him were clear. "Ax for Insurgents," was the way the *Washington Post* described the bloodbath. Chairmen Fowler, Cooper, and Gardner, insurgents all, were removed from their chairmanships. At the same time, Cannon rescinded his previous grant of authority to the minority leader to make committee appointments for the Democrats. Cannon assigned the Democrats himself, making sure those who had aided him were rewarded. Champ Clark, still smarting at his loss on the rules fight, thought Cannon was asking for more trouble, "pickling a rod for his own back." Former Chairman Fowler did land a few heavy blows. "Do you suppose that I was not aware of your ignorance, prejudice, inordinate conceit, favoritism, putrid preferences...?" he demanded of Cannon in an open letter published in the *Chicago Tribune.* "You revel in a glut of brutal power like Nero to terrorize your subject."

The reaction of members to Cannon's appointments was easily matched by the public outcry over the tariff. He was blamed for it, blamed for the Republicans not living up to their promise to lower duties. Even conservative publications began to attack him. "He belongs to a past generation of sordid politicians and has outlived his usefulness," *Harper's Weekly* editorialized. "The clock has struck for Uncle Joe," declared the *Wall Street Journal.* Surveying the growing number of Uncle Joe's enemies, William Allen White concluded, "Emma Goldman, in her palmiest days, never made so many anarchists as Cannon."

For his part, the Speaker was no longer in a mood for conciliation. Instead, he became increasingly defiant. "Behold Mr. Cannon, the Beelzebub of Congress!" he shouted at an audience in Elgin, Illinois.

"Gaze on this noble, manly form—me, Beelzebub—me, the Czar!" Told of such outbursts, Robert LaFollette called them "the snarlings of a grim old wolf who hears the beaters in the woods and scents them closing in."

The insurgents in the House were inclined to agree, and in January 1910 the fiery Gifford Pinchot gave them a chance to test their strength. When he became convinced that Secretary of the Interior Ballinger was not acting in the interests of conservation, he launched a public attack on him, accusing him of being in the pocket of big business. When President Taft subsequently dismissed Pinchot, a resolution was introduced in the House to investigate the matter. George Norris, an insurgent from Nebraska, decided to offer an amendment that would give the House rather than the Speaker the power to appoint the committee. A savvy, independent-minded legislator given to wearing string ties, Norris could hardly resist using the issue to attack the Speaker, since the conservation focus of it would help coalesce anti-Cannon forces. He waited until John Dalzell, Cannon's sharp-eyed lieutenant, who was presiding at the time, took a lunch break. With Walter Smith of Iowa, a more trusting soul, in the chair, Norris made his move, and as he thought would happen, his amendment carried. By a vote of 149 to 146, the Cannon forces were defeated. One reporter called it the most "stunning rebuke" dealt a Speaker since 1789.

The investigating committee would eventually find in favor of Ballinger, but to Norris that was probably less important than the assurance he now had that there were enough votes to overturn the Speaker. For a long time he had been carrying around in his pocket a resolution that he believed undercut the most noxious part of the Cannon regime by expanding the Rules Committee, removing the Speaker from it, and taking away his power to appoint its members. Now Norris believed that if there were only a way to introduce his worn and tattered resolution, it would succeed. But the opportunity was unlikely to occur since Cannon was aware of his vulnerability and would be wary of giving the insurgents an opening.

Then on Wednesday, March 16, 1910, Edgar Crumpacker, a Republican from Indiana, took to the floor and called for consideration of a House Joint Resolution on the census. The Democrats and insurgents were immediately irritated. This was Calendar Wednesday, they objected, and therefore the bill was out of order. But Cannon overruled them, arguing that because the census was mentioned in the Constitution, the motion enjoyed constitutional privilege. The contentious Democrats and insurgent Republicans once more showed their muscle by voting to overturn his ruling. The next morning, however, when Crumpacker introduced his motion anew, the House was more favorably disposed toward it. Perhaps because it was no longer Calendar Wednesday or perhaps because they recognized the necessity of getting on with the census, the members voted overwhelmingly to consider the resolution.

To an observer in the gallery all of this would have seemed fairly routine, if a little willful. Even on the floor, there was no hint the fuse had just been lit on an explosive series of events. Norris's attempt to get recognition was the first indication: "Mr. Speaker, I have a privileged resolution. . . . Mr. Speaker, I have a matter of privilege. . . ." Finally Cannon looked his way. "Mr. Speaker, I present a resolution made privileged by the Constitution." Norris sent a tattered paper from his pocket to the clerk. It was his proposal to sever the Speaker's ties to the Rules Committee.

As soon as the resolution was read, Dalzell jumped to his feet: "I make the point of order it is not in order. It is not privileged."

Norris countered that the House rules, like the census, are mentioned in the Constitution. "I submit, Mr. Speaker, if the action of the House . . . makes a census bill privileged because of the Constitution, then any proposal to amend the rules must be privileged by virtue of the same instrument."

Suddenly everyone was aware of what was going on. The battle had finally been joined to determine the power of the speakership. Word spread throughout the Capitol, and the galleries began to fill. Soon the whole city heard what was happening, and the corridors were choked with people waiting a turn to watch.

Cannon's tactics were not at first very dramatic. When a motion to adjourn failed, making clear that he and his loyalists did not have the votes to sustain a ruling against Norris, he decided to stall. Throughout the afternoon and evening, his forces telephoned and telegraphed frantically to members who were back in their districts for Saint Patrick's Day. They were heartened by news that four regulars would be on the midnight train, and they waited anxiously for them through the evening and on into the early hours of the morning. But when they appeared on the floor and another motion was made to adjourn, the Cannon forces lost again. Still they didn't have the votes.

At some point during the long night, the stalwarts began disappearing from the chamber. When enough of them had gone, Joseph Tawney, the chairman of the Appropriations Committee, made the point of no quorum, but instead of allowing a recess, the insurgents and Democrats insisted upon a "call of the House." The sergeant-at-arms and his assistants were sent out in taxicabs to round up members.

And so the stalwarts were reduced to filibustering with speeches. The Democrats heckled them unmercifully as they stood to defend the Speaker. When William Reeder of Kansas declared, "These proceedings are absolutely unfair," they yelled at him, "What do you know about fair dealing?" He answered, "I am inclined to think—" "Why don't you?" they shouted, vigorously applauding their own joke.

At other times, the Democrats shouted at the Speaker, "Rule! Rule!"

Instead, Cannon would recognize another regular. "The gentleman from Ohio!" he shouted at one point.

"Rule! Rule! Rule!" the Democrats continued to insist, whereupon the Speaker smiled genially, kissed the tips of his fingers toward his opponents, and recognized Warren Keifer of Ohio, who spoke at length in his support.

Realizing the Speaker was not going to rule until he was ready, the insurgents made a few speeches of their own. One of the most stirring was by first-term Congressman Hamilton Fish, who described how he had been unable to get even a hearing on a parcel-post system. Henry Cooper of Wisconsin rose to give an exhaustive list of Cannon's sins. He began his speech while Cannon was in the Speaker's room—he had gone there after twelve straight hours in the chair—but before Cooper concluded, Cannon was back on the floor, and when he heard the Wisconsin congressman list all the wrongs he had done, he felt obliged to defend himself. He was particularly interested in having Augustus Gardner of Massachusetts tell why he had not been reappointed to his committee chairmanship. The good-humored Gardner obligingly explained that he had asked Cannon for another assignment because to take a chairmanship would have convinced his friends, the insurgents, that he was disloyal. Gardner's admission brought a hearty round of applause, but was scarcely a victory for the Speaker. As the long night passed and morning came, it was increasingly clear he could not get the votes to win. His lieutenants began to confer with the insurgents to see if a compromise was possible. The most the stalwarts would offer, however, was to enlarge the Rules Committee; the Speaker was adamant about remaining a member of it. "If I must get off the Committee," he said, "I prefer to fight it out." Since the insurgents were as determined to have him off the committee as he was to stay on it, no agreement could be reached.

The strain began to tell on Norris. The *Washington Post* reported that he was "worn and haggard," that his unshaven face was drawn and pale, his eyes red and swollen. The seventy-four-year-old Cannon, by contrast, looked fit and spry. He had a red carnation in his buttonhole and let it be known that he had told his daughter (who had acted as his hostess since his wife's death many years before) not to cancel any of his social engagements. Had Cannon been asked for the secret of his endurance, he would probably have pointed out the benefits of eating abstemiously. He had small breakfasts and dinners, and for more than half a century he had not eaten any lunch at all. Once he berated a colleague who was under the weather by saying, "Why in hell don't you quit eating and go to living on tobacco."

At 4:00 P.M. on the afternoon of March 18 he announced he was ready to rule. The insurgents, confident of victory, but tired and dirty after the all-night session, agreed to adjourn until noon the next day when they would hear Cannon's ruling.

It was, of course, against Norris, and as soon as the assembled representatives heard Cannon deliver it, Norris appealed. The House joined him in voting to overrule the speaker by a vote of 182 to 163. Next came the vote on the Norris resolution itself. By 193 to 153, the House voted to change its rules and remove from the speakership one of the sources of its power. Up in the gallery, Cannon's daughter burst into tears and was promptly joined in weeping by the wife of one of the insurgents. On the floor there was confusion. Focused so long on the challenge to Cannon, the insurgents had not planned what to do when they won. Norris moved to adjourn, but the silver-bearded Speaker, who *had* made contingency plans, asked him to withdraw his motion for a moment. Three days ago, he had begun working with former Republican whip James Watson on a ringing defense of his past actions, and he delivered the speech now in calm, measured tones. There was a new majority in the House, he said. It was composed of Democrats and insurgent Republicans, and he was not in harmony with it; nevertheless, he would not resign: "A resignation is in and of itself a confession of weakness or mistake or an apology for past actions. The Speaker is not conscious of having done any political wrong."

There was long and loud applause, and when it had died down he continued: "The real majority ought to have the courage of its convictions and logically meet the situation that confronts it." Therefore, though he would not resign, the chair was ready to entertain a motion to declare the speakership vacant. With that, he handed the gavel to floor leader Sereno Payne and left the chamber.

Although there had been confusion among the insurgents before, now there was chaos. Much of it swirled around Democrat Albert Burleson, who was trying to make just the motion Cannon had dared his opponents for: a declaration that the speakership was vacant. Doubting their ability to hold their coalition on such a vote, insurgents were screaming at him, "It is untimely! It is suicidal!" Joseph Sherley of Kentucky was shouting that the motion to adjourn had priority, while Norris stood in front of the Speaker's desk demanding a vote on adjournment. Democrats who wanted a vote on the Speaker were bawling at Norris, "Withdraw it! Withdraw it! Let's put him out now!" A Republican, William Rodenberg of Illinois, was elbowing his way to the front intent on the same thing. "Vote on it!" he was yelling. "Show your true colors!" Other regulars were screaming at the clerk, "Read! Read!" They too wanted a chance to vote on Burleson's resolution.

And they got it. As the clerk called the roll, the Democrats applauded each insurgent who voted against Cannon; but there were not many of them. For one thing, it was impossible to overlook the spirit and dignity with which Cannon had conducted himself during the battle. Even the Democrats had to praise him. "Mr. Speaker Cannon," wrote Champ Clark, "throughout that bitter contest, bore himself with the utmost dignity and decorum, never appearing to better advantage in his life." In addition, it was much easier for the insurgents to vote with the Democrats on a procedural matter than to join them in removing a Republican from the Speaker's chair.

Even Norris, who wanted to make it clear the battle had not been about personalities, voted for Cannon. "You're not going to elect a Speaker today," a Republican shouted across the aisle at the Democrats. When all the votes had been cast, it was 192 to 155 in favor of Speaker Cannon. He returned to the chamber to face a hysterical ovation, with the regular Republicans yelling themselves hoarse and throwing their hats into the air. A representative from Pennsylvania produced an American flag and waved it happily above the tumult.

But although the victory salved Cannon's ego, it did not end his difficulties. Within a few months other reforms would be instituted, including a discharge rule that allowed any member backed by a majority of the House to take bills away from committees that refused to report them. Presented as a way of undercutting both the Speaker's power of recognition and the influence he gained from appointing committees, the rule passed by a voice vote.

Uncle Joe's beloved party also suffered serious reverses, and in some ways they were his fault. Although it was apparent by now that he did the party no good, he stubbornly insisted that if the Republicans controlled the next House, he would run for Speaker again. Only when the voters saw to it that the Republicans were in the minority was he willing to announce that he had no plans ever again to seek the office.

Taft was also hurt by the battle over Cannonism. Happy as he had been to see the Speaker's powers curtailed ("Well, Archie," he said to his aide, "I think they have got the old fox this time"), his unwillingness to join the insurgents in their fight embittered them and convinced many that Taft was a "stand-patter" himself. This stereotype helped a bored Theodore Roosevelt decide he ought to challenge Taft for the presidency in 1912, and the result was a Republican disaster. The Democrats gained control of both the Congress and the White House, and among the Republicans who lost their seats was Joe Cannon.

At the next election, however, the voters of Danville returned him to the House, and he remained there until 1923, when, at age eighty-seven, he retired voluntarily. As he left the House for the last time, the members who stood to honor him gave living testimony to the remarkable length of his service: half of them had been born while he was serving in the Congress. Another way of appreciating how long Uncle Joe had been in the House was to consider the many changes he had witnessed in the country since he had first become a congressman. He had seen the beginnings of telephone and radio, the development of a nationwide rail network, the start of manned flight. "When . . . I take down a map of the United States and a volume of the census reports," he said, "I find there the realization of the finest dreams of the greatest optimists who ever lived."

But he had also witnessed a change that must have saddened him. He had seen the speakership grow weaker and weaker, not only during his own term in the chair, but during that of his successor, Champ Clark. The revolution Cannon catalyzed took years to run its course, and Clark was forced to relinquish a prerogative Speakers had always enjoyed: the right to appoint standing committees. By the time Joe Cannon left the Hill, the office that had made him famous was as powerless as it had been in the nation's beginnings.

7

SLICK NICK LONGWORTH'S
FIST OF IRON

In 1905, when he was still secretary of war, William Howard Taft decided to take a congressional delegation to the Orient. One of the first members he invited was his own congressman from Ohio, a handsome, wealthy first-termer named Nicholas Longworth. Also included in the party—indeed, probably the most famous member of the entourage—was Alice Roosevelt, the pretty, twenty-one-year-old daughter of the president of the United States. Her cigarette smoking, public pranks, and general rebelliousness had shocked the nation; but apparently the thirty-five-year-old Ohio congressman was charmed, for when the two-month trip was over he and Alice announced their engagement. Alice wired her aunt: "I always told you that old Nick would get me and he has."

It was a fairy-tale wedding, making front-page headlines across the country. The French government sent the couple a Gobelin tapestry; King Edward, a blue and gold enamel snuffbox; the government of Cuba, a perfectly matched set of pearls. At some point, the bride's father decided it was all too much and announced there should be no more foreign presents for the couple—which caused his friend Henry Cabot Lodge to comment, "How like him to make that decision when the gifts were already on the way." Longworth, even nearer at hand, observed, "My first job is to start living down a noble father-in-law."

It was not universally assumed he could manage it. A year later, an observer in the House gallery noticed everyone pointing to Longworth and whispering, "There's Alice's husband." "I wonder," she wrote in her diary that night, "if he will ever live down that title."

It was a formidable task, but Longworth proved himself more than equal to it. Not only did he rise through the ranks of the House to become one of its best-loved Speakers, but he restored that office to its former position of power. And in the process he helped change the stereotype of the American politician. For decades observers like Lord Bryce had been pointing out that "the best men do not go into politics." These observers, invariably wealthy and well-born, had an unfortunate habit of confusing class with capacity; but once that was understood there was validity to their observation. Men of inherited wealth and high social position did not choose political careers. John Adams, Henry's eldest brother, had, according to Henry, "all he wanted; wealth, children, society, consideration; and he laughed at the idea of sacrificing himself in order to adorn a Cleveland cabinet or get cheers from an Irish mob." When young Theodore Roosevelt informed his friends of his intention to go into politics, they discouraged him, saying that "politics were 'low'; that the organizations were not controlled by 'gentlemen'; that [he] would find them run by saloon-keepers, horse-car conductors, and the like."

But if ever there were a gentleman politician, it was Nicholas Longworth. Polished and suave, he was descended from distinguished Ohio forebears. The apple of his family's eye, he was particularly adored by his mother and sisters, and after his father's death all three women moved to Boston to be near him while he attended Harvard. (This was not an unheard-of Victorian phenomenon; ten years later Douglas McArthur's mother, Pinky, would accompany him to West Point. At about the same time, Sara Delano Roosevelt would move to Boston to be near her son Franklin, who was at Harvard.) When Longworth finished law school—one year at Harvard and three at Cincinnati "for the sake of old traditions"—he became involved in politics, an activity that sent the women who hovered over him into a flutter of concern. Their friends solemnly warned them that he "could not touch pitch without being defiled," but when they passed the message along, Longworth assured them the business was not as black as it had been portrayed and made them laugh, if somewhat nervously, with stories of his experiences. A favorite, and one he continued to tell for years, was about marching in the Young Men's Blaine Club:

> My train was late. The parade had started long before I arrived and the best I could do was to fall in at the end of the line. There were about two thousand men participating, and only one band which, naturally, headed the procession. We wound in and out of streets, unable to see further than the next block ahead, and what was worse, quite unable to hear the music.
>
> Finally I turned to a grizzled old veteran who was trudging silently beside me.
>
> "Pretty tough, isn't it?" I grumbled, "here we are in the very last rank, unable to see where we're going, and unable to hear the music of the band. All we do is follow the men ahead."
>
> "Hell!" said the old fellow. "I've been marching in these parades for the last twenty-five years, and I ain't heard the music yet."

Not only was young Longworth willing to roll up his shirt sleeves, but he enjoyed doing it, a characteristic that stood him well in Theodore Roosevelt's opinion. The president wrote of his future son-in-law, "He has worked his way along in politics and has shown that he has good stuff in him." But the president also liked Longworth's having gone to Harvard, his own school, and belonging to the right club there, the Porcellian. It too was his own (though not Franklin Roosevelt's; he was not asked to join, which may, one reviewer speculates, have helped "make him a radical"); arrangements were made for a "Porc" meeting to be held during Alice and Nick's wedding reception.

The Longworths had been married only a few months when there were portents of just how hazardous it could be to have Theodore Roosevelt for a father-in-law. On a European trip with Alice, Nick arranged for them to have lunch with his aunt and uncle, the Bellamy Storers. But what should have been a pleasant family gathering turned out to be spectacularly awkward, because the Storers were locked in a fierce quarrel with the president. Longtime supporters of Roosevelt, they had been the ones to persuade McKinley to appoint him assistant secretary of the navy, and he, in turn, when he became president, appointed Bellamy Storer ambassador to

Austria. When Mrs. Storer, a converted Catholic and an extremely energetic woman, began to plan a way to get a certain Archbishop Ireland elevated to the College of Cardinals, Roosevelt at first fell in with her schemes; but then she began to circulate around the Vatican personal letters he had written her, and Bellamy Storer approached the pope himself. Soon Roosevelt was writing telling them either to refrain from dabbling in church politics or to retire from the diplomatic service. Hurt and angry, the Storers were in the process of compiling a book about the quarrel when Nick and Alice arrived for lunch. "It was," said Alice, with unusual understatement, "a rather strained occasion."

And then came what Alice called "one long lovely crackling row between the White House and the Capitol." A frustrated Roosevelt had suggested that the Congress was restricting the Secret Service in order to protect members from investigation, and in the outrage that followed, Nick found himself in a most embarrassing position. His colleagues roundly condemned the president on the floor of the House, and during one particularly rough excoriation, the *New York Times* noted, "Representative Longworth sat through the speech without making any sign, though his face was crimson."

But all of this was merely prelude to 1912. When liberal dissatisfaction with Roosevelt's hand-picked successor, Taft, led to talk about Roosevelt running again himself, Longworth advised his father-in-law against it. At first Roosevelt agreed with him, but the siren call became increasingly seductive. Sensing the direction in which Roosevelt was heading, Longworth announced he was solidly for Taft. He represented Taft's own district, after all, and the feeling in Cincinnati for Taft was strong. "I think you are right," Roosevelt wrote him, "as to your saying that you are for Taft. In my judgment it would be a mistake for you not to say so."

But having his son-in-law in the Taft camp did not prevent Roosevelt from plunging ahead with plans to challenge the president for the Republican nomination. "I have got to come out," he wrote to Longworth in February, adding by way of comfort, "You let me know how matters are in your district and I will try to smash up any Roosevelt creature who antagonizes you." But there was little either Roosevelt or Longworth could do about the fact that Alice's heart was with her father. After Roosevelt lost the Republican nomination and decided to run on a third-party ticket, the two men took her aside at Sagamore, the Roosevelt estate on Oyster Bay, and told her she simply could not go to the Progressive convention. "We sat on the piazza," Alice recalled, "Father and I in rocking chairs, both rocking violently, while they held a sort of court of justice on me. It was decided that it would not be fair to Nick for me to go to the convention. They were both simply angelic, really, so sorry for me, and I may say that I was so sorry for myself that I was sniffling."

Roosevelt was less successful arguing with certain hard-core Progressives who maintained it was a test of true faith to run someone against the apostate son-in-law, and a Progressive candidate was entered against Longworth. "Nick . . . was having such a dreadful time," observed Alice, who was off at Oyster Bay again getting the latest prognostications from the Bull Moose himself. Longworth's troubles were compounded when his mother and sisters threw themselves into the fight for Taft with an ardor that almost matched Alice's for her father.

In the end, they all lost. Taft and Roosevelt split the Republican vote, thus insuring Woodrow Wilson's victory, and the Progressive candidate in Ohio's first district attracted enough Republican support for the Democratic candidate to squeak out a victory over Longworth. Bitter at first, Longworth found some comfort in a hobby he pursued with almost professional skill. He was a splendid violinist, and now there was more time for the chamber music he loved. Guests would come to Rookwood, the ivy-covered family home in Cincinnati, and after a leisurely dinner, play string quartets. In her memoirs, Alice, who had earlier observed that the name of Nick's "Cremona" violin reminded her of a cigar, wrote that even she began to enjoy the music. But all was not harmony in the Longworth household. About this time the first of many rumors about Nick and other women began to circulate. One had Alice literally stumbling over him and a woman friend in a Cincinnati park. Alice told her family she wanted a divorce, but they talked her out of it. "The whole thing would have caused too much of a hullabaloo apparently," she remarked in her old age. "In those days people just didn't go around divorcing each other."

Thus Nick and Alice were still together at the next election, when he retook his seat easily. The Longworths returned to Washington, and at the same time Nick was reappearing on Capitol Hill, Joe Cannon came back after being involuntarily retired for a term. The coincidence provided the Gridiron Club with ample material for a skit. On the one hand, there was Longworth, a man of sartorial splendor, to whom manicured nails and spats came as naturally as his love of fine wine and classical music; on the other, there was Cannon, whose clothes, one observer noted, "though scrupulously neat, looked as if they had accidentally dropped upon him out of a tree" and whose manners could make hostesses shudder. They were both exceedingly well liked, though not necessarily by each other. Right in the middle of his battles with Theodore Roosevelt, Cannon had given to Longworth one of the coveted seats on the Ways and Means Committee, and he regarded it as a personal betrayal when, after the 1910 rules fight, Longworth announced that he would oppose Cannon for Speaker at the next caucus.

For the Gridiron dinner, they good-humoredly put their differences aside, as they did for another roast, where much was made of the contrast between Cannon's whiskery face and Longworth's shining pate. "Nick, naturally his own advocate," his sister recalled, "quoted the dialogue in the *Comedy of Errors* on all that the bald man gains in time and comfort by not having to brush his hair, and "avoiding it in his porridge," adding that, whereas, in his case, nature was alone to blame, in that of 'Uncle Joe,' who willfully produced such whiskers, taste and not nature should be called into question."

Longworth was again assigned to the Ways and Means Committee. Although this was his third term in Congress, he still ranked at the bottom; but there were other ways of being influential, and when it appeared that the Republicans had a chance of controlling the House in the Sixty-fifth Congress, he was made a member of the committee to devise a strategy. Elected were 215 Democrats, 215 Republicans, and 5 independents. Writing to his family in early March 1917, Nick explained that the chances of getting three of those independent votes looked good, and if the Republicans could do that, and hold every one of their own, they would organize the House.

The war in Europe disrupted these plans. The United States had come into possession of the Zimmerman telegram, in which the German government sought to gain alliance with Mexico by promising her Texas as booty. On March 1 the telegram was released to the press, and the same month German submarines torpedoed five

American merchant vessels. The inevitability of United States involvement in the war undercut the appeal of open partisan opposition. Longworth lost the independents he had been counting on. One of them, Thomas Schall, a blind member from Minnesota, was even persuaded by the Democrats to nominate Champ Clark, their candidate for Speaker. Schall, who was rewarded for his efforts with a seat on the Rules Committee, argued that the Democrats ought to control the House, so that with a Democratic president and Senate the country could present a united front for battle. Clark was elected, receiving twelve votes more than James Mann, the Republican candidate.

As the war progressed, Longworth publicly joined in the call to lay aside partisan politics, but according to Alice's memoirs, there was much private "snarling," a pursuit no doubt encouraged by Theodore Roosevelt. The former president's hatred of Woodrow Wilson bordered on the pathological, and as he frequently stayed with the Longworths in Washington while he tried to get into the war and back into politics, his tirades would have echoed through their home at 1736 M Street. For his part, Wilson declared politics "adjourned" for the duration of the war, but then broke that pledge in spectacular fashion right before the congressional elections of 1918. He issued a statement accusing the Republicans of being "anti-administration" and declared that the voters must return Democratic majorities to the House and Senate. It was no time, he said, "for divided counsel or divided leadership." Republicans accused Wilson of making the war a partisan issue, and aided by escalating prices at home, managed to eke out a narrow majority in the Senate and a comfortable one—forty-eight seats—in the House.

James R. Mann, who had been the minority leader for the past four terms, was regarded by many as the logical successor to the Speaker's chair. But to Longworth, Mann was too much in the mold of the last Republican Speaker, Joe Cannon. He had been Cannon's right-hand man when Uncle Joe was Speaker and, indeed, even looked a little like Cannon, with his silver hair and beard. He was an exceedingly thorough legislator, whose penchant for doing everything himself had once led Longworth to declare: "The gentleman from Illinois undertakes to play the role of Hamlet in this House, and does it with skill, grace and tact, and I think no one will begrudge that role, but when . . . he undertakes not only to play Hamlet, but the fair Ophelia and the King and the Queen and the first grave digger and sometimes, as now, carries a spear, he might be criticized for carrying the thing too far." Now, however, the attack was less genial. The anti-Mann forces, with Longworth as one of the leaders, adopted Frederick Gillett as their candidate. They declared themselves opposed to the seniority system and denounced Mann as "reactionary." The chairman of the Republican National Committee supported the reformers by declaring that electing Mann would revive the specter of Cannonism and do the Republican party great harm in the 1920 presidential election. Mann's cause was further damaged when a Federal Trade Commission investigation and Senate hearings revealed that large meat-packing interests had given him "a horse and on occasions, choice cuts of beef." The disclosure gave the Gillett forces a rallying cry: "Can, can, the Packers' Mann."

On February 27, 1919, the Republican conference (so called because some members disliked the connotations of the word *caucus*) met in the hall of the House. It was not clear as the meeting opened who would be the victor, but as the roll call proceeded, Gillett looked more and more likely. By the time Mann's name was reached, it was certain he had lost, and so he stood and asked that the vote be made unanimous for Gillett.

The next step was for the conference to decide how standing committees were to be appointed. Like the Democrats, the Republicans had decided to take that power away from the Speaker, and the plan of the Gillett forces was to have a committee of seventeen make the appointments. This committee, which would consist chiefly of Gillett's supporters, would also appoint a five-man steering committee for the House and select a floor leader. That was the position to which Longworth aspired, quite realistically now, since his candidate had been elected Speaker.

One of Gillett's supporters stood to offer the resolution creating the seventeen-man committee, but before the members could vote on it, Mann asked for recognition. He offered a substitute proposal, a "master stroke," one of the members there declared it, and it certainly proved that Mann had learned his lessons well at Joe Cannon's knee. He proposed a much larger "Committee on Committees," one consisting of one member from each state, that member to be selected by the Republican delegation from the state and to have voting strength equal to the delegation. The plan was greeted with enthusiasm, not only by senior members who felt confident they would be more influential under its provisions, but by others who had a better chance of being included on the committee simply because it was larger. Mann's proposal passed overwhelmingly. The reformers had won the Speaker's chair, but the old guard dominated the party organization, a mechanism now more powerful than the speakership. Longworth tried to stop the steamroller by requesting a delay in selection of majority leader, but his motion was defeated, and the Committee on Committees picked Mann first, and then when he declined, Frank Mondell of Wyoming, a longtime supporter of both Cannon and Mann. Although Longworth was appointed to the five-man Steering Committee, it was dominated by Mann backers, and Longworth was beside himself. He told a reporter:

> The performance of the Republican Committee on Committees of its important duty, that of selecting the Steering Committee, the Floor Leader, and the Whip, was exactly what ought to have been expected from the men and under the methods controlling. Its net result was to make Mr. James R. Mann the dominating figure in the next House of Representatives. It is the most complete sort of triumph for reactionism. . . . If it had been deliberately planned to restore the conditions existing in the House ten years ago, as a result of which the Republican majority became a minority, the plan could not have been more successfully consummated.

Mann, who knew a thing or two about name-calling himself, suggested to the *New York Times* that Longworth was a sore loser, a man who had wanted to be Speaker, "but no one else was for him," who wanted to be chairman of Ways and Means, "but nobody else could see his special qualifications." Mann suggested that Longworth had been placed on the Steering Committee "as a sort of tribute to Colonel Roosevelt" (who had died two months before), and concluded by asking rhetorically, "What has he ever done outside of attenting social functions?"

It was true that Longworth was an inveterate party-goer. The war had done nothing at all to slow down his social life and may have even enhanced it. First there were special war missions to Washington—the British, the French, the Italian—and Nick and Alice were invited to many events for each of them. The missions were followed by high commissions from the Allied powers, which were composed of members who, as Alice described them, worked hard during the day, but at night "were equally hard at play." It was a formula Nick was long familiar with and fond of. Since his earliest days in Washington, he had preferred to dance rather than sleep through the night. "Mr. Longworth comes into his most gorgeous bloom after dark," one newspaper reported. In his later years, Nick preferred stag parties, but they didn't get him home any earlier. He would stay playing the piano (or the pipe organ, if one was available) until finally someone dragged him away. In the words of one Washington observer, "He knew the milkmen of Washington by their first names."

When he went out socially, Longworth refused to discuss politics, an eccentricity by Washington standards, and one that probably added to the impression that he was a dilettante congressman. "Agreeably indolent," is the way one social acquaintance described him, and although she quickly added, "It is the fact that he was agreeable rather than the fact that he was indolent which should be stressed," there was, nonetheless, an impression abroad in the city that Longworth should not be regarded with complete seriousness. Too bright to be unaware of this attitude, he was apparently undaunted by it. He continued to enjoy himself and to be the delight of those with whom he socialized. "Merely to gaze upon his smiling face was to make one smile in return," one wrote. Commented another, "No matter what group he entered, he added something to it—a sparkle, a charm, a touch of gaiety, a vibrant and gallant spirit."

Adding to the impression that Longworth didn't care about his congressional duties as much as about his night life was that his public statements were seldom as memorable as his off-the-cuff remarks at social gatherings. His speeches on the floor were dry and businesslike, and only occasionally did the kind of humor that made him such a boon companion shine through. One such time was in February 1917. Watching his fellow congressmen load up a bill with special provisions for their districts, he was moved to present them a poem:

> *Dig, brothers, dig with glee,*
> *Dig to the bottom of the treasuree.*
> *Shovel out the shekels for the Kissimmee,*
> *Millions for the nitrates on the Tennessee;*
> *The South is in the saddle, you bet, by gee!*
> *Dig to the bottom of the treasuree.*
>
> *Dig, brothers, dig with glee;*
> *Why leave a nickel in the treasuree?*
> *Leave the accounting to William G.*
> *He can fake up a balance to a t.*
> *The voters are plunged in lethargee—*
> *Dig to the bottom of the treasuree.*

Declared the *New York Times*, "Pork has its laureate."

The idea that Longworth was a lightweight no doubt worked against him in his attempt to become majority leader, but he was also bested by a worthy foe in the person of Frank Mondell. An orphan, Mondell had as a young man decided to seek his fortune in the Rocky Mountain West. After helping discover coal in northeastern Wyoming, he became one of the founders of a town there, Newcastle, and its first mayor. Within a few years, he had managed to get shot in the back by a drunken hotelkeeper (he carried the bullet lodged near his spine for the rest of his life) and elected president of the state senate. In 1894 he was elected to Congress, and although he was defeated in his first bid for reelection, largely by free-silver sentiment, he won again in 1898.

When he became majority leader, Mondell was in his twelfth term, and he set about molding the new organization of the House in a way that testified not only to his experience, but to his political savvy. He also had the advantage of having no assignment besides the majority leadership. Previously the floor leader's duties had fallen to the chairman of the Ways and Means Committee; but a decision had been made to establish a separate office, and the square-jawed, hawk-nosed Mondell could devote all his considerable energy to being his party's leader in the House. He met with the Steering Committee every morning to set immediate agendas and long-term policies. He coordinated their activities with the Rules Committee's and saw to it that both the Speaker and the membership were kept informed of decisions and schedules. Perhaps most important, he worked to consolidate the appropriations power of the House in the Appropriations Committee. He was among those who believed that ever since Reed had accomplished the division of that power in 1885, appropriations had been uncoordinated and excessive. With the power to spend consolidated once more, a system for budgeting was possible.

In his second term as floor leader, Mondell became chairman of the Committee on Committees as well as of the Steering Committee. He was thus far more powerful than the Speaker, who wasn't even a member of either group. Speaker Gillett didn't seem to mind. He liked being Speaker, according to Sam Rayburn, because it felt "fine to go in first to dinner. Gillett didn't really enjoy the power." The committee chairmen who lost their appropriations authority under Mondell probably did mind the Wyomingite's enthusiastic reorganization, but they were noticeably silent after the Committee on Committees disregarded seniority in picking a new chairman of Appropriations. When James Good of Iowa announced he was retiring, Martin Madden of Illinois was moved to Appropriations and then elevated to the chairmanship some months later.

Little public attention was paid to what House Republicans were doing because the battle over the League of Nations had everyone's attention focused on the Senate. Alice Longworth, for example, who might have been expected to have a passing interest in the House, was spending every day in the Senate gallery and committee rooms, working to kill the League. So anonymous were Mondell's activities that his position as floor leader wasn't even listed in the Congressional Directory. In his autobiography, he explained that he had "suggested to the gentlemen responsible for the publication of the Directory the propriety of having the names of the two floor leaders appear..., but these two conservative gentlemen doubted the propriety of such action in view of the fact that these offices had not been heretofore thus recognized."

Perhaps because he was weary of so much work and so little glory, Mondell decided to run for the Senate in 1922, and once more Longworth was a candidate for Republican floor leader. This time he had little opposition. A third-termer, William Graham of Illinois, was the only one to announce against him, and Graham's motive seems to have been to insure that the West and Midwest were represented on the Steering Committee. When three slots were given to representatives from those regions, he withdrew. The near unanimity of opinion for Longworth was particulary noteworthy since he was an avowed "wet," and most of his fellow Republicans were "drys." His opinion on Prohibition (which had been in effect since January 1920) apparently bothered them less than his swanky dress—at least according to one account. Reporter William Hard told how a group of congressmen, early advocates of Longworth for floor leader, approached him with a problem.

"You won't mind if we talk to you on a serious subject?" they asked.

"I'd like you to," said Longworth.

"It's this," they said. "We find there is a great deal of criticism about your clothes and particularly about those spats. Now we want to ask you: wouldn't you be willing to give up wearing spats? It would help us a lot."

Instead of agreeing to change his style of dress, Longworth sent the group on an errand. "Go over to the Senate and see LaFollette," he told them. One look at the Wisconsin insurgent told them why Longworth had wanted them to visit the Senate side. LaFollette too wore spats—a fact that effectively countered any argument that such dress was effete.

As majority floor leader, Longworth was immediately more visible than Mondell had been. The celebrity status he still derived from his marriage, though it was now in its sixteenth year, was part of the reason, but probably more important was a dispute that broke out almost as soon as he was chosen. The Republican majority was so narrow that progressive Republicans were able to prevent the election of a Speaker by refusing to vote for Gillette, the regular Republican candidate. For two days and eight roll calls, there was deadlock, until Longworth, late in the evening, decided to break it. He arrived in formal clothes ("In evening clothes, he appears as if he had just walked out of . . . a Gibson illustration," one correspondent wrote) to meet with John Nelson, the rough-hewn progressive leader, and the two men cut a deal. Nelson would get a seat on the Rules Committee, which many insurgents felt was a stumbling block to progressive legislation, and the House would be given a chance to revise its rules—an opportunity the insurgents used to make it easier to force legislation out of committees that bottled it up. In return, the progressives would vote for Speaker Gillett.

Thus the House was able to organize, but the Senate was paralyzed for more than a month by the conflict between the regular and progressive Republicans. Longworth didn't hesitate to contrast their continuing turmoil with the more orderly situation in the House wing of the Capitol:

> We are preparing to go ahead and do business. We are going ahead and doing business now. . . . A far different situation exists on the other side of the Capitol. It reminds me of what the farmer said to the city man about "after I am through work, sometimes I sit and think, but most of the time I sit."
>
> I have no criticism to make of any branch of this government, least of all the Chamber on the other side of the Capitol, but I am rather glad the situation exists, because I think now we have an opportunity to put the House in the position it used to be and ought to be, the premier of the two legislative branches of this government. . . . We can go ahead and do the business of the people so satisfactorily that it will be admitted from now on that the House is the real medium for the translation into legislation of the hopes and desires of the American people.

Longworth continued with the idea of restoring the House to preeminence when the secretary of the Treasury, Pittsburgh's Andrew Mellon, brought a tax-reduction plan before the Congress. Struggling mightily to get some form of the bill through the House, Longworth was asked why he was going to so much trouble when it was clear that Democrats and progressives in the Senate were going to hack the bill to pieces. "I am putting the House of Representatives back on the legislative map," the majority leader replied. After the Senate had dismembered the bill, Longworth helped work out a compromise plan, and when Mellon demanded to know what was wrong with the bill as he had originally proposed it, Longworth responded with a bit of doggerel that delighted the practical politicians in the House who understood how moguls from Pittsburgh were popularly regarded. "Mary had a little lamb," the floor leader told the secretary of the Treasury:

Its fleece was white as snow.
It followed her to Pittsburgh one day,
And look at the darn thing now.

Longworth had been majority leader less than a year when Speaker Gillett was elected to the Senate. There was no question that Longworth was exceedingly well liked by his fellow Republicans, but was he tough enough, they asked themselves. Was he serious enough for them to elect him Speaker? When he announced he was indeed a candidate for the Speaker's chair, he was also battling precedent in that the majority floor leader had never been elevated to the speakership before. The typical path up in recent years had been the chairmanship of the Appropriations Committee.

The 1924 election, the same one that sent Gillett to the Senate, gave Longworth a chance to show his mettle. That year Robert La-Follette had run for president on the Progressive ticket and the Wisconsin congressional delegation had supported him rather than Coolidge. Party-bolting was a matter that got the affable Longworth's adrenaline running—it had, after all, cost him his seat when his father-in-law had done it in 1912—and the fact that regular Republicans won enough seats in 1924 so that they no longer needed Progressive votes enabled him to take strong action. In January 1925 he read the rebels out of the party. "Of the 247 Republicans [in the House] at least twelve openly supported the third-party candidate. . . .," he explained in a speech. "Some of them even went so far as to leave their states and campaign against Republican candidates for Congress and in favor of Democratic candidates. These men cannot and ought not to be classed as Republicans in the next Congress."

One of the Wisconsin rebels took to the floor of the House to protest such "torture" and "execution." Longworth replied, "I want at the outset to correct the impression that I or anyone I know of has any intention of torturing or punishing anybody, much less of executing them. Punishment and torture imply a hostility, a feeling of rancor, and . . . I have no feeling of hostility toward any Member of this House from Wisconsin or anywhere else who supported the La-Follette-Wheeler ticket in the last campaign. On the contrary, I admire many of them very greatly." But personal feelings were one thing, and politics another, and although the rebels had a perfect right to do what they had done, they also had to be willing to live with the consequences. "Surely," Longworth declared, "no sane man could have believed that the consequences of defeat should have involved anything less than divorce, temporarily at least, from any advantage to be gained by membership in the victorious Republican party." He hoped they would decide to rejoin Republican ranks, but in order to do so, they would have to give up high-ranking committee assignments and start over again at the bottom.

The regular Republicans who applauded Longworth no longer had any doubts about whether he was tough enough for the job of Speaker. The press too began to think that for all his velvet gloves, he did indeed possess a first of iron. "In a manner he is so light and airy," wrote one correspondent, "that he might be said to have the specific gravity of feathers. In action, when the favorable moment for action has come, he has the weight of a lead shot."

Nor did it hurt Longworth's campaign for Speaker when in the middle of it he became a father. Paulina, the Longworths' only child, was born after they had been married eighteen years, and the occasion caused Nick's colleagues to cheer him when he walked onto the floor. Red-faced, he accepted their handshakes, while Alice continued to keep all of Washington entertained with her razor-edged observations on the event. On first discovering she was pregnant, she had told a friend, "I have just called up the Henry Whites [a couple well into their eighties]. I have told them what has happened to me and I have warned them that they had better be careful." When gossips whispered about the Longworth marriage and speculated about the child's paternity, Alice disingenuously observed that the baby really did bear a strong resemblance to Uncle Joe Cannon.

At the gathering of the Republican conference in February 1925, Longworth defeated the plain-spoken, silver-pompadoured Martin Madden, chairman of the Appropriations Committee, in the contest to be the Republican nominee for Speaker. The Wisconsin progressives, excluded from the conference, refused to vote for Longworth when members of both parties cast their votes in December at the beginning of the Sixty-ninth Congress; but he was elected without them, and by pointedly referring to the "unanimity" of his party's vote for him, served final notice that they were no longer Republicans.

He came to be sworn in as Speaker wearing a beautifully tailored morning coat, patent leather shoes, and brown spats. Up in the gallery was Alice in a fur-trimmed coat, white gloves, and carrying a large, gray silk bag. It was her habit to sit in the Senate gallery and watch that body in action. She had become a Senate watcher during the League of Nations battle, and while there were some who said it was not national policy but William Borah, the square-jawed senator from Idaho, who commanded her interest now, she had on this winter day in 1925 come to the House, Nick's House, to watch him being sworn in. He stood in the rostrum, an American flag behind him, and when he addressed the members, he struck on what was now a familiar theme. "I want to effectively assist you," he told the gathered representatives, "in bringing about universal recognition of the fact that this House, closer as it is to the people than any similar body and more directly responsive to their will, is in very truth, as it ought to be, the great dominant legislative assembly of the world."

Longworth's strategy for bringing this about involved making the House work more efficiently, a feat he was able to accomplish despite having relatively few formal powers. He did not have the authority to appoint standing committees, as had every Speaker prior to 1912. He was not even a member of the Committee on Committees, which did have that authority. Nor was he a member of the Rules Committee. But he had dominated his party's organization as floor leader, and he did not loosen his grip when he moved to the Speaker's chair. This was demonstrated on his first day when he managed to undo the liberal discharge rule that had been adopted as a concession to the Progressives in 1924. He had set the stage by using his influence with the Committee on Committees to purge the Rules Committee of most of the Republicans who had framed the more liberal discharge petition rule. The new committee proposed a much more stringent method for discharge, one that Mr. Crisp, a Georgia Democrat and the son of Tom Reed's foe, declared would "hermetically [seal] the door against any bill ever coming out of a committee when the Steering Committee or the majority leaders desire to kill the bill without putting the members of this House on record on the measure." But the regular Republicans heeded the Speaker's wish, and the House adopted the new rule, thus strengthening Longworth's control over what legislation came before the

House. He was immediately attacked for his role in the new rule's formulation and passage. The *New York World* pictured him as "Czar Nicholas" in crown and ermine. The *Louisville Courier Journal* declared editorially that, although Joe Cannon might be retired, his spirit lived on in the new Speaker: "Cannonism—with all that it connotes—becomes canonized now." The *Wall Street Journal* approved, however, complimenting the House on its "growing good sense and efficiency."

Indeed, the House under Longworth seemed to work better than it had in years. One example of its smooth operation had to do with the claim of constitutional privilege. This issue, which had provided the opening for the attack on Speaker Cannon, came up again in 1926 when a California congressman claimed privilege to bring up a reapportionment bill. Fifty years of precedent supported his claim, but Longworth maintained the precedents ought to be overruled. Otherwise, any member of the House, at any time, could bring forward a proposal and, by relating it to the Constitution, claim that all regular business of the House should be set aside while his resolution was considered. "To the mind of the Chair," Longworth told the members, "the logic of this whole question is that the rules of the House ought not to be set aside at all times and under all conditions by merely bringing up a question claimed to be of high constitutional privilege." Although Longworth's interpretation clearly enhanced the power of the House leadership, the members supported him overwhelmingly, 265 to 87.

Contributing to Longworth's success was the warm regard that members on both sides of the aisle had for him. "Longworth has the human affection of the House of Representatives as really no other Speaker in our times has had it," wrote veteran journalist William Hard. "If Longworth should ever die, there would be more cheeks wet with true physical tears for him than for any other public man that Washington to-day knows." Part of why his colleagues liked him, Hard explained, was that he so obviously liked them and the institution in which they all served. Calling him "the great Washington Defender of the prerogatives of the House and its arduous labors," Hard declared, "Longworth loves the House as much as the House loves him."

One of Longworth's minor efforts—or perhaps it was Alice's—to defend the House's prerogatives caused a great stir in Washington society. When Charles Curtis became Herbert Hoover's vice-president, it was announced that his sister, Mrs. Gann, would be his official hostess. When the Eugene Meyers decided to give a dinner party and it was learned that Mrs. Gann, rather than Mrs. Longworth, would be the ranking female at the event, the Longworths declined to attend. Although Alice later maintained that the main reason Nick did not want to go was that the dinner was "dry," the newspapers played it as a protocol war, and for weeks the Gann-Longworth feud was the talk of Washington.

Such magnification of small events was the price of celebrity, and an indisputable aura of glamor did hover around Nicholas Longworth. He was even profiled by a movie magazine, and though he was the only Speaker in history to whom the klieg lights were so attracted, there was no egoistic pretension about him. To everyone, he was "Nick," and comfortable being so. He might love classical music, but he also enjoyed playing his "fiddle" at the raucous parties with which the House celebrated final adjournment in those days. He might love fine clothes, but every Sunday saw him bundled up in a disreputable sweater and hiking through Rock Creek Park with the "Statesman's Sunday Morning Marching Club," of which he was a charter member. Among his friends he numbered sophisticates such as Efrem Zimbalist and his wife, the soprano Alma Gluck, but one of those closest to Longworth was John Nance Garner, "Cactus Jack," the prickly Democrat from Uvalde, Texas. The two of them reigned together over the "Henry Clay room," a small hideaway in the Capitol where they invited other members of the House and an occasional member of the press to sip bourbon and branch water. So much mutual enlightenment came from these sessions that the room gradually came to be called the "Board of Education."

After Garner became minority leader, Longworth insisted on picking him up every morning in the car provided for the Speaker. The ride to the Capitol, like the sessions in the Henry Clay room, gave them an opportunity to work out differences on legislation—disagreements that were, in effect, differences between their parties. Longworth had the upper hand in the negotiations since he had a majority behind him, but Garner was a tenacious soul who could usually extract a concession or two for the Democrats. Although there were many things they couldn't work out—and these issues would be fought out on the floor, hammer and tongs—the agreements they did reach increased the efficiency of the House's operation.

Their morning rides together also gave them time to practice the quick comebacks for which they were both famous. One day Garner noticed big black objects hanging from the trees along Pennsylvania Avenue. "What are those things?" he asked Nick. "Smudge pots for the starlings," Longworth replied. "Oh," Garner instantly responded, "and who is going to teach the birds to set on 'em?"

How precisely Longworth's skills became honed by these exchanges could be seen from an encounter he had with another member, a presumptuous representative who had the nerve to pass his hand over Longworth's bald head and declare, "Feels just like my wife's bottom." Without missing a beat, Longworth passed his hand over his head and observed, "By golly, it does, doesn't it."

In 1928 there was talk of Longworth for president. It became widespread after Coolidge announced he would not run again, but Herbert Hoover quickly locked up the nomination. Longworth seemed unfazed. "I have realized *more* than I ever hoped for. . . ," he had once told his sister. "I have a real horror of the Presidential bee; I have seen it ruin too many good men. Statesmen turn into politicians and lose interest in jobs they were doing well before they got stung. Let's have all the fun we can get out of this Duck-creek business and never think of political ambition."

Longworth simply refused to behave as if the fate of the universe depended on any political event. This attitude, implicit in the phrase "Duck-creek business," was one of the reasons he made so few enemies. Political differences were just that, in his mind, and no more. Fiorello LaGuardia might give him unending grief on the floor, but Longworth often attended the New Yorker's spaghetti parties. His lack of personal animus in dealing with political rivals also made political reconciliation—or at least accommodation—easier. The second time he was elected speaker, even the progressives voted for him, though many had still refused to attend the conference. By the Seventy-first Congress, one of the progressives, John Nelson, had, with Longworth's backing, become a committee chairman.

Longworth's usually unemotional approach to political matters also meant that when he did feel strongly about something he was extremely effective. When President Coolidge, involved in arms-limitations discussions, wanted to hold up building three cruisers, Longworth left the chair to take part in the debate and oppose the president. It was the first time in a decade a Speaker had taken to the floor, and with Longworth in the lead, the cruiser program was finally forced to passage.

Another result of Longworth's characteristic detachment—or cynicism, some called it—was to endear him to newsmen who had been born knowing that life would go on no matter what the Congress decided. Many of them became enthusiastic fans of Longworth, and they tendered him the kind of praise few politicans have ever enjoyed. "Nick to the Rescue," a crusty Baltimore columnist headlined when Longworth worked out a plan to provide veteran's benefits. The truth was a rescue operation had been needed because Nick had been somewhat inattentive. While he had been entertaining out-of-town friends, who had come for the Gridiron dinner, the Democrats loaded down a veterans' benefits bill with so many extras that its original sponsor disowned it. But an overwhelming majority of the House and Senate found it irresistible, and it sailed through both houses despite a presidential promise to veto it. Longworth, now back at the office, arranged for a Republican conference where repentant members agreed to sustain the president's veto and then pass a more reasonable measure. "The result," wrote Baltimore's Frank Kent, "is a triumph not only for Mr. Longworth personally but for the body over which he presides. By contrast, the Senate appears sordid and cheap and puny. Here, at the close of the session, by an exhibition of political sense and leadership, the House stands out as entitled to some public respect. The once superior Senate is on a much lower level. When this achievement of Nick's is fully appreciated, it makes him easily the outstanding man of the session." The idea Kent conveys of the supremacy of the House was one Longworth stressed again and again. Once he even made a public fuss about a reference to the House as the "lower body." The esteem in which newsmen held him gave credibility to his ideas about the House's preeminence and made certain they were distributed across the nation.

At the end of the Seventy-first Congress, it was not at all clear if the Republicans would maintain control when the new Congress convened. The country's worsening economic plight lost them many seats in the 1930 elections, leaving them a margin of only two. The House doctor reported that, on the average, eleven members died each session, so it was quite possible the numbers could shift to favor the Democrats. Longworth wired Garner, "Whose car is it?" When the House was about to adjourn, he told the members, "Perhaps this is the last time I will address you from this rostrum.... The decision lies with none of us here. It is a decision which lies with an all-wise Providence."

Longworth had a cold when he left Washington. His destination was the home of Mr. and Mrs. James Curtis in Aiken, South Carolina. There had been rumors about Longworth and Mrs. Curtis, and the *Washington Herald*, a newspaper run by Cissy Patterson, a rival of Alice's, gave prominent display to a large picture of the Speaker with Mrs. Curtis on his arm. Nick was smiling and looked healthy enough, but within a week he was ill with pneumonia. Front-page stories announced he was in critical condition and reported that the president had asked to be kept informed. The *Herald* ran the picture of him with Mrs. Curtis again, while Alice hurried down to the Curtis home from Cincinnati. An oxygen tent was brought in. Specialists were consulted, extra nurses hired. But the frantic activity was futile, and on April 9, 1931, a doctor signaled from a bedroom window to let the waiting newsmen know that Longworth was dead. "I have lost one of the best friends of a lifetime," John Nance Garner mourned.

"There is grief today," the New York *Herald Tribune* editorialized, "not only for an irreplaceable public official, but for a man whose personal attractions were unique and who, by reason of them, had gained an extraordinary hold upon the affections of his countrymen."

He had also had an extraordinary hold over the members of the institution where he had spent most of his adult life. He had served them well by being a strong Speaker, and he had nurtured in them a fierce pride in being part of the House of Representatives.

For Republicans of upcoming generations, his death would come to have an added poignance, for it signaled the end of a long era in which their party dominated. During the next six decades, they would control the House of Representatives a total of four years.

8

MR. SAM SURVIVES

On a muggy Saturday night in August 1941, a short, bald-headed man walked through the arched marble entrance of Washington, D.C.'s Union Station and headed for the ticket windows. He didn't look like a person of consequence, and the ticket seller would have given him no more than a glance as he took his money, but within hours people all over the city would be looking for this stocky, fifty-nine-year-old congressman. The House of Representatives was locked in a battle that would determine the country's preparedness for war, and this man—who was leaving town, who was leaving the scene of the battle—was the Speaker of the House, Sam Rayburn.

Rayburn knew how crucial the battle in the House was for the country. Within the last two years, Nazi Germany had smashed through Poland, overrun Scandinavia, conquered the lowland countries, and rolled her tanks through the streets of Paris. Just two months before, Hitler had ordered his troops into Russia. Meanwhile the Japanese were moving aggressively in the Pacific. No one could know that within four months, they would bomb Pearl Harbor, but it was clear that the Selective Service Act had to be extended if the United States were to be ready to meet a challenge from the Axis powers. Rayburn also knew that the fight over the draft would have personal consequences. He had been Speaker less than a year, and whether he won or lost such a crucial vote would determine whether he was considered effective or not. He had been working hard for the extension, lobbying his fellow representatives and calling in favors he was owed, but isolationist sentiment was strong in the House, and as the vote approached the outcome was in doubt. In the last few days Rayburn had been casting around for help. He called the White House, but Franklin Roosevelt was meeting with Winston Churchill on a ship off Newfoundland. He turned to Secretary of State Cordell Hull, but Hull's only contribution was an open letter to members, which few found very persuasive.

It looked more and more as if Rayburn could lose this fight, and this terrified him. At a time when every hour and every word to a wavering colleague might make the difference, he had to get away. Two days before the voting, he was leaving Washington.

One can imagine the phone calls the next day. It was a Sunday, and so it was probably late morning before someone from the whip organization tried to call Rayburn's apartment. When there was no answer, he would have waited a half hour or so and tried again. Still no answer. Where was Rayburn? Members of the whip organization would have begun telephoning each other with that question. Where could he possibly have gone just forty-eight hours before such a crucial vote? They probably began calling his personal staff at home to see if they knew, and finally someone came up with the answer. Rayburn was in Tennessee. He had taken a train to his birthplace in Roane County, and while switchboards all over Washington were lighting up with calls looking for him, he was wandering through the log cabin where he had been born, visiting relatives, and attending a country picnic. At one stop he asked for a "wash pan and an old sack towel like I used to use," and when he had washed his hands and gazed at the Tennessee hills awhile, he got himself on a train back to Washington.

Once there, he was magnificent, personally persuading four more Democrats to vote for extension. As bells rang for the roll call and he climbed to the rostrum to preside, there was no hint of doubt or timidity about him. Ignoring the flag-carrying soldiers' mothers who had crowded into the galleries, he instructed the clerk to call the roll. "Mr. Andrews, Mr. Angell, Mr. Arends, Mr. Arnold." The meter with which the clerk counted the votes made a clicking sound. In the background was a buzz of conversation as Democratic whips pleaded with their wavering colleagues. When the clerk finished the alphabet, he read the names again to pick up those who hadn't answered previously: As the last vote was cast, Rayburn looked at the tally sheet; it was a tie. Members who wanted to change their votes crowded into the well, with Rayburn watching closely, and as soon as the total favored draft extension, he took the tally sheet from the clerk and pounded his gavel. "On this vote," he announced, "203 members have voted aye, 202 members have voted no." Before anyone else could change his vote, the Speaker's gavel fell again: "The bill is passed."

Opponents jumped to their feet to demand the vote stay open. When Rayburn refused, one of them demanded a recapitulation, a procedure for reviewing a close vote. The moment it was concluded, Rayburn declared, "No correction in the vote, the vote stands, and the bill is passed and without objection a motion to reconsider is laid on the table."

As the gavel fell, opponents were on their feet again, demanding reconsideration. But the motion had been tabled—so fast that one member claimed it hadn't happened. "The Speaker did not announce a motion to reconsider had been tabled," said Anderson of Minnesota.

"The Chair has twice stated that he did make the statement," Rayburn replied.

"I beg to differ with you—"

"The Chair," said Rayburn, bringing the matter to an end, "does not intend to have his word questioned by the gentleman from Minnesota or anybody else."

It was one of his finest moments, but he had not relished it as a Clay or a Reed would have. Rayburn found risk hard to tolerate, and once he became Speaker he shied away from it when he could. He preferred to avoid battles unless he was certain of the outcome. He did not desire dramatic confrontations, and since they were usually necessary in order to redesign the power structure of the House, Rayburn did not seek to bring about great institutional changes. But his cautious approach still allowed him to gather a great deal of personal power. It gave him long years to devote to the House—years to learn its lore and history, to explore its rules and procedures; years to store away the names of his colleagues' children and the composition of their districts; years to help other members whenever he could. Unmarried and childless, he devoted himself to his work in a way that became legendary, and his power grew bit by bit with every day of that intense dedication, with every tale about it. "Mr. Sam is terribly convincing," a congressman who served under him said. "There he stands, his left hand on your right shoulder, holding your coat button, looking at you out of honest eyes that reflect the sincerest emotions. He's so damned sincere and dedicated to a cause and he knows his country and his job inside out so well that I would feel pretty dirty to turn him down and not trust him, knowing he would crawl to my assistance if I needed him."

Rayburn shied away from risk once he became Speaker because of the enormous psychological investment he had in the office. By his own account, he decided to be Speaker when he was twelve or thirteen years old, a country boy from Flag Springs, Texas, where his parents had moved when he was five. One day in 1894 or 1895, he heard that Congressman Joseph Weldon Bailey was going to speak in Bonham. He knew about Bailey, a famous orator, who could be Speaker of the House if the Democrats won control, and Rayburn wanted so much to hear him that he rode his mule in the rain over eleven miles of dirt roads into town. He hadn't been in Bonham much, and intimidated by all the townspeople "in store-bought clothes," he couldn't bring himself to go into the tent where Bailey was to speak; but he found a flap where he could stick in his head, and for two hours, despite the rain dripping down his neck, he was spellbound. "I was so carried away with what I heard, that I vowed that one day I would be Speaker."

When he had finished school at Flag Springs, he convinced his father, a hard-working, gentle-souled Confederate veteran, to let him go off to college. As Sam left, his father gave him twenty-five dollars. "God knows how he saved it," said Rayburn. There were ten other children and never any extra money. "It broke me up, him handing me that twenty-five dollars." Rayburn took the train to Mayo College, where the motto was "ceaseless industry" and where he could support himself as a janitor and bell-ringer for the school. Three years after graduation, he ran successfully for the Texas legislature, and although he went to law school at the same time he was serving in the red-granite statehouse in Austin, his studies did not, apparently, take away from his legislative work. Four years after his first election, he was chosen Speaker of the Texas house.

His next step was to run for the United States House of Representatives. He opened his campaign in Windom, a few miles from Flag Springs, and closed it at a courthouse rally in Bonham. "When I was a schoolboy I made up my mind that I was going to live to be worthy of your support and to run for Congress when I was thirty years old," he told the crowd. "In this good year of 1912 I have reached that age and am running for Congress." Then lest the gathered farmers and storekeepers think him pompous, he declared, "I will not deny that there are men in this district better qualified than I to go to Congress, but, gentlemen," he added pointedly, "these men are not in the race." He won the seven-man Democratic primary by 490 votes, a victory that in the fourth district of Texas was tantamount to election.

Almost as soon as he got off the train in Washington, he was taken in hand by another member from the Texas blacklands, John Nance Garner. "Cactus Jack" invited Rayburn to share his office until he got a decent one of his own, and when Rayburn decided he wanted to serve on Interstate and Foreign Commerce—a committee being made increasingly powerful by Joe Cannon's old ally Jim Mann—Garner helped him out again. He was on the Democratic Committee on Committees, and one of his good friends was William Adamson of Georgia, the chairman of Interstate and Foreign Commerce. Young Rayburn got the assignment he wanted.

The new congressman from the fourth district also paid heed to other senior members. Several of them lived at the old Cochran Hotel, where he had taken a room, and "each night after supper," as Rayburn remembered it, "most of these men would pull their chairs together at the end of the big old lobby and for several hours they would explore together in serious candor the great issues of the day." The stocky young man with thinning hair who joined them was exactly where he wanted to be. "I cannot live without this life," he wrote his mother, "for it is my very self, for as you know, my every effort all though life has been towards the ends I am now attaining."

Champ Clark, who was Speaker during Rayburn's early years in the House, also interested himself in the young Texan's future. One day in 1916 Clark, a huge man with a splendid physique, beckoned the much smaller Rayburn to take a seat beside him in the private corridor outside the House chamber. He told Rayburn that, though he had all the native talent necessary to rise to leadership in the House, he lacked historical perspective. He should read biographies of the country's great men: Washington, Adams, Jefferson, John Quincy Adams. He had him jot down a reading list, which included works on Polk and McKinley, whom Clark considered among the most effective legislators the House had ever seen. "This was," Rayburn said, "some of the best advice anyone ever gave me." Until he was an old man and his eyesight failed, he read historical biographies, alternating them with another genre he loved—the wild west magazine. Whenever he got on the train for Texas, he was well supplied with slick western thrillers.

But Rayburn did not attract powerful mentors by being the sort who always passively heeded advice. When he felt strongly about a matter, as he did about railroad regulation, he chose his own path and launched himself down it until he had arrived at his goal. He first tried to get a railroad securities bill enacted in his freshman term, and although it passed the House (with Garner voting against it), it was killed in the Senate. No less an observer than Woodrow Wilson was impressed with young Rayburn's moxie. "I want to make my humble contribution to the congratulations you must be receiving," the president wrote. Rayburn submitted the bill again in the next Congress, but by now the war in Europe was changing the president's priorities, and Wilson turned down Rayburn's request for administration support of stock and bond regulation. The bill never came to the floor, but Rayburn submitted it again in the next Congress and then again in the next until finally, in 1920, it became law.

But as the years passed, he did not find the kind of success he had been counting on. That wasn't how he described his career to his constituents, of course. He put the best face on things for them. In 1922 he told a Bonham audience, "I went to Congress, the youngest man in the body, and for eight years I have led such a life before my colleagues on the Democratic side that when the Democratic caucus met in March, 1921, when they looked about for a Chairman of the Democratic Caucus, the biggest body of Democrats in the Nation, my name was the only name presented for the Chairmanship of the Caucus." What he didn't say was that the caucus that had elected him was poorly attended. His name had been slipped in and voted on before many members of it knew what was going on. Nor was the chairmanship all that important: the caucus had fallen on hard times and served little purpose except electing the Democratic leadership.

The truth was he was getting discouraged. He had been in the House now twice as long as he had been in the Texas legislature, and the speakership seemed farther away than ever. The Democrats did not even control the House any longer, having lost it, with Wilson's help, in 1918. Being in the minority was unpleasant, and having run for Congress five times now, Rayburn was also finding it irksome to have a campaign every two years. For a few weeks, he toyed with the idea of running for the Senate, but it would be a difficult race, and he was losing the sense he once had that he could accomplish anything, if only he worked hard enough. He no longer had the relentless optimism of the young man who has attained everything he has worked for, and even when he had put the idea of running for the Senate behind him, he was plagued with doubts. On one long, lonely Sunday, Rayburn, now thirty-six, sat down and in a painfully self-conscious letter poured out his feelings to his brother-in-law:

> I have all of my life worked toward the position that I now hold. Every move since I have been old enough to think has been a part of a dream that I am now realizing in part. Probably I have got as high here as I will ever get, but I hope not. . . . I have sacrificed everything, and many that would have been sweet and dear, to live this life. I have not let anything come between me and the darling of my dreams, and that is fame. I would rather link my name indelibly with the living, pulsing history of my country and not be forgotten entirely after while than to have anything else on Earth. If, in the providence of God, I can win this, I must, and I hope that all of my friends, will realize that this race means everything to me. It would be a tragedy to me that no one else could realize if it should be decreed otherwise.

Those who worked with Rayburn in Washington would have been astonished at such a heartfelt outpouring. They knew him as a reserved, taciturn man. His ambition for the speakership might also have surprised his colleagues since he was so unlike the men who had risen to the top of the House during the last twenty years. There was no genial camaraderie about him, but rather an air of withdrawal. His hard, round face seemed to fall naturally into an off-putting scowl. He didn't have the physical presence or dramatic style of a Champ Clark. He didn't have Joe Cannon's knack for telling jokes to win friends and press attention. "I tried telling a joke once in a speech," he said, "and before I got through I was the joke." What he was good at was hard work. One of his colleagues noted that "the House soon spots the men . . . who attend a committee session where there isn't any publicity, who attend during the long grind of hearing witnesses. . . . Men will come in and out of an executive session, but there are only a few men who sit there and watch every sentence that goes into the bill and know why it went in." Sam Rayburn was one. He had patience and discipline, undramatic traits, but they gave him a reputation for dependability. They would also serve him well in the years ahead, because the speakership would take longer to reach than he had ever imagined. Many men would have given up, but Rayburn, like James Polk, whom Champ Clark had told him to read about, had a stubborn determination at the core of him. A constituent once compared Rayburn to a scarred old bronc rider who wouldn't quit the rodeo. "The only way he could be stopped," explained the constituent, "was to cut off his head and hide it."

During these long years, Rayburn was a regular at the Board of Education meetings where Garner and Longworth reigned. After a day's session, he would head down the corridor connecting the House and Senate and turn left down a side passage when he came to the statue of Stephen Austin. When he reached the small, dark hideaway where Longworth and Garner presided, he would fix himself a drink ("striking a blow for liberty," it was called in those Prohibition days) and take a seat in one of the black leather armchairs. Laconic as he was, he didn't speak often, and when he did, there was little subtlety. One day the conversation had turned to Frederick Gillett, who was such an unenergetic Speaker that a newsman had said of him he didn't drink coffee in the morning "for fear it would keep him awake all day." Garner and Longworth were complaining about his weakness when suddenly Rayburn blurted out, "I'll tell you what I think—I think someday a man will be elected who'll bring the Speakership into respectability again. He'll be the real leader of the House. He'll be master around here, and everyone will know it." Then, no doubt embarrassed at how much of himself he had revealed, he hastily added. "My guess is that one of you two will be the man."

He must have watched with mingled envy and fascination when Longworth became Speaker and made the office formidable once more. It was even more important to Rayburn, however, when upon Longworth's death Garner succeeded to the speakership. With the

Democrats regaining control, Rayburn, after eighteen years in the House, became chairman of the Interstate and Foreign Commerce Committee. And he became Garner's lieutenant, not only for the speakership, as it turned out, but for Cactus Jack's presidential bid. In the contest with Roosevelt for the Democratic nomination, Garner got the Texas delegation behind him and won the primary contest in California. Rayburn was his agent at the Chicago convention, and as balloting deadlocked three times, with Roosevelt unable to gather the last chunk of delegates to send him over the top, Rayburn dealt with the New York governor's desperate agents, who pleaded for Texas to switch. Finally word came from Garner: he wanted to break the deadlock. Rayburn released his delegates and persuaded the howling, near-hysterical contingent from Texas to switch to Roosevelt. Then when Roosevelt offered the vice-presidency to Garner, Rayburn helped convince his fellow Texan to accept.

For a short time, it looked as if his own ambition would be fulfilled. With Garner moving on, the House would be electing a new Speaker, and why shouldn't it be Sam Rayburn? There were a heady few months as he imagined himself about to realize the dream that had been driving him for more than three decades, but then his rivals began to point out the extent to which Texas dominated the House. They had five committee chairmanships; surely the speakership ought to go to another state. It was a powerful argument, and not even Garner's help could save the day. Rayburn withdrew in favor of John McDuffie of Alabama, who was also Garner's choice after Rayburn withdrew. But McDuffie was defeated by the more liberal Henry Rainey of Illinois, who had been majority leader under Garner.

Rayburn's response was to make the position he did have as powerful as possible. When legislation he wanted didn't come his way, he went out and got it, directing the House parliamentarian or even the Speaker himself to send certain bills to his committee. Thus he was at the center of much New Deal legislation. He sponsored a federal securities act; he presided over lengthy hearings that resulted in the Securities and Exchange Commission and the Federal Communications Commission; he sponsored and pushed to passage the Public Utility Holding Company Act; he coauthored the Rural Electrification Act.

Such achievements, one historian of the time has written, made Rayburn's chairmanship of the Interstate and Foreign Commerce Committee a "temporary dictatorship." But that wasn't enough for him. His eye was on the speakership all along. When Rainey died in 1934, he campaigned for the office again. Garner threw himself into the battle on Rayburn's side, but once more they failed to gather the necessary support. Soon it was clear that the new Speaker would be Joseph Byrns of Tennessee, a congressman older than Rayburn, who had been in the House longer, was considered more progressive, and had served as Rainey's majority leader. "I am no longer a candidate for Speaker," Rayburn told a group of reporters he called together. "There are no alibis. Under the circumstances, I cannot be elected."

Less than two years later, Byrns died. By now the tradition of the majority leader moving up to the speakership was so firmly established that Rayburn didn't contest floor leader William Bankhead's right to become Speaker. Rayburn ran for majority leader instead, but here too he faced formidable opposition. John Joseph O'Connor, the red-haired chairman of the Rules Committee, also wanted the job. He had run twice before for Speaker and had already filled in as majority leader when Bankhead moved up. But Garner came to Rayburn's aid once more and secured for him the support of Pennsylvania Senator Joseph Guffey. Guffey had not always been a friend—he had worked to oppose Rayburn when he had run against Byrns for Speaker—but now at a private luncheon at the Mayflower Hotel Guffey entered the contest on Rayburn's side and persuaded the Pennsylvania House delegation to follow him. "I am more than grateful," said Rayburn, who had waited in the Mayflower lobby to hear the news. He was all decked out in a brown suit and brown tie, which, one reporter noted, just matched his cigar. "It will mean a lot in the final windup of this thing," he told the press. As indeed it did. Other delegations followed Pennsylvania's lead, and on January 4, 1937, the Democratic caucus elected Rayburn majority leader. "Frankly," he wrote in a letter, "I now have the position that I have been fighting for for many years."

He began to stand for hours behind the brass rail at the rear of the House chamber, issuing orders, suggestions, and advice to the Democratic troops he now commanded. Remembering Longworth's and

Garner's Board of Education, he set up a hideaway on the ground floor of the Capitol and made it his own with a portrait of Robert E. Lee. When the telephone had been installed, the furniture moved in, and he had invited Speaker Bankhead, John McCormack, committee chairmen such as Carl Vinson, and younger members he favored such as Lyndon Johnson, he settled back in his black leather armchair, surveying with satisfaction the domain to which the majority leadership entitled him.

But there were some who questioned the value of his new job. In the *New York Times*, Arthur Krock declared that "the House leadership isn't much these days," and suggested that the Rules Committee, where O'Connor was still chairman, represented a potent counterforce. The events of the next few years demonstrated just how powerful the Rules Committee was and established a pattern that ran through the rest of Rayburn's career. Time and again, the Rules Committee would challenge his authority, and time and again, he would show little inclination to take measures that would permanently diminish its power.

The Rules Committee had been growing in power since Reed had seen its potential in the 1880s, and it had become an effective instrument for controlling debate. Before a bill went to the floor, it came to the Rules Committee, where a special rule was drafted for it. The special rule determined how much debate there would be, even whether amendments would be allowed. Without some such control, a legislative body of 435 members could not function, but the same power that could facilitate legislation could also block it. In 1937, that began to happen. The four Republicans on the committee and several of the Democrats had been suspicious of Roosevelt to begin with, but after he attempted to pack the Supreme Court, they decided it was their job to protect the country from him. They began to vote together to bottle up legislation the administration desired and the House leadership supported. They refused to vote the special rule that was necessary if a labor standards bill were to be considered before the end of the first session of the Seventy-fifth Congress, and faced with their hostility, Roosevelt had to lay aside his plans for a time. In the same Congress, Rules dealt a harsh blow to the president's plan for executive reorganization by refusing to put any limitations on debate. Once the bill was on the floor, Rules

Chairman O'Connor helped lead the charge against it, and despite Majority Leader Rayburn's taking to the airwaves to defend the proposal, the bill was killed.

Roosevelt was furious. "For weeks and months afterward, I found him fuming against the members of his own party," Jim Farley reported. Finally the president decided to use the 1938 elections to purge the Congress of Democrats who were thwarting him. High on his list was Chariman O'Connor. Rayburn did not think a purge was wise. What if the plan failed? "Our trouble of last session with [O'Connor] would be a small affair compared to what we would have next session," he argued. In fact, most of Roosevelt's efforts to rid himself of nuisances in the House and Senate did fail. O'Connor was his one success. With the White House backing his primary opponent and sending in aides to work full-time against him, the Rules Committee chairman went down to defeat. But Sam Rayburn didn't like the whole idea. "This purging was one of Roosevelt's mistakes," he said, "and I regret it very much."

Such attitudes, some believed, revealed a lack of fortitude. Harold Ickes, Roosevelt's secretary of the Interior, was one who thought the majority leader wasn't tough enough. "Sam Rayburn is not a strong, effective leader. . . . He doesn't want to offend anybody because he hopes someday to be Speaker," Ickes wrote in his diary. Jack Garner seemed to imply that he also found his protégé too timid when he told him, "You've got to get your knuckles bloody once in a while, Sam." But Rayburn's cautious ways finally brought the culmination of his dream. When Speaker Bankhead died in September 1940, Rayburn reached the goal he had set almost half a century before. The day after Bankhead's death, while his body still lay in state in the well of the chamber, the House voted unanimously for Rayburn for Speaker. Back in his office, waiting nervously to be sworn in, Rayburn decided to shave and with a trembling razor cut himself. Blood ran down onto his shirt and ruined it; frantic aides scrambled to find him a new one; finally, looking his best, he strode into the chamber. Forty-six years after he had decided he wanted to be Speaker, twenty-seven years after he had entered the Congress, eight years after he had first run for the office, he was sworn in as Speaker of the House of Representatives.

He had been in office only a few months when Roosevelt made it clear that he also worried Rayburn wasn't enough of a fighter. In what may be the most condescending letter ever sent by a chief executive to a congressional leader, Roosevelt told Rayburn:

> I myself must, as you know, be guided by the recommendations of the Democratic leaders in the House, and while in no sense of the word do I want the advice of "yes men," I do want the advice of fighting leadership, with the adjective "fighting" underscored. . . .
>
> You and I and John McCormack [who had been elected Majority Leader] are facing a very difficult session. On the success of that session will depend the future reputation of the President and the Speaker and the Majority Leader. It will not help any of the three to meet with a series of defeats in the next Congress.
>
> That is especially true if the three of us, or any one of the three, accepts the prospective defeat tamely. Therefore, I renew my ancient feeling that it is better to be defeated while going down fighting than it is to accept defeat without fighting. . . .
>
> I know you agree and I know that John McCormack agrees.
>
> What I want to get across to both of you before the new session begins is that good fellowship for the sake of good fellowship alone, an easy life to avoid criticism, an acceptance of defeat before an issue has been joined, make, all of them, less for Party success and for national safety than a few drag-down and knock-out fights and an unwillingness to accept defeat without a fight.

How those words must have grated. The *idea* that he wasn't tough enough! He, who had picked cotton day after day under the hot Texas sun; he, who had worked his way up from hardscrabble poverty, sacrificing everything along the way, enduring long years of loneliness. He had fallen in love once. Her name was Metze Jones, and she was the sister of Marvin Jones, with whom Rayburn shared an apartment in the Washington Hotel. They were married in 1927, when he was forty-five and she was twenty-seven, but the marriage lasted only a few months, and then he was alone again—alone Sundays in his apartment, alone mornings, when the restaurant across the street brought him his breakfast. Since he wasn't much for small talk, the social life of Washington had little attraction for him. And he wasn't interested in foreign travel. During his entire congressional career, he left the country only twice, once to inspect the

Panama Canal and once to vacation in Mexico. He had centered his life on the House of Representatives, sacrificed everything to rise to the top of it—and now there was this talk he wasn't tough enough.

Those who had seen his temper knew he could be mean. "When he would say 'She-e-e-et,' drawing the word out, I knew he was still good-natured," House Doorkeeper Fishbait Miller remembered. "But if he said it fast, like 'I don't want to hear a lot of shit from you,' I knew I was in trouble." And congressmen who crossed him must have laughed at the idea that the stocky, bull-like Rayburn wasn't tough. A Texas congressman who violated Rayburn's rule about wearing cowboy clothes on the floor of the House carried scars of the tongue-lashing the speaker administered for months. Robert Caro tells of another representative who voted against Rayburn, then later came up to explain that he was surely sorry, but supporting the Speaker would have cost him at home.

"You *could* have voted with me," Rayburn said angrily. "I've known that district since before you were born, and that vote wouldn't have hurt you one bit. You didn't vote with me because you didn't have the guts to." The top of his bald head was turning red. "So don't you come crawling across the room telling me you wish you could have voted for the bill. 'Cause it's a damn lie. It's a damn lie. And you're a damn liar."

Having a temper, though, was different from having a thirst for battle. "A man doesn't learn his job in the House until he's had his head damn near well bloodied a couple of times," Rayburn once said, "but a leader may as well quit if his head is bloodied too often." The idea that he would lose once too often haunted him, and so he would seek accommodation rather than confrontation. During the war years, he made no effort to undercut the Rules Committee's power. Instead he tried to work with Gene Cox, the handsome, volatile leader of the committee's conservative Democrats, to get what he wanted. "Do you really need this one?" the tall, gray-haired Cox would ask, and if Rayburn said he did, the committee usually gave it to him. Rayburn responded in kind. Once when Roosevelt started talking about purging Cox, Rayburn told the president, "Hell, Mr. President, you can't go after Cox. He's at least five votes on the Rules Committee." Rayburn's primary message—that he and Cox had reached a useful accommodation, which it would be foolish to ruin by getting rid of Cox—had an underlying warning. If

Roosevelt went after Cox and failed to get him, five votes on Rules would be forever lost to the administration. You might not win, Mr. President, Rayburn was saying. And, therefore, you'd better not try it.

Occasionally the Rules Committee would overplay its hand so egregiously that it looked safe to enter the skirmish against it. In 1944 the Committee on Banking and Currency reported a bill that would prolong the life of the Office of Price Administration (OPA), one of the war agencies that most irritated conservatives. One member of the Rules Committee, Virginia's Howard Smith, had recently concluded an investigation of OPA and proposed a number of restrictions on the agency. Banking and Currency had rejected his suggestions, but now he managed to get a rule on Banking and Currency's bill that would permit his proposals to be added to their bill as an amendment. When the rule came to the floor, Rayburn strode into the well: "I take this time to warn the Members of this House [that] the Committee on Rules was never set up to be a legislative committee. It is a committee on procedure." The House turned down the rule by a vote of 177 to 44.

But victory on a single rule did little to affect the larger battle, and the very next year the committee refused to let a bill reported by the Banking and Currency Committee go to the floor unless alterations that the Rules Committee desired were made. The same year they also refused Truman administration requests for rules to permit the House to vote on fair-employment legislation. In 1946, they refused clearance to the administration's labor-relations legislation, reporting instead an antilabor measure of their own. And so it went, time after time, and Rayburn simply coped.

The committee was blocking legislation he wanted to see passed, but to force a showdown was to risk too much. He couldn't be positive of commanding a majority—the House seldom overturned the committee's rules, after all—and if he tried and failed, everything he had worked for since he was twelve years old could slip away. He'd read the histories of the great legislators of the past. He knew how Reed had prepared himself to resign when he undertook his great battle, how he had resigned after he had become alienated from his party. Rayburn had served in the Congress with Joe Cannon after he had lost his fight over the Rules Committee, and the sight of the much-diminished former czar would have impressed him. Deep down in Rayburn's psyche there was an even more devastating vision of what it meant to lose, a picture burned there by his Confederate cavalryman father's experience in the Civil War. The elder Rayburn had told the stories again and again of battles lost and pain endured. As a child, Rayburn had seen the devastated countryside and watched as desperate people fled the ruined land. He had experienced the hard, narrow circumstances that were the lot of those who lost the war, and the thought of any battle would have touched the chords of these old memories. "I hate like hell to be licked," he said once. "It almost kills me."

The risk of a Rules Committee showdown could be avoided, but there were other ways to lose the speakership, and as the elections of 1946 approached, it looked increasingly as though Rayburn would fall victim to an electorate that wanted a Republican Congress. As early as April 1945, William S. White had a sense of what that meant to Rayburn. He was with him in the Board of Education when word came that Roosevelt had died, and he saw the sixty-three-year-old speaker weep, heard him talk about following his leader in death just as he had in life. "It was," White observed, "at least to some of us who stood and looked, a scene with a certain touch of elegy for more than one man. Mr. Rayburn was in his fourth term as Speaker; already, if one looked at history, his power was running on borrowed time, for another Democratic capture of the House, in the election of the following year, looked most unlikely."

When the Republicans did win control, a bitter Rayburn said he wanted no part of being minority leader. "I don't want to step down from the Speakership and be expected to be replying from the Floor at all times to every little 'yelping' Republican that gets up," he wrote. His decision was final, he repeated many times. He even advised John McCormack on how to go about getting the minority leadership for himself. But on the day before the caucus, Democrats were still lining up in his office to press him to take the party leadership, and finally he gave in, moving his belongings from the Speaker's office into the smaller quarters of the minority leader. For two years, he chafed at his position and groused at the Republicans. Then Truman beat Dewey, there was a Democratic House once more, and Rayburn moved all his belongings back.

Hardly had he done so, when he found himself facing a familiar kind of problem. A number of House members had been among the southern conservatives who bolted from the Democratic convention over the platform's civil rights plank. They had formed their own party and supported Strom Thurmond for president rather than Harry Truman. To many Democrats who had been loyal to the ticket, it seemed obvious that Rayburn should do what Longworth had done in a similar situation: strip the defectors of their seniority. "What incentive was there," asked Congressman Richard Bolling, who entered the House in 1949, "for a Southern Democrat in Congress to be loyal to his party and his party's Presidential nomination—much less to his party's program—if the Mississippians could walk out of the Democratic convention planning to defeat the party's nominee? Then when the nominee, despite their efforts against him, was reelected to the Presidency and the party they had deserted was once more in control of the Congress, they were permitted to return with impunity to share in the power they had tried to prevent their party from regaining."

But Rayburn made no move against the "Dixiecrats." "No doubt Speaker Rayburn did not want to rock the boat," Bolling suggests. Part of his motivation may also have been his agreement with the Dixiecrats on civil rights. "Some newspaper correspondents," he had written in February 1948, ". . . printed that I said many of the Southern Congressmen would cool off. I think they will, and should, but this does not mean I support the President's so-called Civil Rights Program. Although I would be for the repeal of the poll tax by the voters of Texas, I have always voted against it here as I have voted against the Anti-Lynching Bill." And a month later he told another correspondent, "I am going to do everything I can for my state to protect our segregation laws. I think we can work out our local problems without any interference from the outside, and especially interference from people who do not know what the racial problem is."

He had to find some way to assuage the animosity of liberal Democrats, however. Their feelings of betrayal were running so high that not placating them had become a high-risk course. The result was Rayburn's first effort to curb the Rules Committee. He directed the House parliamentarian to write a rule providing that any piece of legislation reported by a legislative committee that the Rules Committee either acted on unfavorably or failed to act upon within twenty-one days could be called up on the floor by the legislative committee chairman. Rayburn took the new rule into the Democratic caucus and saw that it was passed. After it had also passed on the floor, eight bills, which would otherwise have died in the committee, were brought forward, and seven of them approved.

But Sam Rayburn was not particularly happy. It was true that the Rules Committee had been curbed, but the power of committee chairmen had grown as a result. Rayburn knew what Rules would do, and while they might occasionally block legislation he thought should come to the floor, he could count on them not to report out legislation he didn't want to have considered. Chairmen were not so reliable. John Rankin of Veteran's Affairs, for example, had a fondness for budget-busting veterans' bills. Because of the vocal constituency they affected, even the most fiscally conservative members had a hard time voting against them, and with the twenty-one-day rule in effect, there was no way to keep such measures off the floor. Rayburn understood that, and when a move was made to rescind the rule in 1951, he did not attempt to save it.

He was sixty-nine years old now, and his ways were pretty well set. He'd traveled to Texas and back by train his entire career, and although it took two nights and a day, it was hard for him to change to the airplane. He also had his own method of politicking, an old-fashioned one that meant knowing the people of his district the way a man would know his own family. When friends of his, trying to help, took a poll in the fourth district, he was furious. "What if word got out that I was having some of these polling fellers come in from outside to traipse around over my district? My folks wouldn't like it one bit," he fulminated, "and I wouldn't blame 'em. It's prying into their business. Tear up both copies!"

He handled the press in the same straightforward way he had since they first started paying him attention. The reporters who came to his office got five minutes for their questions. His answers were short, to the point, and off the record. "You'll have to go somewhere else to get your quotes," he told them. When Lawrence Spivak asked him to be on "Meet the Press," the Speaker replied, "I never go on programs such as yours because some twenty or more years ago I did go on a panel program on the radio and all the folks on the panel got in such an argument that I had enough." Never having had a very high opinion of publicity, he wasn't going to change his mind about it now. One of the greatest compliments he could pay a colleague was to say, "He doesn't run around getting his name in the newspapers all the time."

And he still ran the House in the same way, dealing with members one-on-one, helping where he could, saying where he couldn't, and never getting the two confused. Franklin Roosevelt once asked him how he could remember all the different pledges he made. "I always tell the truth the first time and do not need a good memory to remember that," Rayburn replied. A man who needed a favor could find him in the late morning in his formal office, an ornate room with a gilded mirror over the fireplace and a huge crystal chandelier hanging from the high ceiling. Afternoons, when the House had gone into the Committee of the Whole, he could often be found leaning on the brass rail at the back of the chamber. Joe Martin, who had led the Republicans in the House almost as long as Rayburn had led the Democrats, was often there with him, for out of their rivalry had come a deep and lasting friendship. That made it a little easier when, in 1952, the Democrats lost the House again and Rayburn had to turn control over to the Republicans. Once more he moved his belongings out of the Speaker's suite and into the minority leader's office, and even though Democratic victories in 1954 gave him the right to move back, he decided to stay where he was. "Ah'm tired of all this shiftin' around," he told Martin. "What do you say we keep the same room we got now."

Every year there was a new crop of freshmen to educate, and the Speaker didn't grow any more tactful with the passage of time. "You got to go along to get along" was his message. Do what your leaders tell you and you'll get what you want, whether it's a dam for your district or an important committee assignment. Chester Bowles, who as a freshman representative heard the Rayburn lecture, reported that it offended many of his fellow newcomers—and that those most offended soon learned that Rayburn's words weren't to be taken lightly. What he lacked in formal authority over committee appointments, he made up for with informal influence, and the recalcitrant freshman (particularly if his recalcitrance extended to doubts about the oil-depletion allowance) was never going to get on Ways and Means. One anonymous member put his frustrations into verse:

I love Speaker Rayburn, his heart is so warm,
And if I love him, he'll do me no harm.
So I shan't sass the Speaker one little bitty,
And then I'll wind up on a major committee.

What it took the freshmen a while to realize was that Rayburn himself practiced what he preached. He had learned to get along by going along with Democratic presidents. During the Roosevelt years he had urged his colleagues to support the president by telling them, "I have found that those members who submerge their own wills to the leaders of the nation are the ones who survive." This attitude led to the charge that he was a rubber stamp, an accusation he vehemently denied. Toward the end of his life, when a reporter mentioned he had served under eight presidents, he snapped, I never served *under* any President, I served *with* eight." It was true that his suggestions and assessments were often crucial in structuring executive proposals, but once a measure had been decided on, he usually worked the chief executive's will whether it accorded precisely with his own or not. Even when the president was a Republican, there were areas, such as foreign policy, where he did what he could to help. He supplied Eisenhower with more votes on reciprocal trade than Joe Martin did. On the Formosan resolution, he managed to get the president every Democratic vote but one. A study in *Congressional Quarterly* showed that only eight members in the entire House supported Eisenhower more frequently than Rayburn did, and this pattern of cooperation troubled some of his Democratic colleagues. A large delegation who believed the Formosan resolution unnecessary stormed into his office one day, only to be turned away by a stone-eyed stare and a firm command: "I don't want one word said against this resolution when it gets to the floor."

Discontent was also growing about the Rules Committee once more. After the 1954 elections put Rayburn back in the Speaker's chair, there were eight Democrats and four Republicans on Rules, but voting often deadlocked at six-six, with the two southern Democrats on the committee joining the Republicans. Since a tie vote meant a bill was lost, the committee, under the chairmanship of Virginia's courtly Howard Smith, was an effective block to legislation. Rayburn had a friendly relationship with the thin, slightly stooped Smith, who sometimes wore wing collars and a pince-nez, and the Speaker could frequently bargain with the Virginian to get legislation out of Rules, offering to cooperate in killing housing and TVA bills, for example, if Smith would release a bill dealing with minerals. In an emergency, Rayburn could also turn to his friend Joe Martin and get the minority leader to help him put pressure on Rules. But at times Rayburn was helpless. When Smith violently opposed a measure, he was known to disappear from the Capitol entirely so that the committee could not meet. On one occasion, when his excuse was that a barn had burned down on his Virginia farm, Rayburn was moved to a rare bit of humor. "I knew Howard Smith would do most anything to block a civil rights bill," he observed, "but I never suspected he would resort to arson."

Liberal Democrats grew increasingly restive. In 1959, after Democrats had increased their margin in the House by forty-nine, members of the Democratic Study Group repeatedly insisted that Rayburn do something. One of them, Richard Bolling of Missouri, went to him again and again, arguing that action had to be taken, until finally Rayburn snapped, "I've heard all I want, and that's the end of it." Strong as their feelings were, these liberals could not get him to engage in a battle when there were no guarantees he would win and when a loss could threaten his speakership. The idea of such a loss had not grown more acceptable with the years. To the contrary, as his brothers and sisters in Texas died one by one, the speakership became even more important in giving his life purpose and binding him to other human beings. Without the speakership, would presidents call him? Without the speakership, could he persuade aides to come into the Capitol on Sunday to do make-work and keep an old man company?

Nor did he share fully in the young liberals' indignation. There were times when Smith's tactics suited him. On measures with which it was awkward for Rayburn to have to deal, Smith did him a favor by keeping them off the floor. The question of whether House sessions should be televised was one example. Rayburn thought the cameras would cause members of the House to posture rather than attend to business, and he hated the way the lights made his bald head look. He had been known to sit through an entire televised interview with his hat on. Civil rights legislation was a more serious example. Although Rayburn had helped with the voting rights effort of 1957, his constituents were not fond of civil rights measures, and his letters to them indicate he wasn't either. "I have always thought," he wrote to one, "we were making good progress in race relations in the south without laws made by legislation or court decisions."

Rayburn did finally make the Democratic Study Group a promise, however. He would use his influence to get from the Rules Committee the legislation they considered imperative. But then his friend Joe Martin lost the Republican leadership. He was beaten by Republicans who had grown tired of cooperating with the Democrats, and the new man, Charles Halleck of Indiana, was chosen specifically for his combative style. Thus Rayburn's influence was diminished and he was unable to fulfill his pledge to the Democratic Study Group. "I could always manage to get a bill out of the Rules Committee while Joe Martin was the Republican leader," he complained. "I could work along with Joe. . . . Charlie Halleck is different, a hard man to deal with."

The liberals tried using the rules of the House to pry legislation from Howard Smith's committee. They filed a discharge petition to get a civil rights bill to the floor, and when it had almost the required number of signatures, Rules released it. When they threatened to use Calendar Wednesday procedures to get an aid-to-education bill out of Rules, that bill also came to the floor and passed the House. The Senate passed a slightly different version, however, and the Rules Committee killed the bill by preventing it from going to conference. A minimum-wage bill suffered a similar fate. The Rules Committee would not allow it to go to conference until the House conferees promised not to compromise the more conservative House version. Operating under this stricture, conferees could not reach agreement, and the measure died.

Each new frustration enraged the liberals further, and although Rayburn was aware of their anger, he still had no intention of moving against the Rules Committee. "The boys are serious this time," he told a reporter shortly before the Democratic convention in 1960. "Of course, they won't get anywhere."

And then a Democratic president was elected. Rayburn had some doubts about the new man. In the first place, he wasn't Lyndon Johnson, whom the Speaker had labored mightily to put into the White House. And for another, John Kennedy had not been a very effective member of the House of Representatives. But the Speaker was impressed with the way Kennedy campaigned in Texas and impressed further when he conferred with him in Florida after the election. The new man was clever. "You don't have to draw a map for him," Rayburn observed. The Speaker was also given a full dose of the potent Kennedy charm. When he went fishing, Jacqueline followed him with her camera. "The fish haven't got a chance," she wrote on the photograph she sent to Rayburn. "And neither has the House of Representatives," the president-elect added.

From the beginning of his campaign to the end, John Kennedy had advocated measures such as raising the minimum wage and providing federal aid to education, legislation of exactly the kind the Rules Committee specialized in blocking. It was important to him, therefore, that the power of the committee be curbed, and the seventy-eight-year-old Rayburn's inclination was to help. As Speaker, he had been helping presidents for almost two decades. It was the way a man survived and prospered, he believed; but in order to help this president, he would have to break out of a pattern just as firmly ingrained as his habit of aiding the White House. He would have to set out on a course of high-risk confrontation with congressional conservatives.

Rayburn agreed to move against the Rules Committee. The decision was far from easy for him, however, and understanding its difficulty, placing what he agreed to do in the context of the very different way he had operated for almost half a century, explains the uncharacteristic hesitancy he exhibited in the struggle that followed. "His customary sure touch was lacking," Richard Bolling has observed.

On January 2, 1961, Rayburn indicated that he would move to restrain the Rules Committee by "purging" one of its conservative Democratic members, William Colmer of Mississippi, who had not supported Kennedy in 1960. But nine days later, he told reporters that he would expand the committee instead: "I decided that the painless way and the way to embarrass nobody who didn't want to be embarrassed was to raise the Committee from twelve to fifteen." Some have maintained that Rayburn was forced to reverse himself by southern conservatives who threatened to bolt the Democratic party if he purged Colmer. Others have argued that Rayburn never intended to purge at all. How could he punish Colmer when Adam

Clayton Powell had not been made to pay for supporting Eisenhower rather than Stevenson in 1956? Rayburn may have been using the purge simply as a tactical maneuver to win support from southerners: in order to dissuade him from striking a blow to the seniority system, as the purge of Colmer would do, they would agree to support his expansion proposal. But if that were the plan, it was only partly successful. In the end, nearly two-thirds of his southern Democratic colleagues would vote against him.

Deciding to expand rather than purge the Rules Committee made Rayburn look like a leader unsure of whether he wanted to win the battle. His ability to prevail on a purge was certain. The matter would be decided in the Democratic caucus, where fewer than a hundred of the 261 Democrats in the House would vote against him. But to expand the committee required changing the rules of the House, and that required a vote of the whole membership. Conservative Democrats would be joined by Republicans, who had picked up twenty seats in the 1960 elections. "We're going to have to be reckoned with," Minority Leader Halleck had warned, "not just as roadblocks, but for sanity in government. I'm not going for a lot of radical, wild-eyed spendthrift proposals that will do the country severe damage."

Once the decision to expand the committee was behind him, Rayburn had to decide on the role of the Democratic caucus. He hadn't used the caucus much as Speaker, declaring it a "waste of time," but now he decided to have a "binding" caucus, which was an event Democrats hadn't witnessed in more than a decade. Newer members had to have the idea explained to them: if two-thirds of the party voted to support expansion of the Rules Committee in the caucus, then all members had to support the plan on the floor. Otherwise they would lose their seniority and committee assignments.

If the Democrats were all pledged to support him, there was no way Rayburn could lose on the floor. But the day before the caucus was scheduled, he backtracked again: he announced the caucus would not be binding. "Supporters of Rules changes were staggered," Richard Bolling wrote. It may be that Rayburn was unsure whether he could command a two-thirds majority, or it may be that negotiations with Chairman Smith changed his mind. He continued to talk with the Virginian, and Smith had a trump card. If the Rules Committee chose, it could prevent the proposal for enlargement from coming to the floor. Once the Democratic caucus was declared to be nonbinding, however, Smith pledged to have the committee report the resolution out.

Whatever the reasons for Rayburn's backtracking, both friends and foes took it as a signal of weakness, and he did little to counteract that impression. "On tough decisions, Mr. Rayburn became a loner," Carl Albert has said, and he wasn't given to meeting with his troops to buoy their spirits. Indeed, when the Democratic Study Group asked to hear his plans for expanding the Rules Committee, he growled, "I don't want to talk to them." Republicans were as encouraged as Democrats were demoralized by what looked like hesitancy on the Speaker's part. Although they had defectors too (like former Minority Leader Martin, who, still smarting from his ouster by Halleck, had signed on with Rayburn), their tally sheets showed a win was possible, and the Democratic leadership's tentativeness buoyed their hopes. Minority Leader Halleck, naturally pugnacious, could taste the victory and became furious with Republicans who were going to vote with the other side. When a certain Nebraska delegate wouldn't commit to him, his anger erupted, and he grabbed the Nebraskan by the lapels and shook him—thereby insuring the loss of his vote. The other side, too, was cutting deals, making promises and threats. "Tell him," one of the Speaker's allies said of an Annapolis congressman, "that if he doesn't come with us, we'll move the Naval Academy." One Democrat bridled when his committee assignment was threatened and sent word that "neither Jack Flynt nor Georgia wants any assignment that badly." Outside forces were mobilized from labor groups to the Chamber of Commerce, and they began telephoning and visiting congressmen. Under all this pressure, one especially susceptible representative changed sides five times.

Rayburn himself was approaching members. "We've got to give this young man in the White House a chance," he would say. Or, "You're going to stay with me on this one, aren't you?" But a few representatives he spoke to had already signed on with Smith, and after the Speaker had been turned down once or twice, he wanted no more to do with attempted conversions. "I won't call them up," he said, "and have them tell me no." Far from reassuring his forces, he had to be reassured by them. In his book *House out of Order*, Richard Bolling tells of a gathering in the hideaway shortly before the

January twenty-sixth vote. Rayburn was "unaccustomedly worried and unconfident," Bolling writes, and instead of arguing with a doubter in the room, left it to Bolling and Frank Thompson to convince him the Speaker's forces could win. Rayburn's own spirits seemed to revive as he listened.

Then he sent another signal, this one the most demoralizing of all. He postponed the vote from January 26 to January 31, a move widely interpreted to mean he didn't have the numbers. "It looks," Charlie Halleck crowed, "as though the New Frontier is having trouble on its first roundup." Describing the delay as "disturbing," Bolling writes, "I wasn't certain at the time how to explain Rayburn's unwonted insecurity."

One explanation was the White House, which had a different idea of how things should be done than Rayburn did. The young men there had fresh in their minds a convention where each delegate had been catalogued and placed on file, whereas Rayburn had once described his method of leadership by saying, "You feel your way, receptive to those rolling waves of sentiment." His inclination was to run the House by instinct and intuition, "out of his back-ass pocket," in Lyndon Johnson's words. No less august an observer that Joseph Alsop agreed that with the numbers of people involved and the forces brought to bear on them it was next to impossible to get a hard count in the House, but Kennedy's men wanted one anyway and were appalled at what seemed to them vagueness on Rayburn's part. Larry O'Brien, who handled congressional relations for Kennedy, did his own count and concluded that the Speaker's side was going to lose. He and the president insisted upon a delay to give them a chance to get into the fight, and a reluctant Rayburn acceded.

It is highly doubtful if the postponement helped. It was based, first of all, on a head count of questionable value. Richard Bolling, who was closer to the action than O'Brien and counting himself, thought the Speaker had the votes. And administration efforts during the five days seemed to hurt as much as they helped. Secretary of the Interior Stewart Udall, who had been a member of Congress and should have known better, managed to offend four members by threatening Interior Department projects important to them. All four ended up voting against the expansion of the Rules Committee. Over Rayburn's objections, Kennedy himself insisted on calling

Harold Cooley, the dean of the North Carolina delegation, but Cooley didn't waver in his support of Judge Smith. Meanwhile, the terms in which some of Kennedy's men were couching the battle provided a certain amusement to House members who had been around awhile. How would the president be able to deal with Khrushchev if he lost this fight? White House aides were asking. "I do not think Khrushchev started it," Howard Smith observed.

On Friday, January 27, Rayburn sent ripples of concern through his ranks once more by negotiating with Judge Smith again. But Smith's final offer—to clear the five major bills Kennedy had announced if Rayburn would call off the fight—was unacceptable. "The President may have forty bills!" Rayburn fumed, and negotiations broke off. The next day the Speaker held a press conference to reassure his troops that he was in the fight for the duration.

On the following Monday, the day before the voting, a review of the tally sheets showed that 216 or 217 representatives were committed to expanding the Rules Committee. Just one or two votes short of a majority of the total membership, Rayburn's forces had reason to be confident of victory; because there would be absences, the commitments they had should be enough to win. Still, it must have been a long and agonizing day for the Speaker, particularly if his staff told him how the press was playing the impending vote. "A crucial test of power, especially for Speaker Rayburn," the *New York Times* was calling it. "Speaker Rayburn has invested the whole of his own prestige in the effort to enlarge the Rules Committee," the *Washington Post* editorialized.

On Tuesday, at 12:30, an aide pushed open the swinging door between the Speaker's lobby and the House chamber. Although Rayburn strode through it with a firm step, the strain he had been under showed on his face, and the assembled representatives seemed at once to be struck by a need to show the old man their respect and affection. One by one they rose and began to applaud until finally the whole gathering, spectators as well as members, was standing, cheering for the man from Texas. He nodded a few times to acknowledge the tribute, then banged down his gavel: "The House will be in order."

The debate that followed was not meant to persuade. The members knew the arguments by now, and this presentation was explanatory. They were telling the country why they had fought as they had. They were leaving a record for history. First came Smith of Virginia. Peering over his spectacles, he defined the battle as a matter of conscience. He had, he said, made a pledge when he first became chairman of the Rules Committee: "That is, I will cooperate with the Democratic leadership of the House of Representatives just as long and just as far as my conscience will permit me." His words struck some of his colleagues as funny; Smith bridled at their laughter: "Some of these gentlemen who are laughing maybe do not understand what a conscience is. They are entitled to that code, and I think I am entitled to mine." He renewed his offer to compromise, to see that the five bills at the heart of Kennedy's program came to the floor. But that was as far as he would go. "When I am asked to pledge aid to the passage of any resolution or bill in this House that I am conscientiously opposed to, I would not yield my conscience . . . to any person or any Member or under any conditions."

Then Minority Leader Halleck took to the floor. He had received a mountain of mail from people opposed to expansion of the Rules Committee, he said. "And why are they opposed to it? They are concerned about rash and reckless platform promises repeated in the campaign. . . . As I read that mail from the people of this country, right-thinking people by the millions, I am convinced they are afraid that this effort signals a collapse of the opposition to such unwise measures. They are afraid the floodgates will be let down and we will be overwhelmed with bad legislation."

The next speaker was Rayburn himself. When he entered the well, there was another standing ovation, tribute to the man who had held the speakership so long he was practically synonymous with it. In just a few months he would have served twice as many days as Henry Clay, the Speaker who until Rayburn had the longest service. When the applause had faded, this stubborn, patient survivor, who had avoided battles whenever he could, explained why he had fought this one: "The issue, in my mind, is a simple one. We have elected to the Presidency a new leader. He is going to have a program that he thinks will be in the interest of and for the benefit of the American people. . . . Let us move this program. Let us be sure that we can move it. And the only way that we can be sure this program will move . . . is to adopt this resolution today."

The voting that followed was wonderfully dramatic. Journalist Neil MacNeil described its conclusion superbly:

When the clerk completed the first call of the roll, Rayburn leaned forward and in a whisper asked Lewis Deschler, House Parliamentarian, how the vote stood. "214 to 209," Deschler whispered back. It was still exquisitely close and not yet over. Eleven members had failed to answer the first call, and now the clerk called out their names again. Clarence Cannon of Missouri was called, and he voted "aye." Rayburn had 215 votes. Another member was called, and he voted "no." The people in the galleries sucked in their breath at this, making a low, whistling sound. George Fallon of Maryland was called, and he voted "aye." Rayburn had 216 votes. Then came another "no" vote, and then another. At each, the people in the galleries again made that same low whistling sound, an involuntary response. It was obvious that the galleries were for Mr. Sam. Fred Marshall of Minnesota was called, and he voted "aye." Rayburn had 217 votes. Now he could not be beaten, for even if the conservatives could tie this vote, Rayburn's vote would break that tie.

When the final tally was announced—217 ayes to 212 nays—there was loud cheering from the floor and the galleries. Rayburn had won. It wasn't a fight he had wanted—the tentativeness with which he had waged the battle testified to that—but he had won. He had survived once more.

What the victory meant beyond that was at first as uncertain as Rayburn's tactics had been. There was talk among students of government that the vote had restored to the speakership some of the power Joe Cannon had lost; there was hope among liberals that Kennedy's program would be enacted. It would be neater history had it worked that way, but the House subsequently turned down New Frontier proposals for federal aid to education, Medicare, and tax revision, and Rayburn was able to do little to help. He was no more powerful because of the Rules Committee vote and may have even been less so. The personal power he had cultivated over the years was very much a matter of perception, and now that the Rules Committee was no longer keeping off the floor bills that would be defeated there, the Speaker looked less potent.

Nor was any Speaker after Rayburn significantly more influential because of the vote to expand the Rules Committee. The committee's power did not move to the speakership; it simply dissipated— and in some ways, that may be neat history after all. Rayburn, who had never sought to bring about the kind of institutional change that would make the speakership more powerful, managed to win a dramatic victory that, in the end, changed the office very little.

But if the Rules Committee vote did not make it more likely that the Speaker would have his way, it would eventually make the House less able to prevent liberal administrations from having theirs. A roadblock had been cleared, a defense mechanism removed, some would say, and while John Kennedy didn't gain much as a result, the way was opened for other administrations working under different circumstances. Sam Rayburn would never know it—in the spring he would become ill and eight months after the Rules Committee fight he would die of cancer—but his victory in January 1961 would ultimately benefit his protégé, Lyndon Johnson. Although the New Frontier profited little from Rayburn's final battle in the House of Representatives, without it, the Great Society would have been impossible.

9

SPEAKER NEWT

The first thing he wanted to achieve, the representative from Georgia told the reporter, was a Republican-dominated House of Representatives. Then, he continued, he wanted to use the power of majority status to set the nation on a new path. "The Congress in the long run can change the country more dramatically than the president," he said. "I think that's healthy. One of my goals is to make the House the coequal of the White House."

Newt Gingrich made this declaration in 1979, his freshman year in the House of Representatives. It is hardly uncommon for new members of Congress to have grand aspirations and even to state them publicly, but it is unusual for such pronouncements to become reality; and while scores of members with lofty goals have faded from public view, Newt Gingrich has done much of what he said he would: achieved a Republican majority and, as Speaker, made the House of Representatives into the clear rival of the White House in terms of setting the national agenda.

Behind his success is a fertile mind that keenly appreciates the technology that is transforming our times. When we first wrote *Kings of the Hill* in 1983, we noted that many Speakers became powerful by focusing on the institution of the House itself. Speakers like Sam Rayburn, we wrote, gave us the model of the leader as "the 'inside' man, who seeks little attention outside the House, avoiding the media in particular." But in the future, we speculated, the pattern would probably be different: the next strong Speaker would likely make "use of the media, since it is increasingly the instrument that shapes national debate," and employ it to build "a nationwide constituency for [his] viewpoints." We did not know as we wrote that we were describing Newt Gingrich—though perhaps we should have suspected. Even then the former history professor from Georgia was writing about the "information revolution" and praising C-SPAN. Even then he was given to quoting Alexis de Tocqueville and Alvin Toffler in the same breath.

Equally important to Gingrich's accomplishments has been his remarkable persistence. "I think of myself as a turtle rather than a hare," he said after becoming Speaker:

> I just keep coming. I may not win every round, but pretty soon, you'll go to sleep and I won't. Over time, if I just keep coming, I'll win. It's inexorable.

The pattern Gingrich describes certainly applies to the way he became a member of Congress: he ran and lost twice before he finally won. The economic costs of defeat for a person of modest means, as Gingrich, a history professor, indisputably was, are enormous—and so, for anyone, are the psychological costs; but he lost once, then lost again, and still kept going. His first race was in 1974, which turned out to be the year of Watergate, a miserable time for Republican candidates everywhere. Still, he came within two percentage points of his opponent, longtime Democratic Congressman John J. Flynt, and immediately geared up to run again—only to have 1976 turn out to be the year that fellow Georgian Jimmy Carter was at the top of the Democratic ticket. "I remember looking at the news the morning after the Wisconsin primary when Carter came from behind with rural votes and beat Udall," says Gingrich. "I realized that I would probably lose and that I had to run from April to November as hard as I could to lose as well as I could so that I could run a third time." One of those apparently impressed by this tenacity was Congressman Flynt, who decided to retire rather than face Gingrich a third time. In 1978, Gingrich beat the Democratic nominee, Virginia Shapard, by almost fifty thousand votes and was on his way to Washington.

As a freshman, he talked about winning a Republican majority within eighteen months, and the 1980 elections, with Ronald Reagan at the top of the ticket, did bring the Republicans up to 192 members. While that was short of the 218 needed for a majority, it was a number that they had not achieved since 1972, when they had also won 192 seats. Not since 1952, the year Eisenhower won the presidency, had a sufficient number of Republicans been elected to put them in the majority. They had, in fact, been the minority longer than any other party in American history.

The success that Republicans enjoyed in 1980 was followed by disastrous off-year elections in 1982. The Republicans lost twenty-six seats, and Gingrich decided to organize. As he saw it, too many Republicans in the House were too willing to compromise, to go along with the Democrats. Henry Hyde of Illinois and Jack Kemp of New York were models for what he had in mind. "They have achieved power in the House and in the country that very few other Republicans . . . have . . . ," he said, "and they have both done it by being mavericks, by being very stubborn, by getting outside their zones." Gingrich approached a number of newer members, including Vin Weber of Minnesota, Bob Walker of Pennsylvania, and Connie Mack of Florida, who seemed to him to have the maverick instinct he saw in Hyde and Kemp, and met with them weekly. The group worked on honing ideas and rhetoric. They wanted their message to be progressive and hopeful, not backward looking and grim, so they called themselves the Conservative Opportunity Society (COS). Everything they opposed was lumped together under a bleak umbrella term: the Liberal Welfare State.

By the fall of 1983, Gingrich and his colleagues were ready to go public. They organized a conference in Baltimore, where they told their fellow Republicans, "Either we change or remain doomed for our lifetime as a permanent minority." Gingrich recommended that as members thought about changing, they read writers he found insightful: Peter Drucker, Daniel Bell, and Alvin Toffler. Vin Weber told a reporter that the aim of the conference was to challenge "the concept of being a congressman as we have been taught it." For Republicans, he said, that meant no more being "good little cogs in a machine that is set up by the Democrats."

Bob Walker had shown the way to throw sand in the gears and at the same time go around the machine in taking the COS message public. The Republicans had learned over the years that it was important to have one of their members on the floor at all times to monitor the Democrats. By making use of the right to object, this member could inquire into such matters as the scheduling of votes or the contents of bills, or he might make specific points about legislation. Toward the end of a session, when the Democratic leadership tried to pass a spate of legislation by unanimous consent, the "unofficial objector" (as the member who filled this role came to be called) played a particularly crucial role. He decided what the minority party would let go by and what it would stop.

Those who filled this role were self-appointed. H. R. Gross of Iowa had done it for a time, often assisted by Durward Hall of Missouri. In the late 1970s, the "unofficial objector" was Robert Bauman of Maryland, with John Rousselot of California and John Ashbrook of Ohio often helping out. In the early eighties, all three of these congressmen left the House, and Bob Walker took up the role. Because of C-SPAN, which first televised the House in 1979, he quickly became a celebrity. When other members traveled to New York or Wyoming or Georgia, one of the first questions people asked them was if they knew Bob Walker.

With C-SPAN's coverage of Congress, the floor of the House had become a center of the electronic network stretching across the nation, and COS members took advantage of it. They might meet early in the morning, then walk over to the House floor and, taking advantage of the time at the beginning of the day set aside for one-minute speeches, deliver a series of observations on subjects that mattered to them, such as balancing the budget. They had another opportunity to take the floor after the House had finished its business for the day and was operating under "special orders," which permit members to speak for up to an hour on any subject. Since few members are present during special orders, speeches made then were, in the days before the Conservative Opportunity Society came along, "strictly for home consumption," as Tip O'Neill once put it, strictly aimed at a member's home district. But COS members knew that with C-SPAN, a House chamber literally empty was virtually full; and they spoke on subjects of national import.

In May 1984, that subject was foreign policy, specifically "What's the Matter with Democratic Foreign Policy," as a report by Republican staffer Frank Gregorsky was entitled. Bob Walker read from the report for an hour during special orders, and then Newt Gingrich took it up, continuing with the theme that the radical Left in the United States tended to put the Communist world in a positive light while maintaining that "America does nothing right."

Democrats responded furiously to the reading of the Gregorsky report. David Obey of Wisconsin took to the floor and called Walker and Gingrich "modern descendants of Joe McCarthy." But nobody was angrier than Speaker of the House Tip O'Neill. He had been watching C-SPAN in his office when Gingrich read a quotation by Congressman Ed Boland, one of O'Neill's best friends and for many years his Washington, D.C., roommate. "Newt Gingrich was taking advantage of special orders to attack Eddie Boland's voting record and to cast aspersions on his patriotism," O'Neill later wrote. "Anybody watching at home would have thought that Eddie was sitting there, listening to all of this . . . but Boland had left hours ago, along with everybody else in the place." The next day, as Bob Walker was making a special orders speech, a still furious O'Neill ordered the camera crew to pan the chamber so that viewers could see that it was empty. "When they showed the empty hall, Walker looked like a fool," O'Neill wrote in his autobiography.

But he no doubt regretted where his temper led him next. A few days after this episode, Gingrich took to the floor of the House during a regular session on a point of personal privilege and defended the reading of the Gregorsky report. To point out that Democratic members of Congress had a terrible record on foreign policy was not to question their patriotism or imply that they were un-American, he declared: "It is perfectly American to be wrong. . . . It is perfectly legitimate for people to believe in a philosophy which does not work."

As word spread that Gingrich was answering his critics, members began to stream onto the floor—among them Speaker O'Neill. "Will the gentleman yield," he said.

"I am always delighted to yield to our distinguished Speaker," Gingrich responded.

"Red-faced and roaring," in the words of the *Washington Post*, O'Neill turned on Gingrich: "You deliberately stood in that well before an empty House and challenged these people, and you challenged their Americanism," he declared; "and that is the lowest thing that I have ever seen in my thirty-two years in Congress."

An alert Trent Lott, the Republican whip at the time, jumped to his feet: "I demand that the Speaker's words be taken down."

Joe Moakley, a colleague of O'Neill's from Massachusetts who was presiding over the House, had no desire to declare the Speaker's words out of order. A trusted O'Neill aide was dispatched to the Republican leadership desk to see if Lott couldn't be persuaded to withdraw his objection, but the Republican whip stood his ground; and when the parliamentarian advised that the word "lowest" was out of order, Moakley had no choice but to reprimand the Speaker: "The Chair feels that that type of characterization should not be used in debate."

It was the first time anyone could remember a Speaker being declared out of order, and the dramatic sequence of events provided perfect footage for network television. Thanks to Speaker O'Neill's having lost his temper, Gingrich, still a junior member of the House, suddenly had an audience of millions.

Gingrich and his fellow COS members used the new visibility to push ahead with their agenda, most notably at the 1984 Republican convention in Dallas, where they used the hearings on the party platform to argue for lower taxes, school prayer, and a balanced budget. With such activities, COS members managed on a regular basis to irritate their congressional colleagues. Senator Bob Dole of Kansas dubbed them "the young hypocrites." "They think they can peddle the idea that they've taken over the party," he said. "Well, they aren't the Republican party and they aren't going to be." One of the authors of this book, a member of Congress at the time and generally supportive of the COS, was once quoted calling the future Speaker a "pain in the fanny."

Gingrich's fame also brought a level of press scrutiny that he had not experienced before. A November 1984 article in *Mother Jones* magazine noted that Gingrich had emphasized family values in order to win his seat in Congress and had distributed campaign literature full of photos of him and his wife, Jackie, who had been his high school math teacher, and their two daughters. The successful 1978 Gingrich campaign had also run an ad claiming that his opponent, Virginia Shapard, would leave her husband and children behind in Georgia if she were elected, while "Newt will keep his family together." But within eighteen months of being elected to

Congress, amid rumors of various affairs, Gingrich had asked his wife for a divorce, wrote David Osborne in the *Mother Jones* article. Quoting a Gingrich acquaintance, Osborne offered details of a messy divorce that would be repeated thousands of times in the years ahead.

Democrats took delight in the *Mother Jones* article, circulating it so widely that it became what one reporter has called a "shadow dossier," and it enjoyed a certain popularity in Republican ranks as well. But for all the hesitation that many of his GOP colleagues had about Gingrich, there was also growing sympathy for his confrontational tactics—particularly after a 1985 dispute over a congressional seat in Indiana.

Initially it had appeared that Democrat Frank McCloskey had won the congressional race, but a recount gave a slim margin to his opponent, Republican Rich McIntyre. When Democrats protested that a large number of votes had been unfairly disallowed, a House task force was created with a membership of two Democrats and one Republican. The two Democrats on the committee decided that McCloskey had won by four votes, leaving even the most moderate Republicans in a fury. Representative Bill Frenzel of Minnesota declared that McIntyre had been beaten by "McCloskey's Democratic cronies." Republicans staged a walkout, marching out of the House en masse. "I don't think the Democrats should rest on the idea that it ends today," warned Representative Olympia Snowe of Maine. "If anything, it's just beginning."

Newt Gingrich saw the outcome of the McCloskey-McIntyre dispute as yet another example of how the Democrats had been corrupted by their long reign of power, a theme he had been exploring —and exploiting—since his days as a campus politician at Emory University in Atlanta. When Tip O'Neill retired as Speaker and was succeeded by Jim Wright of Texas in 1987, Gingrich took up his longtime theme with a vengeance. He began labeling Wright "the least ethical Speaker of the century"; and a *Newsweek* magazine story in June 1987, which detailed Wright's efforts to intercede with regulators on behalf of Texas savings and loan operators, gave some force to his accusations. Three months later, the *Washington Post* reported that Wright had received unusually high royalties on a book that had been published by Carlos Moore, a friend of Wright's, whose printing company had received hundreds of thousands of dollars for services to Wright's campaign. Gingrich added the stories to the negative newspaper clippings on Wright that he had begun routinely to circulate to media and watchdog groups.

Wright was not as congenial as his predecessor Tip O'Neill had been, and many Republicans regarded him with antipathy. On October 29, 1987, a day that Republicans would call "black Thursday," Wright's methods for insuring passage of a controversial budget reconciliation bill fueled their animosity. The rule governing the bill, which Wright had helped craft, was structured in such a way that an aye vote automatically attached nine Democratic amendments to the bill, including a $6 billion welfare provision. That structure, added to the fact that the bill itself increased taxes and was full of special-interest, pork-barrel provisions, convinced all the Republicans and dozens of Democrats to vote against the rule. By a vote of 203 to 217, the House handed Wright a stunning defeat.

Wright and his lieutenants decided that eliminating the welfare provision would be enough to rally the Democrats, but rather than seeking the two-thirds vote that returning the bill to the floor on the same day would require or waiting until the next day, Friday, to vote on the bill, they executed a maneuver that created two legislative days in one. At twenty minutes before three o'clock, Majority Leader Foley moved to have "the House adjourn today"—in order to reconvene at 3:15. Republican William Dannemeyer jumped to his feet:

> Genesis tells us our Lord created the world in seven days. We are now witnessing the creation of an eighth day. I just ask the gentleman: Does he have a name for this new creation?

Responded Majority Leader Foley, "Yes; it is called the Guaranteed Deficit Reduction Reconciliation Act."

Angry as they were at this parliamentary legerdemain, Republicans became even more furious when the fifteen minutes allowed for voting on the bill had passed. Their side was ahead by one vote—but Wright held voting open so that his side could search frantically for someone to switch from nay to yea. The Speaker and his allies engaged in various legislative maneuvers while Democratic whip Tony Coelho and Wright aide John Mack threatened and cajoled freshman Democrat Jim Chapman of Texas into changing his vote. Finally Mack rushed down the aisle with Chapman, and as soon as his vote had been changed, the Speaker brought down the gavel and announced that the bill had passed, 206 to 205.

Speakers had often used fast gavels, but in the context of everything else that had happened on the budget reconciliation bill, this instance caused the floor to erupt in boos, taunts, and hisses. An angry Trent Lott of Mississippi slammed his fist down so hard on the wooden lectern in front of him that the lectern cracked. The way Speaker Wright had handled the bill was, said one of the authors of this book at the time, "the most arrogant, heavy-handed abuse of power I've ever seen in the ten years that I've been here. You have a Speaker who . . . will do anything he can to win at any price, including ignoring the rules, bending the rules, writing rules, denying the House the opportunity to work its will."

This budget reconciliation package was, in the view of Republicans, a particularly egregious example of the Speaker's ongoing effort to control the House by taking away the power of other members to have any impact on legislation. Even Democrats were beginning to chafe at the increasing use of rules that prevented members on both sides of the aisle from offering amendments; and late in 1987, seventy-nine of them wrote to the Speaker to complain.

All the while, Newt Gingrich continued his attack on Wright's ethics. As he traveled around the country, he gave interviews to local newspapers in which he called Wright "a genuinely bad man," "a genuinely corrupt man." He continued his letter-writing campaign, suggesting that newspaper editors assign reporters to investigate Wright. Several times he wrote Fred Wertheimer, president of Common Cause, urging him to press the House ethics committee for an investigation of Wright. In December 1987, Gingrich wrote to every member of the House, recommending that the Committee on Standards of Official Conduct, as the ethics committee was formally titled, begin an ethics investigation of Wright.

Information continued to surface about the Speaker's dubious business dealings, some of them involving his longtime friend and business partner, George Mallick, Jr., others concerning his book. The *Wall Street Journal* reported, for example, that the Teamsters union had bought a thousand copies of *Confessions of a Public Man*. Despite this, and despite the heavy-handed way in which

Wright dealt with the minority, many Republicans were nevertheless hesitant about the idea of Gingrich's bringing formal charges against the Speaker. Minority Leader Bob Michel asked Gingrich to allow two of his fellow congressmen, Robert Livingston of Louisiana and James Sensenbrenner of Wisconsin, to examine the materials he was circulating about Wright to see if they justified a formal complaint. After spending several weeks reading through the clippings Gingrich had gathered, Livingston and Sensenbrenner agreed that while Wright's activities often gave the appearance of impropriety, there was no evidence of illegality.

Gingrich held off on filing the ethics complaint but kept up the campaign against Wright. He seemed to suffer a setback when the *Washington Post* ran a lengthy story reviewing Wright's S&L ties but noting there was no evidence that the Speaker had benefited personally from them. Two days later, however, the *Wall Street Journal* ran an editorial demanding an investigation of the Speaker. On May 18, 1988, Fred Wertheimer of Common Cause joined in pressing the ethics committee to investigate the Speaker and specifically urged that an outside counsel be appointed. On May 26, Gringrich formally filed a complaint against the Speaker with the ethics committee. His complaint was accompanied by a supporting letter from seventy-three House Republicans. Every member of the leadership had signed the letter except Bob Michel.

By fall, however, even Michel had turned against Wright. In September, Wright, who had tried to carve out a foreign policy role for himself, accused the CIA of provoking antigovernment demonstrations in Nicaragua, a charge that a "knowledgeable source" told the *Washington Post* was a twisted version of information contained in classified briefings. More disturbed by this incident than by any of Gingrich's charges against the Speaker, Michel cosigned a complaint with one of the authors of this book that asked the ethics committee to investigate the possibility of unauthorized disclosures of classified information.

As the ethics committee undertook its inquiry, Wright's support among rank and file on both sides of the aisle was weakening. Particularly damaging to the Speaker's reputation among members was his inability to hang tough in the face of public demands for a House vote on a 51 percent pay raise for members. The Congress, having been bedeviled from the beginning of its history by the political awkwardness of members voting their own pay, had finally managed to get a plan in place that would allow an outside commission to set salaries. If the commission recommended a raise, it would automatically go into effect unless both houses turned it down. The Senate, in a move that House members privately derided as cowardice, had voted to reject this particular increase, with many senators—or so representatives believed—fully expecting the House to insure the raise by refusing to vote. Indeed, most representatives thought this was what would happen; but Wright, in the face of a public firestorm about the salary increase, declared that he would conduct a poll among members about whether the issue should come to a vote, thereby dooming any possibility that it would not—and dooming the pay raise. As had happened many times before in the House of Representatives, the matter of how much members would be paid had significant political repercussions. The *Washington Post*'s David Broder wrote of Wright, "He let the whole political world see he could not take the heat," and that demonstration, Broder wrote, "almost certainly will speed his own exit from the speakership."

Both inside and outside the House, Wright's speakership was increasingly perceived as doomed; and as his star fell, Newt Gingrich's rose. In March, an unexpected opening occurred in the whip's position, the second highest leadership post in the Republican hierarchy, and Gingrich began running for it almost immediately. His victory was a narrow one: just two votes. But the fact that he gained important support for his race from the moderate wing of the party—Marge Roukema of New Jersey and Steve Gunderson of Wisconsin were among the first he enlisted—was testimony to how deeply radicalized the Republicans had become.

Having led the charge against Speaker Wright and having become by virtue of his ascension to the whip's post the next likely Republican leader, Gingrich provided an irresistible target for Democrats. He had publicized his book, *Window of Opportunity,* with financial support from outside backers, and in April 1989, Representative Bill Alexander of Arkansas filed a ten-count complaint with the ethics committee that focused on this arrangement. Gingrich claimed that his book deal was quite a different matter from Jim Wright's. He and his second wife, Marianne, had, Gingrich said, written "a real book for a real company that was sold in real bookstores.'' The ethics committee investigation went on for over a year, costing the Gingriches $145,000 in legal fees and, according to Gingrich, nearly destroying their marriage. "Every time Marianne tried to get a job," Gingrich remembers, "she had to say, 'I'm under investigation by the ethics committee.' When it got too much for her, she'd go off to Ohio. We were separated on and off for a couple of years."

Gingrich talks about this episode as one of the many times in his life when, as he puts it, "I got the crap kicked out of me, but I came back." In the end, the ethics committee admonished him for a single error, one that had nothing to do with his book. He should have listed on his financial disclosure forms, the committee said, his older daughter's home mortgage, which he had cosigned.

The Democrats' assault on Gingrich's ethics produced little public result, but it was quite otherwise with his attack on Wright. After an announcement from the ethics committee that it had reason to believe Wright had violated House rules in sixty-nine instances, many of them related to his book and to his dealings with George Mallick, the Speaker resigned. In the same week that Wright announced his resignation, the number three Democrat in the House, Tony Coelho, who had admitted failure to disclose a $50,000 loan used to purchase junk bonds, also announced he was resigning, lending credence to a claim that Gingrich had been making throughout the Wright affair: that the problem was not with just one individual, but with a system of behavior encouraged by one party's being in power too long.

Driving that party out of power, as Gingrich saw it, depended on pressing ideas forward across a broad front. The National Republican Congressional Committee (NRCC), where he had been proposing plans to defeat Democrats since he was first elected to Congress, formed one battle line, the Republican National Committee (RNC) another. GOPAC, a political organization formed by Pete du Pont, former governor of Delaware, and turned over to Gingrich when du Pont ran for president in 1988, had been especially effective at advancing the cause. Funded by large and undisclosed contributors, it financed Gingrich's travels around the country as he recruited and campaigned for Republican candidates for state office. It also brought ideas that Gingrich had been honing for most of his life to those whom he hoped would one day be part of a Republican majority in the House. In training manuals and on audio- and videotape, Gingrich advised candidates to choose words carefully, attaching positive ones like *opportunity* to Republican causes and negative ones like *failed* and *obsolete* to the Democratic agenda. He encouraged persistence, telling tales of tribulations endured and overcome. One of his stories was about Grant and Sherman at the Battle of Shiloh. Grant had been surprised and his army driven back, leading Sherman to think that perhaps the Union should retreat. With the idea of offering this counsel, he approached Grant, who was leaning against a tree, smoking a cigar. "They beat us today," Sherman said. "Yep," Grant replied. "Lick 'em in the morning, though."

Former GOPAC executive director Jeff Eisenach established the Progress and Freedom Foundation to fund a weekly television show cohosted by Gingrich on the conservative National Empowerment Television network and to help underwrite a twenty-hour college course called "Renewing American Civilization," which Gingrich taught, first at Kennesaw College and later at Reinhardt College, both in Georgia. Available on videotape, the course was, as Gingrich saw it, a way of explaining the apprehension many Americans felt about the direction of the culture. "Today," he declared, "the greatest threat to freedom is here at home."

> The decay of American Civilization is undermining our capacity to have economic productivity, have a decent, safe society and to project assistance abroad to help other people. In an America in which 12-year-olds have children, 15-year-olds are shooting one another, 17-year-olds are dying of AIDS and 18-year-olds graduate from high school with diplomas they cannot read, it is impossible, in the long run, to sustain American civilization.

To reverse this trend required both economic and cultural action. American civilization could be renewed, Gingrich explained in the course, by encouraging entrepreneurial free enterprise, cultivating personal strength, and learning the lessons of America's history and heroes.

Gingrich had a number of metaphors for describing how efforts as varied as the NRCC and a college history course fit together. They were forward thrusts on different battlefields in a single theater of war. They were all part of creating "a wave in which those [Republican] candidates who would otherwise lose by three points will win by one."

Gingrich's focus was on the Congress, on helping Republicans get elected; and it sometimes appeared that he didn't care who else lost—and that included George Bush. In 1990, Gingrich was part of the congressional–White House negotiations on the budget, but when the outcome of those negotiations—which included new taxes—was made public, Gingrich denounced it and worked successfully against its passage. He later called the fight against the Bush forces "one of the saddest things I've ever been involved in," but it was, in his view, necessary. He was sure that a Republican majority in the House could not be built on a foundation of more taxes. To the contrary, Republicans needed to focus on tax relief and other issues that gave citizens—not government—greater power. With polls showing that a majority of Americans favored such policies, Gingrich proposed that in the 1992 election, all Republicans run on an agenda composed of them. The Bush campaign showed little interest in resting their candidate's fate on Gingrich's idea, however, and "An Agenda Worth Voting For," as the plan was called, went nowhere.

Anyone who had watched Gingrich closely should have known that this would not be the end of it. He was relentless in his determination to wrest control of the House from the Democrats, and this insurrectionist approach made him the polar opposite of longtime Republican leader Bob Michel. Representing the eighteenth district of Illinois in the House since 1956, Michel was part of a generation more comfortable with comity than conflict. He took a more conciliatory attitude toward Democrats and would have found the prospect of walking away from a president of his own party—as Gingrich had done in the 1990 budget fight—nearly unthinkable. Asked once to describe the attributes of a good congressional leader, Michel listed "patience." That was not one of Newt Gingrich's strong points, and although in many ways Gingrich served Michel as an effective whip, he also made it clear that he was not anxious to stay long in the number two position. Faced with certain challenge from Gingrich for the position of Republican leader, Michel, in October 1993, announced he would be retiring.

With Bill Clinton in the White House, Gingrich started planning for the 1994 campaign. In the spring of that year, he sold RNC chairman Haley Barbour on an updated version of "An Agenda Worth Voting For" and then assigned Congressman Dick Armey of Texas to flesh out the idea. Exactly how Armey developed the document that would become the Contract with America was not, Gingrich says, of much interest to him, as long as the basic thrust of moving power away from Washington was there—and "as long as it worked."

Many people were convinced that the Contract wouldn't work, that it was flawed as a political device. For one thing, it nationalized the 1994 campaign, and to Democrats who had long believed—as Tip O'Neill had once declared—that all politics is local, this seemed a mistake. Moreover, as Democrats saw it, with its promises to cut government and taxes, the Contract gave them an opportunity to accuse the Republicans of wanting to hurt social security recipients and benefit the rich. They gleefully described the Contract as warmed-over Reaganism and called the more than three hundred candidates who signed it on September 27, 1994, puppets, "Stepford candidates," in the words of Charles Schumer, a Democratic member from New York.

With these tactics, Democrats hoped that they could keep Republican gains in the House in the twenty- to twenty-four-seat range. On the morning of Wednesday, November 9, 1994, however, the nation awoke to find that the Republicans had gained over fifty seats, well above the number they needed to gain control of the House. Democratic incumbents lost in every part of the country; not a single Republican incumbent was defeated; and seventy-three new GOP members were on their way to Washington.

It was a historic triumph, and an analysis of the results suggests that Gingrich was right and the Democrats wrong to focus on ideology. Pollster Fred Steeper observes that this emphasis drew into Republican ranks many conservatives who had previously thought of themselves as Democrats: "1994 was a policy election," he writes. "The voters perceived Republicans as representing a conservative direction and Democrats as representing a liberal direction and chose accordingly more than they have ever done in, perhaps, over 60 years." Vote totals showed Republican congressional candidates pulling nine million more voters and the Democrats a million fewer than they had in 1992, the last off-year election.

As soon as the election results were in and it was clear that Gingrich would be the new Speaker of the House, pundits started asking whether he was up to the job. He was a brilliant strategist, as the election outcome proved, but how would he fare as a commander?

Gingrich quickly demonstrated that there can be a synergy between the two roles. Part of his genius as a strategist had been inspirational. When he spoke to potential candidates and donors, he gave the impression that what was at stake was not just an election, but the future of the nation. He often did that by talking about great figures from the past who had shaped history, and that was what he did when the Republican conference formally voted to make him Speaker. The figure he described was Franklin Roosevelt, an odd choice in some ways, since Gingrich was about to lead an effort to undo much of the New Deal. But the Speaker-elect offered these thoughts:

> If you truly love democracy and you truly believe in representative self-government, you can never study Franklin Delano Roosevelt too much. He did bring us out of the Depression. He did lead the Allied movement in World War II. In many ways he created the modern world. He was clearly, I think, as a political leader the greatest figure of the twentieth century. [Think of] his concept that we have nothing to fear but fear itself, that we'll take an experiment, and if it fails, we'll do another one—and if you go back and read the New Deal, they tried again and again. They didn't always get it right and we would have voted against much of it, but the truth is we would have voted for much of it.

His choice of Roosevelt was in part a conciliatory gesture, but he also clearly saw FDR embodying a trait that had characterized his own career. The persistence that he admired in Roosevelt had brought Gingrich from a small college in Georgia to the pinnacle of the House of Representatives.

Gingrich the commander particularly benefited from the work of Gingrich the strategist in having the Contract with America in hand. Even before the election, he had described it as a postelection planning document, and that was exactly what it became. It not only set the agenda for what the House would do during the first one hundred days, it changed the House itself on the very first day. On Wednesday, January 4, 1995, three weeks earlier than the House usually convened, members voted to implement a number of changes, including slashing congressional staff, putting term limits of six years on committee chairmen, and requiring the Congress to live by the same laws that governed the rest of the country.

But the most significant institutional changes happened out of public view. Gingrich moved quickly to assert his authority over House committees, elevating to the chairmanships of three of them members whose seniority did not entitle them to those posts. Nothing personal was meant by this, Gingrich signaled. Gerald Solomon of New York, who had challenged Gingrich briefly for party leader, was allowed to become chairman of the Rules Committee. But the new Speaker expected loyalty to the Republican cause; and Carlos Moorhead of California, one of the few incumbent members who had not answered Gingrich's call to contribute from his own campaign funds to challengers running for the House, found himself bypassed for the chairmanships of both the Judiciary and the Energy and Commerce Committees. Gingrich extracted budget-cutting pledges from members of the Appropriations Committee and let it be known that those whom he had placed in positions of power were expected to perform. When one committee chairman expressed doubts about making a legislative deadline, Gingrich told him, "If you can't do it, I will find someone who will." Meanwhile Gingrich saw to it that freshman members were given plum committee assignments.

In the months ahead, Gingrich would further assert his power over the committees. If one of them should fail in an assigned task —reforming farm programs, for example—Gingrich and his lieutenants simply took over the job, accomplishing it in other ways—such as folding the measure they desired into the budget reconciliation package. Gingrich also appointed task forces on different topics. Members of these groups would build support for certain legislation in their areas rather than letting that be the sole prerogative of committees. Gingrich liked to lecture students on avoiding the constraints of traditional problem-solving. He encouraged them to "think outside the box"—a preachment he practiced when he began privately to discuss the possibility of replacing what he called the "archaic" committee system with task forces.

Republicans had promised to reverse a Democratic practice of which they had long complained: bringing legislation to the floor under restrictive rules that prohibited amendment. From the 95th Congress to the 103rd Congress, the percentage of bills with such rules had increased from 15 percent to 70 percent. When Republicans set out to reverse this trend, they quickly discovered that doing so could bring the legislative process to a standstill since it permitted Democrats to offer amendment after amendment even when they knew those measures had no chance of passage. Subsequently, Republicans began using time-structured rules that limited hours of debate, a practice that had the effect of controlling the number of amendments. Although outside observers found this a fairer method of advancing legislation than Democratic regimes had employed, Democrats nevertheless complained that the House was being run in an oppressive and heavy-handed way.

All of this led to Gingrich's frequently being compared with Joe Cannon, but to equate the two overlooked the way Gingrich often exercised power—which was through delegation. Dick Armey became, by virtue of being placed in charge of executing the Speaker's plans, one of the most powerful majority leaders ever to serve in the House. It was he, for example, who orchestrated the first ninety-three days of the 104th Congress, the period in which all of the provisions of the Contract with America were taken up in the House—and in which almost all of them were passed.

In conceiving and implementing strategy, Gingrich also relied upon a working group of about twenty members; some, like Bob Walker of Pennsylvania, were veterans of the House, but many, like Jim Nussle of Iowa, John Beohner of Ohio, and Jennifer Dunn of Washington, were newer members who had come into the House in the nineties. Gingrich assigned tasks and left it to those in their working group to figure out how best to accomplish them. Not since Henry Clay's early years in the House had so many new members had so much influence.

Another Speaker with whom Gingrich was often compared was, ironically, Jim Wright; and the reason for the comparison was that ethical issues dogged both men. Shortly after the 1994 elections, Gingrich was offered a $4.5 million advance to write a book, an arrangement that generated so much negative publicity that he backed off his initial acceptance and agreed that he would accept royalties only after they were earned. Democrats nevertheles continued to pound on the issue, charging that Gingrich had exploited his position as Speaker to land a book deal that would be lucrative whether royalties were advanced up front or not. They also brought complaints to the ethics committee that the foundation set up to fund Gingrich's course, "Renewing American Civilization," was in violation of the tax code since the course was distinctly political.

The case against Gingrich had obvious vulnerabilities. He was hardly the first politician to write a profitable book while in office. As a senator, Al Gore had done the same. And the notion that "Renewing American Civilization" was political—as opposed to other history courses being taught in tax-exempt colleges and universities across the nation—surely struck anyone familiar with the state of late-twentieth-century history instruction as ludicrous. Nevertheless, it was the college course on which the committee focused. Although its members found a number of grounds on which to reprimand the Speaker (including the book contract, which, said committee members, though in "technical compliance," gave the appearance of impropriety), they dismissed all charges against him except the one relating to "Renewing American Civilization." To help resolve that matter, they hired a special counsel. Meanwhile, the Federal Election Commission sued GOPAC for not having registered as a federal political committee sooner than it did, but early in 1996 a federal judge dismissed this charge.

The accusations against Gingrich and GOPAC added to the extraordinarily negative publicity that Gingrich received during his first year as Speaker. Shortly after it became clear that he would ascend to that post, William Greider, writing in *Rolling Stone*, called him a "world-class demagogue, a talented reactionary in the vengeful tradition of Gov. George Wallace and Sen. Joseph McCarthy." Robert Wright in the *New Republic* posed this as the appropriate way for the media to deal with Gingrich: "I say we beat the noxious little butterball to a pulp." In December 1995, when *Time* declared Gingrich to be "Man of the Year," the magazine used a cover photo that played up his five o'clock shadow and showed him against an acid-yellow background with purple lighting on his face.

Although some in the media claim that their actions have scant political consequence, there seems little doubt that Gingrich's negative coverage helped drive his approval ratings down and his disapproval up among the general public.

Gingrich also made mistakes, as he himself admitted: the book contract, in particular, and, more generally, a tendency to continue to couch his ideas in the fiery rhetoric of an insurgent rather than in the measured language one expected from an established leader. But the nightly news and the major newspapers seldom portrayed the Speaker's full complexity, seldom showed him as the inspirational figure he could be. He was capable of captivating audiences with the descriptions of the poltical changes he had in mind. He had the gift of being able to break through the carapace of daily life to give those listening a sense that they could be part of the larger effort he was leading, part of something that would connect them with history.

He was, as he often described himself, a revolutionary leader, and therein lay the error of comparing him to Joe Cannon or Jim Wright. In contrast with them, Gingrich entered the speakership with a loyal following of men and women who believed as he did and who knew they were members of the House because of his efforts. They were committed to his leadership—as were most of the longer-serving members whom he had led out of the wilderness of the minority. On the eve of the Republican victory in 1994, Christopher Shays, a moderate from Connecticut, put the case for Gingrich this way: "If Newt were not our leader, we would not have a chance for the House majority."

A benchmark of the loyalty that Republican members felt for Gingrich and the agenda he had set—and a measure of his effectiveness as a leader—occurred very early in his term, on April 7, 1995. The House had completed work on the Contract with America a full week ahead of schedule, and while not every measure had passed (term limits was the embarrassing exception), most had—and every measure had been voted on, as the Republicans had promised. Gingrich requested time from the networks to tell the American people what lay ahead, and CBS, CNN, and C-SPAN agreed. As his image entered homes across the nation in a manner usually reserved for presidents, Newt Gingrich accomplished a large part of the task he had set for himself so many years before.

He had not only achieved a Republican majority, he had, for the moment at least, made the House the equivalent of the White House in terms of setting the national agenda.

But enacting that agenda with a president of the opposite party in office would prove enormously difficult, as the budget battle that began in late 1995 illustrated. Republicans passed a bill that would have reshaped government by cutting taxes, slowing the growth of federal spending, and devolving power to the states. Threatened with a veto, Gingrich and his allies hoped to prevail by using their power over the purse: If the president would not accept their budget plans, they would not pass interim spending measures to keep the federal government functioning.

When the crisis came, however, and the federal government closed down twice, it was not Bill Clinton but congressional Republicans who felt the pressure. Rather than crediting them with trying to balance the budget, the public blamed them for the shutdown— as Gingrich quickly realized. Many in the House, from leaders to freshmen, professed not to care that their approval ratings were plummeting, and Gingrich found himself having to rein in the revolution he had created. "I'm here to tell you what the team's going to do," he announced to the Republican conference. "Sometimes you don't agree with the plays that are called. But this is the way we're going." After he described the legislation he had crafted to end the shutdown, there were complaints in the ranks; but the overwhelming majority of Republican members voted for it. "We designed a big bang theory of change, and it failed," he said later. "Now we're going to take an incremental approach and see how much we can get done every week."

Whether the changes he wanted would become law would not be apparent for months or even years, but his accomplishments were historic, nonetheless. Ending forty years of Democratic control of the House, he had set an agenda that required both politicians and the electorate to address difficult questions about spending and taxes and the proper role of government in our lives. He had made the House of Representatives into an instrument that forced us to choose our fate.

CONCLUSION:

Power and the Public Good

Of all the assertions of power we have seen, the most spectacular was Henry Clay's. No one, not even Thaddeus Stevens, managed to do what young Henry Clay did—thrust the nation into war. Audacious and bold, he and his war hawks were exhilarating company as they maneuvered a doubtful president and a divided nation onto a firm and fiery course. "Clay, Calhoun, Cheves and others filled the public attention, and contested the public admiration," wrote William Preston, who visited Washington in 1812. "My heart bounded as I looked upon these gentlemen."

But elation quickly turned to confusion and fear. The nation was not adequately prepared, and the war hawks' prediction of a swift and easy victory was soon proved false by a series of bloody and painful defeats on land. At sea, there were some magnificent victories, as when the *Constitution* defeated the *Guerrière,* but they had little strategic value since American warships were soon blockaded in their home ports. In August 1814 came the greatest humiliation of all as the British entered Washington and burned the president's house and the Capitol. "Those beautiful pillars in the Representatives' Hall," Margaret Bayard Smith reported, "were crack'd and broken, the roof, that noble dome, painted and carved with such beauty and skill, lay in ashes in the cellars beneath the smoldering ruins."

Clay heard the news in Ghent, where he was trying to negotiate a treaty of peace with Britain. Madison had appointed him a peace commissioner, and for more than four and a half months he labored until finally an agreement was reached. It decided nothing very much, except that the fighting would end, and it said a great deal about this war that, after the treaty was signed, but before word of it could reach the United States, this country won her most dramatic victory: Jackson defeated the British at New Orleans.

Clay's role in negotiating a peace was ironic, given his part in bringing the war about (one has to imagine that Madison permitted himself a small smile as he signed the papers appointing Clay to the peace commission), but the negotiator's role was also entirely appropriate to the rest of Clay's career. He would become known as the Great Compromiser, the Great Pacificator, because of his mighty struggles to avoid war. Being able to keep something from happening, he had learned, was often as important as being able to bring something about.

Madison had known this all along. He had discussed at length in *The Federalist* the necessity of impediments to government action. A primary reason for dividing and redividing the government of the United States, he explained in number fifty-one, was so that the separate parts could serve as checks on one another. In number ten, another paper emphasizing the importance of the government's being able to resist pressure to act, he pointed out ways of "curing the mischiefs of faction." A faction, as he described it, was a group of citizens who had a common interest in mind, their own interest rather than the interest of the entire community. If we substitute "pressure groups" for "factions"—and the meaning is the same— then Madison's ideas take on a particularly contemporary flavor. The way in which the Congress is pressured by groups that represent particular interests, whether they are those of the National Education Association or the American Medical Association, trial lawyers or Medicare recipients, has been noted often. While each group may have a persuasive case to present, it cannot have everything it wants, not if the *public good*—that is, the general interest of the entire nation—is to be served.

One solution to the "mischiefs" posed by pressure groups, Madison said, was to elect representatives whose eyes are firmly fixed on the public good, "whose wisdom may best discern the true interest of their country and whose patriotism and love of justice will be least likely to sacrifice it to temporary or partial considerations." But Madison was well aware that governments are composed of men and not angels. "If men were angels, no government would be necessary,'' he wrote. Even the most patriotic and justice-loving member of Congress may wish to avoid martyrdom on election day; and since saying no to special interests can bring the full weight of their political influence to bear, he or she may seek ways to escape full blame for denying them what they want.

In the past, strong leadership provided an escape. Joe Cannon described a letter that congressmen under him frequently wrote their constituents: "I have tried to get your bill passed, but the Speaker would not recognize me." Nicholas Longworth told how he, his majority leader, John Tilson, and Rules Committee Chairman Snell prevented irresponsible legislation from coming to the floor, knowing they would take public blame for it and understanding that was part of their job:

> Often a substantial majority will gladly acquiesce in our quietly "killing" a bad bill, while the same majority would vote for it if it were to come to the floor owing to pressure of what is believed to be public opinion in their respective districts. Such pressure often influences Members of Congress to support certain measures that they know, at heart, to be unsound. It is easy to tell constituents how much their Congressman is in favor of their pet measure but that the "hard-boiled triumvirate" will not let it come up for a vote.

In a lighthearted moment, Longworth put the same thoughts into a poem:

> *If you can't get your bill through our Congress*
> *And the voters at home start to yell,*
> *Just unload all the blame and the cussin'*
> *On Longworth and Tilson and Snell.*
>
> *These guys are legitimate targets*
> *Go to it and give the bunch hell;*
> *Don't blame the whole rout*
> *When bills are thrown out,*
> *Slang Longworth and Tilson and Snell.*

In the absence of a strong leader, another power center can serve the same purpose. In the Sixty-third Congress (1913–15), which the Democrats controlled, the Democratic caucus both set policy and enforced it. The caucus was "binding"—that is, if a measure was approved by two-thirds of the caucus, then all members had to support it on the floor. That members used the caucus as a way of making it easier to say no to different pressure groups is clear from the abuse that was heaped upon "King Caucus." Wrote the secretary of the National Voters League, a progressive organization, "Those actually responsible for not bringing politically dangerous questions before the House for an open vote seek shelter in the failure of the caucus to command them to do so."

From the time of Franklin Roosevelt to the time of John Kennedy the Rules Committee served the same function, though not in the absence of a strong leader. Indeed, it is possible to argue that Rayburn's long reign was possible because the Rules Committee drew blame from him. He did not have raining down on his head the obloquy that destroyed Joe Cannon and King Caucus. In any case, for more than two decades, the Rules Committee was the naysayer. Putting the worst face on this situation was Fiorello LaGuardia, who didn't like legislation to be impeded: "Members alibi themselves behind the rules when pretending to be for certain legislation but not really for it; or in a desire to avoid a vote on highly controversial subjects." Journalist Tom Wicker offered a somewhat more objective description: "The Committee on Rules, composed as nearly as could be of impregnable members from 'safe' districts, was counted upon to keep off the floor bills that would embarrass too many members, bills for which there was vociferous public demand but equally loud opposition, bills of an irresponsible nature that were still hard to vote against."

When we wrote this book in 1983, we noted that for many years the House had had neither strong leadership nor any other well-developed centralized power. Authority was dispersed among a few elected leaders, many committee chairmen, and a multitude, or so it sometimes seemed, of subcommittee chairmen. When that situation was decried, we observed, it was usually because the institution's ability to work its will had been impeded. It was unable to engage in "assertive policymaking," in the words of Lawrence Dodd. But the point we wanted to emphasize was that another equally important power had been just as drastically undermined. It was what Garry Wills called "the power to impede," what Madison called the "tendency to break and control the violence of faction."

In the 1980s it was extremely difficult for members of Congress to say no to the factions that besieged them, with the result that the general interest of the nation, particularly in fiscal matters, was not served. When the Congress gives all things to all people, the sure result, we pointed out, is economic chaos for everyone. The interest groups themselves realize this. Countless are the times when they would begin the presentation of their case to a member by saying, "Of course we want you to balance the budget"—and then there was an embarrassed laugh—"but you understand that our particular program is essential."

When we first made these observations, we looked forward to a time when strong leadership would change this situation and make it politically possible for a majority of members to vote in a fiscally responsible manner. What we did not foresee was how this would happen. Speaker Gingrich does not provide cover for members who wish to reverse the growth of government spending. He does not keep them from having to cast hard votes. That is the old leadership model. What he has done—the new model he provides—makes casting such votes into a cause. He has reframed the issue so that saying no to ever-increasing growth in spending—indeed, to ever-increasing growth in government power—is positive, a way not only of working toward fiscal sanity, but of renewing our country and setting us back on a path from which we have wandered at our peril.

His accomplishment is not just in recasting what should be thought of as positive and negative, but in relentlessly pursuing the election of like-minded citizens to the House until there is now a cadre of members who think according to the new paradigm. There are no guarantees, of course, about how long this new way of thinking will prevail. Indeed, the focus of opposition efforts is now on calling its validity into question, on trying to reassert the old equation that made government action and government spending synonymous with the public good.

One way in which Speaker Gingrich has probably changed the speakership forever is in using the electronic media to advance his cause. Should the Republicans capture the White House, his access to the media will likely diminish as the spotlight reserved for Republicans shines on the Oval Office, but there seems little doubt that he will continue to try to make his case on radio, television, the

Internet—wherever technology beckons—and his successors will no doubt do the same.

But exactly how and to what end would be folly to predict. Power in the House—as this book shows—is shaped by the individual who wields it. Although the obstacles he encounters may be familiar ones, the way he makes his way through them or somehow transforms them is likely to be unique.

As Sam Rayburn observed, the House is high drama, and part of its fascination lies in the continuing mystery of the denouement. No sooner do we think we have seen the resolution of the play than a creative leader steps on stage, picks up plot threads we had barely noticed, and uses them to begin a new act. The next strong leader will likely be as different from Newt Gingrich as Gingrich is from Sam Rayburn, as Rayburn was from Nicholas Longworth and Longworth from Joe Cannon.

However it happens, new leadership will emerge. Power in the House will not be won easily, nor will its possessors find the responsibilities that come with it easy ones. Still, there will be representatives who, loving the House and frustrated by it at the same time, attempt to impose their will upon it. They will try to become Kings of the Hill, and some few of them will succeed.

References

This bibliography, arranged according to chapters, is not intended to be systematic or thorough. It is confined, with a few exceptions, to works cited in the text.

INTRODUCTION

Bibliography

Bolles, Blair. *Tyrant from Illinois: Uncle Joe's Experiment with Personal Power.* New York: W. W. Norton, 1951.

Brown, George Rothwell. *The Leadership of Congress.* Indianapolis: Bobbs-Merrill, 1922.

Bryce, James. *The American Commonwealth.* 2 vols. New York: Macmillan, 1931–33.

DeChambrun, Clara Longworth. *The Making of Nicholas Longworth,* Freeport, N.Y.: Books for Libraries, 1971 [1933].

McNeil, Neil. *Forge of Democracy.* New York: David McKay, 1963.

Wilson, Woodrow. *Congressional Government.* Cleveland: World Publishing Co., 1956.

Notes

xii   "Temple of confusion," Bryce, I, 559.

xii   "Against a rocky shore," Bryce, I, 145.

xiii   "Body of the world," *Congressional Record* 69:1, 382.

xiii   "The Speaker's eye," Bolles, 95.

xiv   "The following outrage," Brown, 88.

xiv   "Seems dark indeed," DeChambrun, 300.

xiv   "Sometimes impetuous," McNeil, 5.

xiv   "Single stand-point," Wilson, 57.

xiv   "This earth today," *Congressional Record* 85:1, 46.

CHAPTER 1 / MR. CLAY'S WAR

Bibliography

Adams, Henry. *History of the United States of America during the First Administration of James Madison.* 2 vols. New York: Scribners, 1909.

Adams, Henry. *John Randolph.* Boston: Houghton Mifflin, 1898.

Annals of Congress. Twelfth Congress.

Benton, Thomas Hart. *Thirty Years View.* 2 vols. New York: D. Appleton, 1854–56.

Binns, John. *Recollections.* Philadelphia: Parry and M'Millan, 1854.

Bradford, Gamaliel. *As God Made Them.* Boston: Houghton Mifflin, 1929.

———. *Damaged Souls.* Boston: Houghton Mifflin, 1923.

Brant, Irving. *The Fourth President: A Life of James Madison.* Indianapolis: Bobbs-Merrill, 1970.

Bruce, William Cabell. *John Randolph of Roanoke.* 2 vols. New York: G. P. Putnam's Sons, 1922.

Clay, Henry. *The Papers of Henry Clay.* 5 vols. Edited by James F. Hopkins. Lexington: University of Kentucky Press, 1959–1973.

———. *The Works of Henry Clay.* Edited by Calvin Colton. 7 vols. New York: Henry Clay Publishing Co., 1897.

Colton, Calvin. *The Life and Times of Henry Clay.* 2 vols. New York: Garland Publishing Co., 1974 [1846].

Follett, Mary Parker. *The Speaker of the House of Representatives.* New York: Longmans, Green & Co., 1896.

Fribourg, Marjorie G. *The U.S. Congress: Men Who Steered Its Course.* Philadelphia: Macrae Smith Co., 1972.

Fuller, Herbert. *Speakers of the House.* New York: Arno Press, 1974 [1909].

Galloway, George B. *History of the House of Representatives.* New York: Thomas Y. Crowell Co., 1976.

Goldman, Perry and James S. Young. *The United States Congressional Directories, 1789–1840.* New York: Columbia University Press, 1973.

Harlow, Ralph V. *The History of Legislative Methods in the Period before 1825.* New Haven: Yale University Press, 1917.

Hooker, Edward. "Diary," *Annual Report of American Historical Association* 1 (1895): 842–929.

Irving, Washington. *Life and Letters.* Edited by Pierre Irving. 4 vols. Detroit: Gale Research Co., 1967 [1863–64].

Josephy, Alvin M., Jr. *History of the Congress of the United States.* New York: American Heritage Publishing Co., 1975.

Kennedy, John F. *Profiles in Courage.* New York: Harper & Row, 1964.

Ketchum, Ralph. *James Madison.* New York: Macmillan, 1971.

Mayo, Bernard. *Henry Clay: Spokesman of the New West.* Boston: Houghton Mifflin, 1937.

Morison, Samuel Eliot and Henry Steele Commager. *The Growth of the American Republic.* 4th ed. 2 vols. New York: Oxford University Press, 1960.

Nevins, Allan, ed. *American Social History as Recorded by British Travelers.* New York: A. M. Kelley, 1969 [1923].

Perry, Benjamin F. *The Writings of Benjamin F. Perry.* 3 vols. Spartanburg, S.C.: Reprint Co., 1980 [1882–89].

Plumer, William. *Memorandum of Proceedings in the U.S. Senate, 1803–1807.* Edited by Everett S. Brown. New York: Da Capo Press, 1969 [1923].

Pratt, Julius. *Expansionists of 1812.* New York: Macmillan, 1925.

Prentice, George. *Biography of Henry Clay.* Hartford, Conn.: S. Hanmer, Jr. and J. J. Phelps, 1831.

Private Papers in Manuscript Division, Library of Congress: Henry Clay; Thomas Jefferson; William Lowndes; James Madison; James Monroe; Joseph Nicholson.

Ravenel, Mrs. St. Julien. *Life and Times of William Lowndes.* Boston: Houghton Mifflin, 1901.

Smith, Margaret Bayard. *The First Forty Years of Washington Society.* New York: Scribner's, 1906.

Smith, William Henry. *Speakers of the House of Representatives.* Baltimore: Simon J. Gaeng, 1928.

Taggart, Samuel. "Letters 1803–1814," *Proceedings of the American Antiquarian Society,* 33 n.s. (1923), 113–226, 297–438.

Tucker, Glenn. *Tecumseh: Vision of Glory.* Indianapolis: Bobbs-Merrill, 1956.

Wiltse, Charles M. *John C. Calhoun, Nationalist.* Indianapolis: Bobbs-Merrill, 1944.

Winthrop, Robert. *Memoir of Henry Clay.* Cambridge, Mass.: John Wilson & Sons, 1880.

Notes

1 Mrs. Dawson's boardinghouse, Goldman, 50–51.
1 Details of parlor life from letters in private papers of William Lowndes. Many of these letters are quoted in Ravenel.
1 Details on Cheves, William Smith, 70–71.
1 Details on Calhoun, Wiltse, 16.
2 Details of Clay's early life and of early Lexington from Mayo.
3 "He usually wins," Bradford, *As God,* 62.
3 "Absolutely astonishing," ibid., 71.
3 "Juvenile indiscretions," Winthrop, 5.
3 "And fewer balls," Mayo, 342.
4 "Solemn stillness," Clay to Monroe, Nov. 13, 1810. Monroe papers.
4 "In the Senate," Kennedy, 49.
4 "Of the People," Mayo, 360.
4 "The Western Star," Ravenel, 84.
4 "Almost every night," Plumer, 608.
5 Clay's mouth, Bradford, *As God,* 55.
5 "Irresistibly captivating," Margaret Smith, 304.
5 "Do and say," Johnston to Clay, July 10, 1829. Clay papers.
5 Glasscock anecdote, Perry, II, 100.
5 "Cast-iron man," Nevins, 186.
5 "I love him," Kennedy, 77.
6 "Savage warfare," Clay, *Papers,* I, 449–50.
6 Madison portrait drawn from Brant and Ketchum.
6 "Apple-John," Irving, 263.
6 "As a statesman," Josephy, 144.
7 "Prime minister," Harlow, 176–77.
7 "Cure the nosebleed," Mayo, 316.
7 "Ridicule and disgrace," ibid., 359.
7 "Concentrating influence," Ravenel, 86.
8 "Ignominious peace," Clay, *Papers,* I, 449.
8 Description of House chamber, Hooker, 927.
8 "Seat of republicanism," ibid.
8 "All he left," Fuller, 30.
9 "Spirit and expectations," *Annals,* 13.
9 Details on Tecumseh from Tucker, 14–15, 93–113.
10 "The greatest excitement," ibid., 113.
10 "The United States," Pratt, 44.
11 "The white people," Tucker, 228.
11 "Had their effect," *Annals,* 425.
11 "Already been shed," ibid.

11 "As adopted brothers," ibid., 426.
12 Randolph's preparations, Binns, 240.
12 "Conquest and dominion," *Annals,* 441, 449–50.
12 "Canada!" ibid., 533.
13 "General welfare," ibid., 450.
13 Details of Randolph's life from Adams and Bruce.
13 Richard Randolph scandal, Bruce, I, 106ff.
13 Acquaintance's comment on Randolph's health, ibid., II, 302.
13 "Idea of my situation," ibid., II, 304.
14 "Infinitely your superior," ibid., II, 321.
14 "Cock of Kentucky," Mayo, 192.
14 "Upstart patriots," Randolph to Nicholson, Dec. 20, 1811. Nicholson papers.
14 Randolph's dogs, Duane to Jefferson, January 25, 1811. Jefferson papers.
14 Other reprimands, Mayo, 425.
15 "As you can," Follett, 81.
15 "Safety at home," *Annals,* 451.
15 "Best treasure, honor," ibid., 596–99.
16 "Cabinet into custody," ibid., 707–08.
16 "Ambition and war," ibid., 884.
16 "Pay the reckoning," Taggart, 384.
16 "Really deserves ridicule," Mayo, 481.
17 Details of Henry papers, Brant, 478–80.
17 "From the continent," Pratt, 54.
17 "The most wicked," Macon to Nicholson, Mar. 24, 1812. Nicholson papers.
17 "For the onset," Prentice, 82.
18 "Our unprepared state," *Annals,* 1263–64, 1590.
18 "Lead to war" and rumors, Mayo, 502–504.
18 Meeting with president, Mayo, 509; Colton, I, 161.
19 "Precursor to war," quoted in Mayo, 513.
19 "Before the wind," Taggart, 393.
19 "And New York," *Annals,* 1461.
20 "Of the House," ibid., 1461–68. In this passage, the indirect discourse of the *Annals* has been turned into direct discourse. Also see account of this incident in Fribourg, 121ff.
20 "In the Nation," Clay, *Papers,* I, 700.
21 "Shines and stinks," Kennedy, 77.
21 For Clay-Randolph duel, see Benton, I, 77ff.

CHAPTER 2 / WHO IS JAMES K. POLK?

Bibliography

Adams, John Quincy. *Memoirs of John Quincy Adams.* 12 vols. Freeport, New York: Books for Libraries, 1969 [1874–77].
Bassett, John. *The Life of Andrew Jackson.* 2 vols in 1. New York: Macmillan, 1931.
Baxter, Nathaniel. "Reminiscences," *American Historical Magazine* 8 (July 1903): 262–70.
Bemis, Samuel Flagg. *John Quincy Adams and the Union.* New York: Alfred A. Knopf, 1956.
Biddle, Nicholas. *Correspondence.* Edited by R. C. McGrane. Boston: Houghton Mifflin, 1919.
Congressional Globe.
Eaton, Clement. *Henry Clay and the Art of American Politics.* Boston: Little Brown, 1957.

Fairfield, John. *The Letters of John Fairfield.* Edited by A. G. Staples. Lewiston, Maine: Lewiston Journal Co., 1922.

Galloway, George B. *History of the House of Representatives.* New York: Thomas Y. Crowell, 1976.

Index to the James K. Polk Papers. Washington, D.C.: Library of Congress, 1969.

James, Marquis. *Andrew Jackson.* Indianapolis: Bobbs-Merrill, 1937.

McCormac, Eugene. *James K. Polk.* Berkeley: University of California Press, 1922.

Mangum, Willie. *The Papers of Willie Person Mangum.* Edited by Henry Shanks. 5 vols. Raleigh, N.C.: State Department of Archives and History, 1950–56.

Meyer, Leland. *The Life and Times of Colonel Richard M. Johnson of Kentucky.* New York: AMS Press, 1967 [1932].

Nelson, Anson and Fanny. *Memorials of Sarah Childress Polk.* New York: A. D. F. Randoph & Co., 1892.

Nevins, Allan, ed. *American Social History as Recorded by British Travelers.* New York: A. M. Kelley, 1969 [1923].

Parks, Joseph. *John Bell of Tennessee.* Baton Rouge: Louisiana State University Press, 1950.

Perry, Benjamin F. *The Writings of Benjamin F. Perry.* 3 vols. Spartanburg, S.C.: Reprint Co., 1980 [1882–1889].

Polk, James K. *Correspondence.* Edited by Wayne Cutler and Herbert Weaver. 5 vols. Nashville: Vanderbilt University Press, 1969–79.

———. *Diary of James K. Polk during his Presidency.* Edited by Milo Quaife. 4 vols. Chicago: A. C. McClurg & Co., 1910.

Poore, Ben Perley. *Reminiscences of Sixty Years in the National Metropolis.* 2 vols. Philadelphia: Hubbard Brothers, 1886.

Private Papers in Manuscript Division, Library of Congress: Andrew Jackson; James K. Polk; Martin Van Buren.

Register of Debates

Schachner, August. *Ephraim McDowell.* Philadelphia: J. B. Lippincott, 1921.

Schlesinger, Arthur M., Jr. *The Age of Jackson.* Boston: Little, Brown, 1953.

Sellers, Charles. *James K. Polk, Continentalist.* Princeton, N.J.: Princeton University Press, 1966.

———. *James K. Polk, Jacksonian.* Princeton, N.J.: Princeton University Press, 1957.

Smith, Margaret Bayard. *The First Forty Years of Washington Society.* New York: Scribner's, 1906.

Sundquist, James. *The Decline and Resurgence of Congress.* Washington: Brookings Institution, 1981.

Van Buren, Martin. *The Autobiography of Martin Van Buren.* Edited by John C. Fitzpatrick. New York: A. M. Kelley, 1968 [1920].

Notes

22 Details on McDowell and his methods from Schachner.
23 Biographical facts, anecdotes, and quotations by and about Polk from Sellers or McCormac unless otherwise indicated.
25 "Greenville, South Carolina," Perry, III, 209.
25 "Are the most," ibid.
25 Polk remembering a face, Baxter, 264.
25 "Them with despair," Nelson, 26.
26 "At New Orleans," Poore, I, 23.
26 "Running mountain high," Van Buren, 666.
26 "Majority should rule," *Register of Debates* 19:1, 634.
26 Jackson's letter, Polk, *Correspondence,* I, 41–43.
27 "[This] excited period," Van Buren, 339.

27 "On one's head," Bassett, 459. The ellipses are the correspondent's. Details and quotations about the Eaton affair are from Bassett unless otherwise indicated.
27 "And narrow path," Smith, 228.
27 "Her ready made," Sellers, *Jacksonian*, 143.
28 Sarah's political astuteness, Jeremiah Harris to George Bancroft, September 17, 1887, quoted in *Index*, vi; Brown to Sarah Polk, January 14, 1844. Polk papers.
28 Sarah joking, Nelson, 34.
29 Adams's sending attack to Polk, Adams, VIII, 512.
29 "Had ever happened," Biddle, 198.
29 "This be had," Polk, *Correspondence*, I, 575.
30 "Without the republic," *Register of Debates* 23:1, 2289.
30 Nullifiers' attitude, Mangum, II, 349–51.
31 "Man of iron," Polk, *Correspondence*, II, 432.
31 Campaign against Bell, Parks, 84–118.
31 "A town meeting," Fairfield, 33.
31 Sessions of Congress, Galloway, 34.
32 "Reach a street," Nevins, 183.
32 Wise's appearance, Poore, I, 78.
32 "Sort of importance," *Congressional Globe* 24:1, 131–32.
33 "God and man," Polk, *Correspondence*, IV, 542.
33 "Way you please," *Nashville Banner*, March 16 and March 25, 1836.
33 "Dead shot," ibid., March 25, 1836.
33 Democratic attitude toward appointments, Sellers, *Jacksonian*, 307.
33 Opposition attitude toward appointments, *Washington Globe*, March 26, 1836.
33 "Through his body," ibid.
34 "*Slaves* and *menials*," *Congressional Globe* 24:1, 652–53.
34 "His uncompromising assailants," Boston *Age* as quoted in McCormac, 103.
34 "Gagged or not," *Register of Debates* 24:1, 4028–30. In this and other exchanges between Polk and Adams some indirect discourse has been turned into direct discourse.
36 "Upon its soil," *Register of Debates* 24:2, 1317.
36 "Over the House," Fairfield, 105.
36 "Of incendiary publications," Polk, *Correspondence*, IV, 511–12.
37 "It is false," Adams, X, 4.
37 "And the world," Fairfield, 233.
37 "Of pure whiskey," Adams, X, 5.
37 "Scoundrel Hop. Turney," Sellers, *Jacksonian*, 335.
37 "Be no fight," Bemis, 378.
38 Jackson's resignation from Senate, James, 141; Gadsden to Jackson, September 15, 1825. Jackson papers.
38 Portrait of Johnson from Meyer.
39 "Affinity to *darkies*," *Congressional Globe* 25:2, appendix 280.
39 "After this success," Polk, *Correspondence*, V, 367.
40 "Be constables even," *Nashville Banner*, March 30, 1841.
40 "To the Presidency," Polk, *Correspondence*, V, 616.
40 "To a President," Jackson to Van Buren, November 29, 1843. Van Buren papers.
40 King's prospects, Sellers, *Continentalist*, 37–38; Brown to Sarah Polk, January 14, 1844. Polk papers.
40 Johnson's prospects, Sellers, *Continentalist*, 37–38.
40 Polk's strategy, ibid., 49; Johnson to Polk, March 10, 1844. Polk papers.
41 "More for shouting," Crockett to Polk, May 28 [29], 1844. Polk papers.
42 "Will wonders cease," *Washington Whig Standard*, May 30, 1844.
42 "Who is safe," Schlesinger, 439.
42 "Iota to them," Eaton, 93.
42 "To the measure," ibid., 94.
43 "Upon reasonable terms," McCormac, 272.

43 "Or coming back," Sellers, *Continentalist,* 148.
43 Our strongest presidents, Sundquist, 19, fn. 5.
44 Polk's lack of vacation, Polk, *Diary,* II, 84.
44 "In this country," ibid., 360.
44 "Shadows we pursue," *Index,* ix.

CHAPTER 3 / OLD THAD STEVENS

Bibliography

Adams, John Quincy. *Memoirs of John Quincy Adams.* 12 vols. Freeport, New York: Books for Libraries, 1969 [1874–77].
Bemis, Samuel Flagg. *John Quincy Adams and the Union.* New York: Alfred A. Knopf, 1956.
Blaine, James G. *Twenty Years of Congress.* 2 vols. Norwich, Conn.: Henry Bill Publishing Co., 1884.
Brodie, Fawn. *Thaddeus Stevens: Scourge of the South.* New York: W. W. Norton, 1959.
Bruce, William Cabell. *John Randolph of Roanoke.* 2 vols. New York: G. P. Putnam's Sons, 1922.
Catton, Bruce. *The Coming Fury.* New York: Pocket Books, 1967.
Congressional Globe.
Cox, Samuel. *Why We Laugh.* New York: B. Blom, 1969 [1876].
Current, Richard Nelson. *Old Thad Stevens.* Westport, Conn.: Greenwood Press, 1980 [1942].
Fairfield, John. *The Letters of John Fairfield.* Edited by A. G. Staples. Lewiston, Maine: Lewiston Journal Co., 1922.
Fessenden, Francis. *Life and Public Services of William Pitt Fessenden.* 2 vols. New York: Da Capo Press, 1970 [1907].
Freemasonry Unmasked; or Minutes of the Trial of a Suit of Common Pleas of Adams County, Wherein Thaddeus Stevens, Esq., Was Plaintiff, and Jacob Lefever, Defendant. Gettysburg: R. W. Middleton, 1835.
Korngold, Ralph. *Thaddeus Stevens.* New York: Harcourt, Brace, 1955.
McCall, Samuel W. *Thaddeus Stevens.* Boston: Houghton Mifflin, 1899.
McCarthy, Charles H. *The Antimasonic Party.* Washington, D.C.: Government Printing Office, 1903.
McClure, Alexander K. *Abraham Lincoln and Men of War-Times.* Philadelphia: Times Publishing Co., 1892.
———. *Old Time Notes of Pennsylvania.* 2 vols. Philadelphia: J. C. Winston Co., 1905.
———. *Recollections of Half a Century.* New York: AMS Press, 1976 [1902].
MacNeil, Neil. *Forge of Democracy.* New York: David McKay, 1963.
Milton, George. *The Age of Hate.* New York: Coward-McCann, 1930.
Morison, Samuel Eliot and Henry Steele Commager. *The Growth of the American Republic.* 2 vols. 4th ed. New York: Oxford University Press, 1960.
Nevins, Allan. *The Ordeal of the Union.* 8 vols. New York: Scribner's, 1947–71.
Nicolay, John G. and John Hay. *Abraham Lincoln: A History.* 10 vols. New York: Century Co., 1917.
Private Papers in Manuscript Division, Library of Congress: Andrew Johnson; Thaddeus Stevens.
Proceedings and Debates of the Convention of the Commonwealth of Pennsylvania of 1837. 14 vols. Harrisburg: Packer, Barrett, & Parke, 1837–39.
Riddle, Albert G. *The Life of Benjamin Wade.* Cleveland: W. W. Williams, 1886.
———. *Recollections of War Times.* New York: G. P. Putnam's Sons, 1895.
Sandburg, Carl. *Abraham Lincoln: The War Years.* 4 vols. New York: Harcourt, Brace & World, 1939.

Schurz, Carl. *Reminiscences of Carl Schurz.* 3 vols. New York: McClure Co., 1907–1908.
Scoval, James. "Thaddeus Stevens," *Lippincott's Magazine* 61 (April 1898): 545–51.
Sellers, Charles. *James K. Polk, Jacksonian.* Princeton, N.J.: Princeton University Press, 1957.
Seward, Frederick W. *Reminiscences, 1830–1915.* New York: G. P. Putnam's Sons, 1916.
Smith, William Ernest. *The Francis Preston Blair Family in Politics.* 2 vols. New York: Da Capo Press, 1969 [1933].
Young, James S. *The Washington Community, 1800–1828.* New York: Columbia University Press, 1966.

Notes

45 Length of service at mid-century, MacNeil, 123.
45 "All the while," Bruce, I, 582.
45 Polk accident, Sellers, 195.
45 Malaria and canal, Nevins, II (*A House Dividing*), 51–54.
46 "A Dutch oven," Young, 45.
46 Details Thirty-eighth Congress, Cox, 172.
46 Fairfield's experience, Fairfield, 21–29, 429–449.
46 Speaker Randall, McClure, *Recollections,* 447.
46 "Of the chair," Blaine, I, 72.
47 Adams' anti-Masonic support, McCarthy, 382.
47 "Underrated by me," Bemis, 283.
47 Adams and Phi Beta Kappa, ibid., 286.
47 "Express his vexation," Brodie, 28. Hereafter, biographical facts, anecdotes, and quotations by and about Stevens are from Brodie, Current, or Korngold unless otherwise indicated.
48 "Of my parentage," *Gettysburg Star and Sentinel,* July 7, 1874. Clipping in Stevens papers.
48 "Prostituted harlot," *Freemasonry,* vii–xii.
49 "Body with women," February 15, 1868. Stevens papers.
50 "Wealth and pride," "Speech on the School Law," April 1835. Copy in Stevens papers.
50 "Been worth living," McClure, *Lincoln,* 264.
50 "Of their freedom," *Proceedings,* III, 694.
50 *"Foe of the South,"* Lancaster Intelligencer, August 29, 1848.
51 Stevens's caustic comments, *Congressional Globe* 31:2, 130, and 298.
51 "Of reproduction," *Congressional Globe* 31:1, App. I, 143.
51 "Assemblage of men," ibid., App. I, 462.
51 "Filthy a beast," ibid., App. I, 767.
51 "Been disposed of," Seward, 83–84.
51 Washington social life, Nevins, II (*A House Dividing*), 54–58.
52 "Of our citizens," *Congressional Globe* 32:1, 582.
52 "Any of them," ibid., 1164.
53 "A deliberative assembly," McCall, 127.
53 Clerk's hesitancy, Catton, 12–18.
54 Dungforks, Riddle, *Wade,* 236.
54 "Pryor to Posterior," Scoval, 550.
54 "The Blair family," Blaine, I, 286.
54 "Take that back," McCall, 311–12.
54 "Things of nights," Riddle, *Recollections,* 180.
55 Intention of members gathering round: McCall, 127.
55 "Servility and meanness," *Congressional Globe* 36:2, 624.

55 "By common consent," Blaine, I, 325.
55 Stevens limiting debate to one hour, ibid., 403.
55 Passing habeas corpus in one day, Nicolay and Hay, VIII, 34.
56 "Our self respect," Brodie, 155.
56 "Three fellers again," Sandburg, 1, 566.
56 "I have indicated," *Congressional Globe* 37:2, 1613.
57 "To the world," McClure, *Lincoln*, 258–59.
57 "Blasted and destroyed," Riddle, *Recollections*, 32.
57 "As Stevens departs," Cox, 173.
57 "Upon its soil," *Congressional Globe* 37:2, 3127.
58 Stevens commending Lincoln, McClure, *Lincoln*, 261.
59 "Our whole system," Smith, II, 237–38.
59 "To the army," Sandburg, III, 24.
60 Declaring Blair's seat vacant, *Congressional Globe* 38:1, 3389.
61 "To ask it," Sandburg, III, 206.
61 "This people reunited," *Congressional Globe* 38:2, 124.
62 "Looked fire," *New York Herald*, February 3, 1865.
62 "Thundering, and uncontrollable," Sandburg, IV, 13.
63 "It will shine," *Congressional Globe* 40:1, 207.
63 "What I am," The *London Sun Times*, March 7, 1865, as quoted in Brodie 221.
     According to Brodie, the version in the *Congressional Globe* was corrected and
     expurgated by Johnson.
64 "Having no pride," Milton, 96.
64 "Was approaching usurpation," May 16, 1865. Johnson papers.
64 "Part of it," July 6, 1865. Johnson papers.
65 "Dead and gone," Schurz, III, 215–16.
65 "Is an outsider," *Congressional Globe* 39:1, 3–4.
66 "Irritation against them," Schurz, III, 175.
67 *"Horse was respectable," Congressional Globe* 39:1, 1308.
67 "Cost him his head," ibid., 536–37.
68 "Victims at Memphis," ibid., 2544.
68 "Not among angels," ibid., 3148.
69 "Labors of earth," Speech "The Pending Canvass," September 4, 1866. Copy in
     Stevens papers.
69 *Nation* on Johnson, Morison, II, 94.
69 "Most of his fellows," McClure, *Old Time Notes*, II, 207.
70 "The proud traitors," *Congressional Globe* 39:1, App. II, 1308–09.
71 "Reconstruction was usurpation," letter to Samuel Shock, August 26, 1867. Pub-
     lished in *New York World*, August 28, 1867.
71 "Unconstitutional legislation," Milton, 544.
72 "Great a hazard," Fessenden, II, 154–55.
72 Grimes on Johnson, Brodie, 353.
73 "For the Republic," McClure, *Lincoln*, 264.
73 "Millions of happy people," *Congressional Globe* 40:2, 3790.

CHAPTER 4 / BLAINE AT BAY

Bibliography

Adams, Henry. *The Education of Henry Adams.* Boston: Houghton Mifflin, 1918.
Barry, David. *Forty Years in Washington.* Boston: Little, Brown, 1924.
Blaine, Harriet. *Letters of Mrs. James G. Blaine.* 2 vols. New York: Duffield & Co.,
     1898.
Bradford, Gamaliel. *American Portraits: 1875-1900.* Boston: Houghton Mifflin, 1922.
Committee of One Hundred. *Mr. Blaine's Record.* Boston, 1884.
Congressional Globe.

226 | REFERENCES

Congressional Record.
Crawford, Theron. *James G. Blaine.* Philadelphia: Edgewood Publishing Co., 1893.
Cullom, Shelby. *Fifty Years of Public Service.* Chicago: A. C. McClurg & Co., 1911.
DePew, Chauncy. *My Memories of Eighty years.* New York: Scribner's, 1922.
Ford, Henry Jones. *The Cleveland Era.* New Haven: Yale University Press, 1919.
Fuller, Herbert Bruce. *The Speakers of the House.* New York: Arno Press, 1974 [1909].
Hamilton, Gail. *Biography of James G. Blaine.* Norwich, Conn.: Henry Bill Publishing Co., 1895.
Hess, Stephen and Milton Kaplan. *The Ungentlemanly Art.* New York: Macmillan, 1968.
Hoar, George Frisbee. *Autobiography of Seventy Years.* 2 vols. New York: Scribner's, 1903.
Hofstadter, Richard. *The American Political Tradition.* New York: Alfrerd A. Knopf, 1948.
Josephson, Matthew. *The Politicos: 1865-1896.* New York: Harcourt, Brace, 1938.
Josephy, Alvin M., Jr. *History of the Congress of the United States.* New York: American Heritage Publishing Co., 1975.
Kennedy, John F. *Profiles in Courage.* New York: Harper & Row, 1964.
Kittridge, Herman. *Ingersoll.* New York: Dresden Publishing Co., 1911.
McClure, Alexander K. *Our Presidents and How We Make Them.* New York: Harper & Bros., 1902.
———. *Recollections of Half a Century.* New York: AMS Press, 1976 [1902].
Muzzey, David. *James G. Blaine: A Political Idol of Other Days.* Port Washington, N.Y.: Kennikat Press, 1963 [1934].
Oberholtzer, Ellis. *Jay Cooke: Financier of the Civil War.* 2 vols. New York: B Franklin, 1970 [1907].
Peel, Roy Victor. "James Gillespie Blaine: A Study in Political Leadership." Unpublished Ph.D. dissertation, Department of Political Science, University of Chicago, 1927.
Private Papers in Manuscript Division, Library of Congress: James G. Garfield.
Russell, Charles Edward. *Blaine of Maine.* New York: Cosmopolitan Book Corp., 1931.
Schurz, Carl. *Reminiscences of Carl Schurz.* 3 vols. New York: McClure Co., 1907-1908.
Sellers, Charles. *James K. Polk, Jacksonian.* Princeton, N.J.: Princeton University Press, 1957.
Sherman, Thomas H. *Twenty Years with James G. Blaine.* New York: Grafton Press, 1928.
Stanwood, Edward. *James Gillespie Blaine.* Boston: Houghton Mifflin, 1905.
United States House of Representatives. Miscellaneous Document No. 176.
Watson, James E. *As I Knew Them.* Indianapolis: Bobbs-Merrill, 1936.

Notes

74 "For the Republican party," Hoar, I, 239.
74 "In the world," Hamilton, 225. Biographical facts, anecdotes, and quotations by and about Blaine are from Hamilton, Muzzey, or Russell unless otherwise indicated.
75 Webster's retainer, Kennedy, 84–85.
76 "Altogether worth knowing," Peel, 101.
76 "Frankly my ideal," Watson, 16.
76 Conkling description, Josephson, 97; Josephy, 252; Barry, 70.
77 "Undeserving public servant," *Congressional Globe* 39:1, 251.
77 "God help me," ibid., 2152.
77 "Controversy with him," ibid., 2299.

77 "In criminal practice," Muzzey, 61–62.
77 Dawes's reticence, Stanwood, 105.
78 "Support for myself," Blaine to Garfield, November 10, 1868. Garfield papers.
78 Dinner at Welker's, Cullom, 115–16.
78 Butler anecdote, Hoar, I, 201–202.
78 "Row of bricks," Harriet Blaine, I, 50.
79 "Is very languid," ibid., 60.
79 Speaker's "despotic" power, *Nation,* April 4, 1878.
80 Blaine's explanation of killing bill, Stanwood, 113; *Congressional Globe* 42:1, 126.
80 Blaine and Butler chatting, Hamilton, 249.
80 How Blaines looked to newspapers, Harriet Blaine, I, 22.
80 "Money is concerned," ibid., 72.
81 "Most fearful embarrassments," Committee of One Hundred, 40.
81 "Carelessly held it," Harriet Blaine, I, 277.
81 1816 pay raise, Fuller, 45–47.
82 Polk's departure from speakership, Sellers, 339ff.
82 "Thronged about him," Stanwood, 110.
82 "Been so popular," Muzzey, 72.
82 Blaine's objection to Wood's motion, *Congressional Record* 44:1, 168.
84 "Organized that murder," ibid., 323–36.
84 "Smartness at last," Schurz, III, 365.
85 "Blaine was right," Muzzey, 82.
85 "In your favor," Hamilton, 383.
85 "Severe pecuniary loss," *Congressional Record* 44:1, 2724–25.
86 "Matter under enquiry," U.S. House of Representatives Miscellaneous Document No. 176, p. 110.
86 Black frock suit, Crawford, 334.
88 "Have suppressed it," *Congressional Record* 44:1, 3603–3608.
88 "Roar of triumph," Hamilton, 392.
89 "Manner be appeased," Oberholtzer, I, 173 and 354.
90 "The large auditorium," McClure, *Recollections,* 426.
91 "James G. Blaine," Kittridge, 80.
91 "An easy triumph," McClure, *Recollections,* 426.
91 Lights at convention, Peel, 193.
92 Bristow's hurt feelings, Hoar, I, 381.
93 "Thrill of loathing," Hess, 106.
93 "President of the United States," Schurz, III, 405.
94 Hoar on Blaine, ibid., 281 and 379.
94 Gifts to Grant, Josephson, 59.
94 "Twice as much," Hofstadter, 169.
94 "Like the Constitution," Adams, 280.
94 "Suspicion of wrong," Hoar, I, 281.
94 "A devoted following," DePew, 141.
94 "Fury of affection," Bradford, 125.
95 "1844–1884," McClure, *Our Presidents,* 245–46.

CHAPTER 5 / REED AND THE RULES

Bibliography

Adams, John Quincy. *Memoirs of John Quincy Adams.* 12 vols. Freeport, New York: Books for Libraries, 1969 [1874–1877].
Alexander, DeAlva. *History and Procedures of the House of Representatives.* Boston: Houghton Mifflin, 1916.
Beer, Thomas. *Hanna.* New York: Octagon Books, 1973 [1929].

Brownson, W. H. "Thomas B. Reed," *New England Magazine,* n.s. 2 (March 1890): 188–93.

Cater, Harold Dean. *Henry Adams and His Friends.* Boston: Houghton Mifflin, 1947.

Clark, Champ. *My Quarter Century of American Politics.* 2 vols. New York: Harper & Bros., 1920.

Congressional Record.

Croly, Herbert. *Marcus Alonzo Hanna.* New York: Macmillan, 1912.

DeCasseres, Benjamin. "Tom Reed," *American Mercury* 19 (February 1930): 221–28.

Dingley, Edward Nelson. *The Life and Times of Nelson Dingley, Jr.* Kalamazoo, Mich.: Ihling Bros. & Everard, 1902.

Dunn, Arthur Wallace. *From Harrison to Harding.* 2 vols. Port Washington, N.Y.: Kennikat Press, 1971 [1922].

Fuller, Herbert. *Speakers of the House.* New York: Arno Press, 1974 [1909].

Leech, Margaret. *In the Days of McKinley.* New York: Harper & Bros., 1959.

Leupp, Francis E. *The Man Roosevelt.* New York: D. Appleton & Co., 1904.

———. "Personal Recollections of Thomas B. Reed," *Outlook* 96 (September 1910):36–40.

Lodge, Henry Cabot. *The Democracy of the Constitution and Other Essays.* New York: Scribner's, 1915.

Lodge, Henry Cabot, ed. *Selections from the Correspondence of Theodore Roosevelt and Henry Cabot Lodge.* 2 vols. New York: Scribner's, 1925.

McCall, Samuel. *The Life of Thomas Brackett Reed.* Boston: Houghton Mifflin, 1914.

McClure, Alexander. *Recollections of Half a Century.* New York: AMS Press, 1976 [1902].

Muzzey, David. *James G. Blaine: A Political Idol of Other Days.* Port Washington, N.Y.: Kennikat Press, 1963 [1934].

Peck, Harry Thurston. *Twenty Years of the Republic.* New York: Dodd, Mead, 1907.

Porter, Robert P. "Thomas Brackett Reed of Maine," *McClure's* 1 (October 1893): 375–89.

Powers, Samuel. *Portraits of a Half Century.* New York: Little, Brown, 1925.

Pringle, Henry. *Theodore Roosevelt.* New York: Harcourt, Brace & Co., 1931.

Reed, Thomas B. "The Rules of the House of Representatives," *Century Magazine* 37 (March 1889): 792–95.

Robinson, William A. *Thomas B. Reed, Parliamentarian.* New York: Dodd, Mead, 1930.

Stealey, Orlando. *Twenty years in the Press Gallery.* New York: Publisher's Printing Co., 1906.

Tuchman, Barbara. *The Proud Tower.* New York: Bantam, 1966.

Notes

96   "Meeting of maniacs": Muzzey, 282.

96   "Desire to win," Lodge, *Democracy* 192.

96   "Of human knowledge," McCall, 248. Biographical facts, anecdotes, and quotations by and about Reed on this page and throughout the chapter are from McCall or Robinson unless otherwise stated.

97   "I ever saw," Lodge, *Democracy,* 195.

97   "Than two hundred," Dunn, I, 299.

97   "Companion ever lived," Lodge, *Democracy,* 207.

98   "Down in Louisiana," *New York Tribune,* April 23, 1899.

98   "His opponents' faces," DeCasseres, 224.

98   "Wish to proceed," Brownson, 192.

98   "Intricacies and secrets," *Congressional Record* 46:2, 480.

99   "The United States," ibid., 47:1, 4307.

99   "Word of command," Alexander, 202.

99   "A monstrous proposition," ibid., 203.

100   "Went with it," Lodge, *Democracy,* 191–92.
100   "Enraptured a Memling," DeCasseres, 222.
101   Refusing free telegraph service, Powers, 268–69.
101   "Matter-of-fact drawl," DeCasseres, 222.
101   "Saw or heard," Clark, I, 277.
102   "Through a quill," *Congressional Record* 48:2, 1288.
102   "Senate and Sam Randall," *Washington Post,* December 1, 1885.
102   Details on Randall, McClure, 441–49.
103   "Of this world," *Congressional Record* 49:1, 210.
103   "Slowly doing nothing," January 19, 1888.
103   "The incapables," January 7, 1889.
103   For Hanna's activities in speakership fight, Croly, 150.
103   "The ten commandments," Leupp, *Roosevelt,* 292.
103   For Roosevelt's activities in speakership fight, Dunn, I, 22; Lodge, *Correspondence,* I, 89–97.
104   "One hundred one are right," Reed, 794.
104   Adams on disappearing quorum, Adams, X, 242–43.
104   "No quorum." Unless otherwise indicated, all quotations from quorum fight from *Congressional Record* 51:1, 949ff.
105   "Brink of a volcano," Alexander, 160.
105   "At a pet lunatic," DeCasseres, 227.
105   "Pond by comparison," January 30, 1890.
106   "Never learned anything," Dunn, I, 34.
106   "Crag to crag," ibid., I, 24.
106   Press caught up in frenzy, Peck, 200.
107   "Counting was being established," Dunn, I, 23–24.
107   "As a highwayman," January 30, 1890.
107   "Over their heads," Dunn, I, 24.
107   "In the least," Powers, 264.
107   "Down and out," Porter, 375.
108   Green persimmon, *Washington Post,* September 17, 1893.
108   "High-handed conduct," Clark, II, 257.
108   "The more unpopular," Cater, 235.
108   "His beauty now," Clark, I, 282.
109   "Who is dead," Lodge, *Democracy,* 191.
109   "Think they will," Brownson, 193.
109   Clark on Reed's reaction to abuse, Clark, II, 258.
110   "Subject of his satire," Leech, 43.
110   "Call him names," Beer, 110.
111   Hanna on Reed, Pringle, 159.
111   Hanna and McKinley organization, Croly, 167.
111   "Unstained and unimpaired," Lodge, *Democracy,* 206.
111   "Is a farce," Pringle, 159.
112   "House-stands-adjourned," Fuller, 234.
112   "Deliver your money," *Congressional Record* 55:2, 1628.
112   "Market for gravestones," Dunn, I, 234.
112   "Dissuade a cyclone," *New York Times,* April 7, 1898.
113   "To beat Hawaii," Lodge, *Correspondence,* I, 302.
113   Note from Dingley, Dingley, 467.
113   Hinds passed word along, Dunn, I, 290–91; *Washington Post,* June 11, 1898.
114   "Me beyond words," Lodge, *Correspondence,* I, 370.
114   "Overthrown the column," February 26, 1899.
115   "Sulphurous language," *New York Times,* April 23, 1899.
116   "Of private society," Leupp, *Recollections,* 39.
116   "Americans had closed," Powers, 272.

CHAPTER 6 / ATTACK ON UNCLE JOE

Bibliography

Bolles, Blair. *Tyrant from Illinois, Uncle Joe Cannon's Experiment with Personal Power.* New York: W. W. Norton, 1951.
Brown, George Rothwell. *The Leadership of Congress.* Indianapolis: Bobbs-Merrill, 1922.
Busbey, L. W. *Uncle Joe Cannon.* New York: H. Holt & Co., 1927.
Butt, Archie. *Taft and Roosevelt: The Intimate Letters of Archie Butt.* 2 vols. New York: Doubleday, Doran & Co., 1930.
Clark, Champ. *My Quarter Century of American Politics.* 2 vols. New York: Harper & Bros., 1920.
"Congress Defying the Big Stick," *Literary Digest* 36(May 9, 1908): 665–67.
Congressional Record.
Crouch, Tom. "December: Diamond Anniversary of Man's Propulsion Skyward," *Smithsonian* 9(December 1978): 36–46.
Dunn, Arthur Wallace. *From Harrison to Harding.* 2 vols. Port Washington, N.Y.: Kennikat Press, 1971 [1922].
———. *Gridiron Nights.* New York: Frederick A. Stokes Co., 1915.
Fitch, George. "A Survey and Diagnosis of Uncle Joe," *American Magazine* 65(December 1907): 185–92.
Fuller, Hubert Bruce. *The Speakers of the House.* New York: Arno Press, 1974 [1909].
"Groping for a Budget," *Nation* 97(July 3, 1913): 4.
Gwinn, William Rea. *Uncle Joe Cannon, Archfoe of Insurgency.* New York: Bookman Associates, 1957.
Hatch, Carl E. *The Big Stick and the Congressional Gavel.* New York: Pageant Press, 1967.
Hechler, Kenneth. *Insurgency: Personalities and Politics of the Taft Era.* New York: Columbia University Press, 1940.
Hoover, Irwin. *Forty-two Years of the White House.* New York: Houghton Mifflin, 1934.
Jones, Charles O. "Joseph G. Cannon and Howard W. Smith: An Essay on the Limits of Leadership in the House of Representatives," *Congressional Behavior.* Edited by Nelson Polsby. New York: Random House, 1971.
Leupp, Francis E. "The New Speaker," *Outlook* 75(November 21, 1903): 684–88.
Lodge, Henry Cabot, ed. *Selections from the Correspondence of Theodore Roosevelt and Henry Cabot Lodge.* 2 vols. New York: Scribner's, 1925.
Longworth, Alice Roosevelt. *Crowded Hours.* New York: Scribner's, 1933.
Neuberger, Richard L. and Stephen B. Kahn. *Integrity: The Life of George W. Norris.* New York: Vanguard Press, 1937.
Norris, George. *Fighting Liberal: The Autobiography of George W. Norris.* New York: Macmillan, 1945.
Pinchot, Gifford. *Breaking New Ground.* New York: Harcourt, Brace & Co., 1947.
Pringle, Henry. *The Life and Times of William Howard Taft.* 2 vols. New York: Farrar & Rinehart, 1939.
———. *Theodore Roosevelt.* New York: Harcourt, Brace & Co., 1931.
Private Papers in Manuscript Division, Library of Congress: Theodore Roosevelt; William Howard Taft.
Roosevelt, Theodore. *The Letters of Theodore Roosevelt.* Edited by Elting Morison. 8 vols. Cambridge, Mass.: Harvard University Press, 1951–54.
Stephenson, Nathaniel W. *Nelson W. Aldrich.* New York: Scribner's, 1930.
Sullivan, Mark. *Our Times.* Vol. 4. New York: Scribner's, 1932.
"Taps for Uncle Joe," *Literary Digest* 91(December 4, 1926): 36–42.

References | 231

"Uncle Joe Quits with Optimism and a Smile," *Literary Digest* 76(March 17, 1923): 573-74.
Watson, James E. *As I Knew Them.* Indianapolis: Bobbs-Merrill, 1936.

Notes

117 "To the people," quoted Gwinn, 162.
117 "Cannon played square," W. H. Taft to Horace Taft, Aug. 11, 1909. Taft papers.
118 Details of Taft's dress and transportation, *Washington Post,* Aug. 6, 1909.
118 "Did defeat Cannon," W. H. Taft to Horace Taft, Aug. 11, 1909. Taft papers.
118 "Artful in the craft," Sullivan, 374.
119 "Niagara-like profanity," Watson, 92.
119 "Foul-mouthed speech," *Congressional Record* 51:1, 9234-38.
119 "Than the fire," William Hard quoted in Sullivan, 376.
119 "Freely and Frequently," Longworth, 170.
120 "Ignorance of Eastern affairs," Butt, I, 341-42.
120 "Common sense intellect," *Congressional Record* 66:1, 7526.
120 "In my hair," ibid., 43:1, 1069.
120 "As 'also spoke,'" Busbey, 131. Biographical facts, anecdotes, and quotations by and about Cannon on this page and throughout the chapter are from Busbey or Gwinn unless otherwise indicated.
121 "A wobbling foundation," Leupp, 687-88.
121 Clark's and Gillett's anecdotes, Clark, II, 366 and 377.
122 "To one another," Dunn, *Gridiron,* 117.
122 "Their being made," "Groping for a Budget," 4.
122 Roosevelt urging attacks on Cannon, Lodge, II, 107.
122 "Enough for him," Busbey, xxxii.
122 Details of aerodrome, "December," 36-40; also "Taps."
123 Members' view of Hopkins, Dunn, *Harrison,* I, 310-12.
124 Reasons for Henderson's retirement, Fuller, 248-49; Clark, I, 379.
124 "Compel that change," *Congressional Record* 57:2, 3058-59.
124 Congresswatchers' evaluation of Cannon's chances, Stephenson, 212-15.
124 Speaker's dinner, Hoover, 292; Theodore Roosevelt to Joseph Cannon, February 2, 1905. Roosevelt papers.
125 "On a hedgehog," Dunn, *Harrison,* II, 87.
125 "In socialistic propaganda," March 15, 1906. Roosevelt papers.
126 Report released by Roosevelt, Pringle, *Roosevelt,* 428.
126 "Cent for scenery," Pinchot, 240.
127 "Against moral regeneration," Hatch, 35.
127 "Least elevating form," "Congress Defying," 665-66.
128 Cannon's desire for presidency, Busbey, xix.
128 "Is largely Cannonism," September 21, 1908. Taft papers.
128 Cannon replacing chairmen, Jones, 205.
128 Insurgents' pride, see Nelson's speech, *Congressional Record* 61:2, 3304.
128 "Two ornamental Democrats," Brown, 157.
129 "Best I can," to Theodore Roosevelt, November 7, 1908. Roosevelt papers.
129 "I can afterwards," to Halvor Steenerson, November 30, 1908. Taft papers.
129 Clark's reaction to loss, Hechler, 57.
130 Commitments on tariff, ibid., 57-63.
130 "Ax for Insurgents," August 5, 1909.
130 "For his own back," Clark, I, 277.
130 "Terrorize your subject," quoted Gwinn, 185.
130 "Outlived his usefulness," August 14, 1909.
130 "For Uncle Joe," quoted Bolles, 201.

130 "Anarchists as Cannon," *Topeka Daily State Journal,* October 20, 1909.
131 "Them closing in," quoted Gwinn, 192.
131 "Stunning rebuke," Neuberger, 37.
131 Norris tattered resolution, Norris, 126.
132 Description of fight in House drawn from Bolles, 214–24; Busbey, 243–69; Hechler, 65–78; Neuberger, 34–40; *Washington Post* and *New York Times* for March 18–20, 1910. Quotations from *Congressional Record* will be found 61:2, 3291ff.
134 "Living on tobacco," Watson, 93.
135 "In his life," Clark, II, 279.
136 "Fox this time," Butt, I, 307.
136 One half members born during Cannon's service, "Taps," 40.
137 "Who ever lived," "Uncle Joe Quits," 47–8.

CHAPTER 7 / SLICK NICK LONGWORTH'S FIST OF IRON

Bibliography

Abell, George and Evelyn Gordon. *Let Them Eat Caviar.* New York: Dodge Publishing, 1936.
Adams, Henry. *The Letters of Henry Adams.* Edited by Worthington Chauncy Ford. 2 vols. Boston: Houghton Mifflin, 1938.
Alsop, Joseph. *FDR: A Centenary Remembrance.* New York: The Viking Press, 1982.
Alsop, Stewart. *The Center.* New York: Harper & Row, 1968.
Authier, George. "The New Speaker of the House," *National Republic* 13(January 1926): 30, 42, and 61.
"Backstage in Washington," *Outlook and Independent* 155(May 14, 1930): 60.
Bolling, Richard. *Power in the House.* New York: E. P. Dutton, 1968.
Brough, James. *Princess Alice.* Boston: Little, Brown, 1975.
Brown, George Rothwell. *The Leadership of Congress.* Indianapolis: Bobbs-Merrill, 1922.
Bryce, James. *The American Commonwealth.* 2 vols. New York: Macmillan, 1931–33.
Chiu, Chang-Wei. *The Speaker of the House of Representatives Since 1896.* New York: Columbia University Press, 1928.
Congressional Record.
Connally, Tom and Alfred Steinberg. *My Name Is Tom Connally.* New York: Thomas Y. Crowell, 1954.
DeChambrun, Clara Longworth. *The Making of Nicholas Longworth.* Freeport, N.Y.: Books for Libraries, 1971 [1933].
Gwinn, William Rea. *Uncle Joe Cannon, Archfoe of Insurgency.* New York: Bookman Associates, 1957.
Hard, William. "Leadership in the House," *Review of Reviews* 64(July 1926): 159–64.
———. "Nicholas Longworth," *Review of Reviews* (April 1925), 370–373.
Hasbrouck, Paul DeWitt. *Party Government in the House of Representatives.* New York: Macmillan, 1927.
Keyes, Frances Parkinson. *Capital Kaleidoscope.* New York: Harper & Bros., 1937.
Kiplinger, W. M. *Washington Is Like That.* New York: Harper & Row, 1942.
Leupp, Francis E. "The New Speaker," *Outlook* 75(November 21, 1903): 684–88.
Longworth, Alice Roosevelt. *Crowded Hours.* New York: Scribner's, 1933.
McArthur, Lucile. "Idle Moments of a Lady-in-Waiting," *Saturday Evening Post* 204(September 19, 1931): 3–5, 137–42.
Manchester, William. *American Caeser.* Boston: Little, Brown, 1978.
Memorial Services Held in the House of Representatives for Nicholas Longworth. Washington, D.C.: Government Printing Office, 1932.
Miller, Nathan. *The Roosevelt Chronicles.* New York: Doubleday, 1979.

Miller, William. *Fishbait, Memoirs of the Congressional Doorkeeper.* Englewood Cliffs, N.J.: Prentice-Hall, 1977.
Mondell, Franklin Wheeler. *My Story.* Published serially in the *Wyoming State Tribune* (Cheyenne) from August 1, 1935 to February 4, 1936.
"Nicholas Longworth, a Contradictory Floor Leader of Congress," *Current Opinion* 76(April 1924): 414–15.
Page, William Tyler. "Mr. Speaker Longworth," *Scribner's* 83(March 1928): 272–80.
Pringle, Henry. *Theodore Roosevelt.* New York: Harcourt, Brace & Co., 1931.
Roosevelt, Theodore. *The Letters of Theodore Roosevelt.* Edited by Elting Morison. 8 vols. Cambridge, Mass.: Harvard University Press, 1951–54.
Roosevelt, Theodore. *Theodore Roosevelt, An Autobiography.* New York: Macmillan, 1913.
Searchlight 4(May 1919).
Slayden, Ellen Maury. *Washington Wife.* New York: Harper & Row, 1962.
Teague, Michael. *Mrs. L., Conversations with Alice Roosevelt Longworth.* New York: Doubleday, 1981.
Teichmann, Howard. *Alice.* Englewood Cliffs, N.J.: Prentice-Hall, 1979.
Timmons, Bascom. *Garner of Texas, a Personal History.* New York: Harper & Bros., 1948.
Ulm, A. H. "Speaker Longworth Takes the Gavel," *New York Times Magazine,* December 6, 1925.

Notes

138 "And he has," Brough, 182.
138 "On the way," Miller, 261.
138 "Noble father-in-law," Page, 278.
139 "Down that title," Slayden, 90.
139 "Go into politics," Bryce, II, 69.
139 "From an Irish mob," Adams, II, 55.
139 "And the like," Roosevelt, *Autobiography*, 63.
139 Details of Longworth's early life from DeChambrun.
139 McArthur's mother, Manchester, 48; Roosevelt's mother, J. Alsop, 37.
139 "Without being defiled," DeChambrun, 181.
140 "The music yet," ibid., 182.
140 "Stuff in him," Roosevelt, *Letters,* V, 149.
140 "Him a radical," *Times Literary Supplement,* March 12, 1982, p. 283.
140 "Porc" meeting, Brough, 194.
140 Storer incident, Pringle, 454–58.
141 "Rather strained occasion," Longworth, 125.
141 "And the Capitol," ibid., 160.
141 "Face was crimson," December 12, 1908; 1:5.
141 "To say so," Roosevelt, *Letters,* VII, 497.
141 "Who antagonizes you," ibid., VII, 503.
142 "I was sniffling," Longworth, 211–12.
142 "A dreadful time," ibid.
142 Rumors about Longworth and other women, Teichmann, 96–7; Abell, 180–81; William Miller, 103–104.
142 "Divorcing one another," Teague, 158.
143 "Out of a tree," Leupp, 684.
143 Longworth's opposition to Cannon, Gwinn, 230–31; *New York Times,* March 1, 1919.
143 "Called into question," DeChambrun, 231.
143 Letter to family, DeChambrun, 240.
144 Schall and Rules Committee, Connally, 79.

144   Private "snarling," Longworth, 262.
144   Roosevelt's feeling toward Wilson, Pringle, 582.
144   "Or divided leadership," *New York Times*, October 26, 1918.
145   "Thing too far," *Congressional Record* 67:4, 1716.
145   "Cuts of beef," *Searchlight*, 3.
145   "The Packers' Mann," Chiu, 26.
145   "Master stroke," Mondell, December 13, 1935.
146   "More successfully consummated," *Searchlight*, 6–7.
146   "Attending social functions," *New York Times*, March 17, 1919.
147   "Hard at play," Longworth, 258.
147   "Bloom after dark," *Washington Herald*, April 9, 1931.
147   "Their first names," *Washington Herald*, April 12, 1931. The observer was George Rothwell Brown.
147   "Should be stressed," Keyes, 160.
147   "Smile in return," ibid.
147   "Vibrant and gallant spirit," *Memorial*, 96.
148   "Of the treasuree," *New York Times*, February 7, 1917. "William G." is Treasury Secretary William Gibbs McAdoo.
148   Details of Mondell's life and leadership, Mondell; also Brown, 200ff.
149   "Enjoy the power," Bolling, 109.
149   "Heretofore thus recognized," Mondell, December 17, 1935.
150   Spats anecdote, "Nicholas Longworth," 415–16.
150   "A Gibson illustration," Authier, 42.
151   Organizing the Sixty-eighth Congress, Hasbrouck, 18–21.
151   "The American people," *New York Times*, December 21, 1923; 30:1.
151   "The legislative map," Ulm, 3.
152   "Darn thing now," Page, 276.
152   "Victorious Republican party," *Congressional Record* 68:2, 2712.
153   "Of a lead shot," Hard, "Longworth," 370.
153   "Better be careful," Keyes, 163.
153   Baby's resemblance to Uncle Joe, Brough, 268.
154   Longworths' dress, *New York Times*, December 8, 1925.
154   "Assembly of the world," *Congressional Record* 69:1, 382.
154   "Record on the measure," 67:1, 388.
155   "Czar Nicholas," December 9, 1925.
155   "Becomes canonized now," December 9, 1925.
155   "Sense and efficiency," December 10, 1925.
155   "High constitutional privilege," *Congressional Record* 69:1, 7148.
155   "Washington to-day knows," Hard, "Longworth," 371.
155   "House loves him," Hard, "Leadership," 164.
156   Gann-Longworth feud, Longworth, 330–33.
156   Garner-Longworth friendship, Timmons, 120–25.
157   "Set on 'em," Kiplinger, 419.
157   "Does, doesn't it," Alsop, 80.
157   "Of political ambition," DeChambrun, 289.
157   Spaghetti parties, Timmons, 124.
157   Longworth backs Nelson, DeChambrun, 305.
158   Nick and Gridiron friends, "Backstage," 60.
158   "Of the session," McArthur, 138.
158   "Lower body," *New York Times*, January 22, 1930.
159   House doctor on deaths, McArthur, 141.
159   "Car is it," Timmons, 129.
159   "All-wise Providence," *Congressional Record* 71:3, 7395.
159   Longworth and Mrs. Curtis, Abell, 180.
159   "Of a lifetime," *Washington Herald*, April 10, 1931.

159 "Of his countrymen," April 10, 1931. DeChambrum identifies the writer as Henry Cabot Lodge, who was the grandson of Cabot Lodge, the friend of Thomas Reed and Theodore Roosevelt.

CHAPTER 8 / MR. SAM SURVIVES

Bibliography

Alsop, Joseph and Robert Kintner. "Never Leave Them Angry," *Saturday Evening Post* 313 (January 18, 1941): 22–23, 76–79.
Bolling, Richard. *House Out of Order.* New York: E. P. Dutton, 1965.
———. *Power in the House.* New York: E. P. Dutton, 1968.
Bowles, Chester. *Promises to Keep.* New York: Harper & Row, 1971.
Caro, Robert. "Lyndon and Mr. Sam," *Atlantic Monthly* 248(November 1981): 41–63. *Congressional Record.*
Coughlan, Robert. "Proprietors of the House," *Life* 38(February 14, 1955): 73–94.
Cummings, Milton C. and Robert L. Peabody. "The Decision to Enlarge the Committee on Rules: An Analysis of the 1961 Vote," *New Perspectives on the House of Representatives.* Edited by Robert Peabody and Nelson Polsby. Chicago: Rand McNally, 1969.
Dickerson, Nancy. *Among Those Present.* New York: Random House, 1976.
Dorough, C. Dwight. *Mr. Sam.* New York: Random House, 1962.
Dulaney, H. G. and Edward Hake Phillips, with MacPhelan Reese. *Speak, Mr. Speaker.* Bonham, Texas: Sam Rayburn Foundation, 1978.
Farley, James. *Behind the Ballots.* New York: Harcourt, Brace, 1938.
———. *Jim Farley's Story.* New York: McGraw-Hill, 1948.
Flynn, Edward J. *You're the Boss.* New York: Collier Books, 1962 [1947].
Hardeman, D. B. "Sam Rayburn and the House of Representatives," *The Presidency and Congress.* Austin, Texas: University of Texas Press, 1979.
Ickes, Harold. *The Secret Diary of Harold Ickes.* 3 vols. New York: Simon & Schuster, 1953.
James, Marquis. *Mr. Garner of Texas.* Indianapolis: Bobbs-Merrill, 1939.
MacNeil, Neil. *Forge of Democracy.* New York: David McKay, 1963.
Memorial Services Held in the House of Representatives and Senate of the United States, Together with Remarks Presented in Eulogy of Sam Rayburn. Washington, D.C.: Government Printing Office, 1962.
Miller, William. *Fishbait: The Memoirs of the Congressional Doorkeeper.* Englewood Cliffs, N.J.: Prentice-Hall, 1977.
Mooney, Booth. *Mr. Speaker.* Chicago: Follett Publishing Co., 1964.
———. *Roosevelt and Rayburn.* Philadelphia: J. B. Lippincott, 1971.
Parrish, Michael E. *Securities Regulation and the New Deal.* New Haven: Yale University Press, 1970.
Patterson, James T. *Congressional Conservatism and the New Deal.* Lexington: University of Kentucky Press, 1967.
Robinson, James A. *The House Rules Committee.* Indianapolis: Bobbs-Merrill, 1963.
Shepsle, Kenneth A. *The Giant Jigsaw Puzzle: Democratic Committee Assignments in the Modern House.* Chicago: University of Chicago Press, 1978.
Steinberg, Alfred. *Sam Rayburn.* New York: Hawthorn Books, 1975.
White, William S. "Sam Rayburn, the Untalkative Speaker," *New York Times Magazine,* February 27, 1949.
Wicker, Tom. *JFK and LBJ: the Influence of Personality upon Politics.* New York: William Morrow, 1968.

Notes

160 Rayburn's trip to Tennessee, Steinberg, 170. Biographical facts, anecdotes, and quotations by and about Rayburn are from Dorough, Dulaney, or Steinberg unless otherwise indicated. All Rayburn letters are quoted from Dulaney.
162 "Or anybody else," *Congressional Record* 77:1, 7075–76.
164 "Of the day," Mooney, *Speaker,* 138.
164 "Am now attaining," June, 1914.
165 "Must be receiving," June 9, 1914.
165 Democratic caucus, see letter to Sister Meddie, April 16, 1921; also Bolling, *Power,* 117.
166 "Be decreed otherwise," to W. A. Thomas, February 19, 1922.
167 "It went in," Caro, 54.
167 Description of Board of Education, James, 111; Alsop, 22.
167 "Awake all day," Steinberg, 164.
167 "Be the man," Alsop, 215.
168 Rayburn's role at Chicago convention, Farley, *Ballots,* 132–53.
169 "Temporary dictatorship," Parrish, 112.
169 "For many years," to Ben Stollenwerck, May 2, 1938.
170 "Much these days," January 6, 1937; 22:5.
170 Labor standards bill and executive reorganization, Patterson, 179; 225–26.
170 "His own party," Farley, *Story,* 95.
170 "Have next session," Patterson, 278.
171 O'Connor defeat, Flynn, 149–50.
171 "To be Speaker," Ickes, II, 174.
172 "Without a fight," quoted from Mooney, *Roosevelt,* 153.
173 "Was in trouble," Miller, 230.
173 "A damn liar," Caro, 58.
173 "Couple of times," *Memorial Services,* 374.
174 "The Rules Committee," Mooney, *Roosevelt,* 164.
174 OPA controversy, Robinson, 39.
174 "Committee on procedure," *Congressional Record* 78:2, 5471.
175 "Looked most unlikely," White, 10.
175 "That gets up," to M. Harrill, November 29, 1946.
176 "Party from regaining," *Power,* 181–82.
176 "Rock the boat," ibid., 178.
176 "Anti-Lynching Bill," to E. L. Covey, February 20, 1948.
176 "Racial problem is," to Victor Smith, March 12, 1948.
177 Twenty-one day rule, Robinson, 34; Bolling, *House,* 202; *Power,* 179–80.
177 "Get your quotes," Mooney, *Speaker,* 163.
177 "I had enough," May 4, 1957.
178 "All the time," Mooney, *Speaker,* 163.
178 "We got now," Coughlan, 73.
178 Bowles as freshman, Bowles, 272–73.
179 "A major committee," Shepsle, 159.
179 Reciprocal trade, Bolling, *Power,* 190–91.
179 *CQ* Study, cited by Hardeman, 237.
180 Housing and TVA for minerals, Bolling, *House,* 205.
180 "Resort to arson," Wicker, 58.
180 "End of it," Bolling, *House,* 207.
180 Rayburn keeping hat on, Dickerson, 33.
181 "Legislation or court decisions," to J. Y. Sanders, Jr., July 22, 1957.
181 "To deal with," to John Smith, January 30, 1961.
181 "Won't get anywhere," Wicker, 52.
182 "Touch was lacking," Bolling, *House,* 214. The account of the Rules Committee fight is drawn from Bolling, *House,* 195–220; Wicker, 25–82; MacNeil, 412–47;

References | 237

Cummings and Peabody. Quotations are from these sources unless otherwise indicated.
185 "back-ass pocket," Hardeman, 243.
185 Alsop on House head counts, *Washington Post,* January 30, 1961.
186 "Khrushchev started it," *Congressional Record* 87:1, 1576.
186 "For Speaker Rayburn," January 31, 1961.
186 "The Rules Committee," January 26, 1961.
186 Rules Committee debate, *Congressional Record* 87:1, 1576-80.

CHAPTER 9 / SPEAKER NEWT

Bibliography

Aldrich, John H. and David W. Rohde. "Theories of the Party in the Legislature and the Transition to Republican Rule in the House," paper delivered at the Annual Meeting of the American Political Science Association (September 1995).
Arieff, Irwin B. "GOP Freshmen: Aiming at a Majority," *Congressional Quarterly* (July 7, 1979): 1340.
Barnes, Fred. "The Executive," *New Republic* (May 22, 1995): 25–27.
Barnes, James A. "Partisanship," *National Journal* (November 7, 1987): 2825.
Barry, John M. *The Ambition and the Power.* New York: Viking, 1990.
Beers, David. "Master of Disaster," *Mother Jones* (October 1989): 30–33, 42–46.
Bibby, John F. *Off the Record: The Candid Analyses of Seven Members.* Washington, D.C.: American Enterprise Institute, 1983.
Bruck, Connie. "The Politics of Perception," *New Yorker* (October 9, 1995): 50–76.
Cohen, Richard E. "Hurricane Newt," *National Journal* (September 24, 1994): 2198–2202.
———. "Team Gingrich," *National Journal* (January 14, 1995): 66–68.
Congressional Record.
Connelly, William F., and John J. Pitney, Jr. *Congress' Permanent Minority?* Lanham, Md.: Rowan & Littlefield, 1994.
Cook, Rhodes. "Gingrich Forced to Defensive by Democratic Allegations," *Congressional Quarterly* (April 15, 1989): 798.
———. "Rare Combination of Forces May Make History of '94," *Congressional Quarterly* (April 15, 1995): 1076–1081.
Evans, C. Lawrence and Walter J. Oleszek. "Congressional Tsunami? Institutional Change in the 104th Congress," paper delivered at the Annual Meeting of the American Political Science Association (September 1995).
Gettinger, Steve. "GOP Keeping Promise to Put It to a Vote," *Congressional Quarterly* (August 12, 1995): 2474.
Gibbs, Nancy, and Karen Tumulty. "Master of the House," *Time* (December 25, 1995–January 1, 1996): 54–83.
Gingrich, Newt. "Introduction to Renewing American Civilization," *Readings in Renewing American Civilization.* Edited by Jeffrey A. Eisenach and Albert Stephen Hanser. New York: McGraw-Hill, 1993.
———. *Window of Opportunity.* New York: Tom Doherty Associates, 1984.
———. Acceptance speech, *Congressional Quarterly* (December 10, 1994): 3522–3524.
Greider, William. "Election Post-Mortem: The Price of Failure," *Rolling Stone* (January 12, 1995): 151–154.
Miller, Mark, and Rich Thomas. "Jim Wright: Pork-Barrel Politician as Statesman," *Newsweek* (November 30, 1987): 26–27.
O'Neill, Tip. *Man of the House.* New York: St. Martin's Press, 1987.
Osborne, David. "Newt Gingrich: Shining Knight of the Post-Reagan Right," *Mother Jones* (November 1984): 15–20, 53.

Peters, Ronald M. *The American Speakership*. Baltimore: Johns Hopkins, 1990.
Samuels, David. "Tinkers, Dreamers & Madmen," *Lingua Franca* (January/February 1995): 32–39.
Steeper, Fred. *This Swing Is Different: Analysis of 1994 Election Exit Polls*. Southfield, Mich.: Market Strategies, 1995.
Thomas, Rich. "The Wright Man to See," *Newsweek* (June 29, 1987): 44–45.
Wright, Robert. "The Gay Divorce," *New Republic* (December 19, 1994): 6.

Notes

190 "The White House," Arieff, 1340.
191 "Information revolution" and C-SPAN, Gingrich, *Window*, 68, 265.
191 "It's inexorable." This and other Gingrich quotations not otherwise attributed are from a September 27, 1995, interview.
192 Duration of Republican minority, Connelly and Pitney, 1, 11. These authors note that no previous stretch of House minority status had exceeded sixteen years.
192 "Outside their zones," Bibby, 25. Like one of the authors of this book and five other members of the congressional class of 1978, Newt Gingrich participated in several roundtable discussions between 1979 and 1982. Comments of members of this group are reported anonymously, but future Speaker Gingrich's observations are in several cases readily identifiable.
192 "A permanent minority" and "set up by the Democrats," Associated Press, October 31, 1983.
193 Robert Baumann lost in 1980, as did John Rousselot in 1982. John Ashbrook was running for the Senate when he died in 1982.
193 "Home consumption," O'Neill, 423.
194 "Does nothing right," *Congressional Record* 130:57, 11429.
194 "Descendants of Joe McCarthy," *Congressional Record* 130:57, 11437.
194 "Like a fool," O'Neill, 424.
194 Gingrich-O'Neill exchange and out of order ruling, *Congressional Record* 130:63, 12201.
194 "Red-faced and roaring," *Washington Post,* May 16, 1984.
195 "Aren't going to be," *New York Times,* September 9, 1984.
195 "Pain in the fanny," *New York Times,* August 11, 1983.
195 Campaign (1978) advertising and Gingrich divorce, Osborne, 18–19.
196 "Shadow dossier," Beers, 32.
196 "Democratic cronies" and "just beginning," *Washington Post,* May 2, 1985.
196 Savings and loan controversy, Thomas, 44–45.
196 Book royalties, *Washington Post,* September 24, 1987.
197 "Black Thursday," *Congressional Record* 133:171, H9156–H9157. Also see Barry, 463–474.
198 "Work its will," James A. Barnes, 2825.
198 Democratic complaints about rules, Barry, 538.
198 "Corrupt man," Barry, 532.
198 On Wright's business dealings see, for example, Miller and Thomas, 26.
198 Teamsters, *Wall Street Journal,* January 29, 1988.
199 Wright's S&L ties, *Washington Post,* May 8, 1988.
199 Editorial demanding investigation of Wright, *Wall Street Journal,* May 10, 1988.
199 "Knowledgeable source," *Washington Post,* September 23, 1988.
200 "Exit from the speakership," *Washington Post,* February 12, 1989.
200 The "unexpected opening" was created when Richard Cheney, one of the authors of this book, was named defense secretary by President Bush.
200 "In real bookstores," Cook, April 15, 1989, 798.

202 "Morning, though," Gingrich quoting Sherman in "History and Leadership" audiotape, May 1994.
202 "Sustain American Civilization," Gingrich, "Introduction," 1.
203 "Involved in," Gibbs, 80.
203 "Agenda Worth Voting For," *New York Times,* December 3, 1995.
203 "Patience," *Roll Call,* May 29, 1995.
204 "Stepford candidates," *Washington Post,* September 28, 1994.
204 "60 years," Steeper, 3–4.
205 Vote totals, 1994, Cook, April 15, 1995, 1076.
205 "Much of it," Gingrich, Acceptance speech, 3524.
206 Carlos Moorhead, Fred Barnes, 26.
206 "Someone who will" and committee assignments, Aldrich and Rohde, 11–12.
207 Replacing committees with task forces, Bruck, 72.
207 Percentage of bills with restrictive rules prohibiting amendment, *Congressional Record,* 140:145, H11278–H11279.
207 Time-structured rules, Evans and Oleszek, 19–20.
207 Fairness of time-structured rules, Gettinger, 2474.
207 Gingrich working group, Cohen, January 14, 1995, 66–68.
208 "Joseph McCarthy," Greider, 151.
208 "To a pulp," Wright, 6.
209 "House majority," Cohen, September 24, 1994, 2200.
210 "Way we're going," *Washington Post,* January 21, 1996.
210 "Every week," interview, January 26, 1996.

CONCLUSION: POWER AND THE PUBLIC GOOD

Bibliography

DeChambrun, Clara Longworth. *The Making of Nicholas Longworth.* Freeport, N.Y.: Books for Libraries, 1971 [1933].
Hamilton, Alexander, James Madison, and John Jay. *The Federalist Papers.* New York: New American Library, 1961.
Hasbrouck, Paul DeWitt. *Party, Government in the House of Representatives.* New York: Macmillan, 1927.
The Presidency and the Congress. Edited by William S. Livingston, Lawrence C. Dodd, and Richard L. Schott. Austin, Tex.: University of Texas Press, 1979.
Preston, William. "Personal Recollections of Eminent Men," *The Land We Love* 5 (August 1868): 337–40.
Smith, Margaret Bayard. *The First Forty Years of Washington Society.* New York: Scribner's, 1906.
Sundquist, James L. *The Decline and Resurgence of Congress.* Washington, D.C.: Brookings Institution, 1981.
Wicker, Tom. *JFK and LBJ: The Influence of Personality on Politics.* New York: William Morrow, 1968.

Notes

211 "Upon these gentlemen," Preston, 337.
211 "The smouldering ruins," Smith, 109.
212 "Or partial considerations," Madison, number ten, in Hamilton, 82.
212 "Would be necessary," Madison, number fifty-one, in Hamilton, 322.
213 "Not recognize me," Hasbrouck, 5.

213 "Tilson and Snell," DeChambrun, 302–303.
214 "To do so," Sundquist, 175.
214 "Highly controversial subjects," *New York Times,* January 29, 1961.
214 "To vote against," Wicker, 38–39.
214 "Assertive policymaking," The Presidency, 59.
214 "Power to impede," ibid., 74.
214 "Violence of faction," Madison, number ten, in Hamilton, 77.

INDEX